THE HAIER WAY

THE MAKING OF A CHINESE BUSINESS LEADER

AND A GLOBAL BRAND

THE HAIER WAY

THE MAKING OF A CHINESE BUSINESS LEADER

AND A GLOBAL BRAND

Jeannie Jinsheng Yi, Ph.D.

Shawn Xian Ye, MBA

HOMA & SEKEY BOOKS

DUMONT, NEW JERSEY

First Edition

Copyright © 2003 by Homa & Sekey Books

Library of Congress Cataloging-in-Publication Data

Yi, Jeannie Jinsheng.
The Haier way : the making of a Chinese business leader and a global brand / Jeannie Jinsheng Yi & Shawn Xian Ye.— 1st ed.
p. cm.
Includes bibliographical references
ISBN 1-931907-01-3 (Hardcover)
1. Haier (Corporation) 2. Electric household appliances industry—
China— History. 3. International business enterprises—China—
Management—History.
I. Ye, Shawn Xian. II. Title.
HD9971.5.E543 H359 2002
338.7'68383'0951—dc21
2002005635

Published by Homa & Sekey Books
138 Veterans Plaza
P. O. Box 103
Dumont, NJ 07628

Tel: (201)384-6692
Fax: (201)384-6055
Email: info@homabooks.com
Website: www.homabooks.com

Printed in the United States of America
1 3 5 7 9 10 8 6 4 2

To my parents,
Ye Bingyan and Zheng Xianghua

—S. X. Ye

To my daughter, Blair Zhou

—J. J. Yi

Contents

Authors' Note

The idea for this book came in late July of 2001, when Shawn read an article in the *New York Times* on the $14 million purchase of a Manhattan landmark building by a Chinese company called "Haier." The name was somewhat familiar to him, from when he had been in China about ten years before. Excited at the news, Shawn did some research, and was so impressed with what Haier had achieved over a relatively short period of time that he decided to write a book about the company.

Another factor that stimulated him to write a book on Haier was that, according to his research findings, there had not been a single book written and published in English about a single Chinese company, although there were loads of books on Chinese business as a whole.

Knowing the importance of having access to first-hand information, Shawn first contacted Haier headquarters in Qingdao, China, and then the Haier America Corporation, in New York, to request arrangements for visiting the Haier facilities and interviewing Haier executives and employees. To add a diverse perspective to the book, Shawn invited Jeannie to join him co-writing the book, and Jeannie graciously agreed.

The book is based partly on our many interviews, as well as extensive correspondence, with Haier executives and employees in China, America and Europe, and the material provided by them, and partly on our research from a variety of publications, both English and Chinese, printed and online. We do not claim to have been exhaustive in sourcing our material, but we have tried to be as inclusive as possible.

A note about the form of Chinese names in the book: we generally use the Chinese order, which puts the family name first, followed by the given name, as in "Zhang Ruimin" and "Yang Mianmian," the names of the Haier CEO and President, respectively.

Jeannie J. Yi
Shawn X. Ye

Acknowledgements

There are numerous people who have helped us in various ways in the process of writing this book, especially the Haier executives and employees whom we have interviewed and contacted in China, America, and Europe. They are the major sources of information and inspiration for our writing, without which this book would not have been possible. There are so many of them that we are unable to name them all here, due to limited space. Our special thanks go to Ms. Su Fangwen, director of the Haier Enterprise Culture Center, in Qingdao, and her staff, who arranged our Haier facilities visits and interviews in Qingdao, and who provided us with valuable company information and data. We also thank Mr. Diao Yunfeng of the Haier Overseas Promotion Division, who lent a last-minute helping hand to secure our China trip. We are indebted to Rebecca Espinueva, Haier America's public relations manager, who was very instrumental in the process, providing requested information and coordinating communications, among other things. We are thankful to Noris Ciccardi, of Haier Europe's head office, who responded very promptly to our request for information.

We are grateful to the Harvard Business School Press (HBSP) and the International Institute for Management Development (IMD) in Lausanne, Switzerland, for allowing us to use their case studies on Haier in our book. Special thanks go to Tim Cannon of HBSP, and Persita Egeli-Farmanfarma and Tanja Aenis of IMD Case Services, for their assistance in the permission process.

We appreciated the help of Judy Kwan of New York Life in Hong Kong, and Amrita Mattoo of the New York Life Insurance Company in New York for providing information regarding New York Life's joint venture with Haier, and for confirming some name-spelling in our writing.

We are much obliged to Professor N. T. Wang of Columbia University for writing the preface for our book. We are thankful to Professor Ming-Jer Chen of the University of Virginia, author of *Inside Chinese Business*, for his encouragement of our writing. We also thank Professor Marshall Meyer of the Wharton School at the University of Pennsylvania for reading some of our manuscript.

Lijian Cai of the United Nations has offered consistent support for our publishing endeavor, for which we cannot thank him enough.

Lastly, Jeannie would like to thank Jishu Zhou, her husband, for all the support he has given her in writing this book. Shawn wishes to say many thanks to Michelle Weiwei Fang, his wife, who was not only a big champion of his effort, but also the first reader of his manuscript with a critic's eye.

Jeannie J. Yi
Shawn X. Ye
January 31, 2003
New Jersey

Preface

In response to the quiet revolution in China's economic system toward the end of the 1970s, Columbia University's Graduate School of Business and School of International (and Public) Affairs jointly established the China-International Business Project. A major objective of the Project is to train a new generation of business people, government officials and scholars to cope with the emerging opportunities and challenges pursuant to the sea-change in question. A new graduate course on China International Business Relations was offered—the first of its kind in the United States, and probably in the world.

A major problem with this new initiative was a lack of adequate instructional materials. There were virtually no serious, relevant case studies, comparable to the ones made famous at Harvard. One remedy was to mobilize all the knowledgeable people in various disciplines and walks of life to share their experiences and insights, often on an off-the-record basis. Another was to encourage all those involved to prepare case studies on Chinese business.

After more than two decades, the problem originally encountered changed from one involving scarcity to one involving an explosion of materials. There is virtually no discipline which does not have some literature related to China-International Business, whether on issues of war and peace, human rights and obligations, environmental degradation and protection, government and corporate governance or cultures and civilizations. Yet, despite this surge in relevant case studies, including those developed by the present writer, most of them fall short of the ideal. Many are based on brief interviews with senior enterprise leaders and on corporate public relations materials. On-the-spot visits are often no more than guided tours. Many documents are considered proprietary information.

The present book-length case study on Haier is thus timely. While it is not the first case study of the now-legendary turn-around Chinese enterprise and the chief architect behind it, this volume is more comprehensive and up-to-date, as compared with the studies by

Harvard and the International Institute of Management Development, and stories reported in the media, such as those presented by the *Financial Times*, the *New York Times*, *Fortune* and *Forbes*.

Furthermore, discourse with the man responsible for Haier's historic rise and transformation, Zhang Ruimin, whether at Columbia, Wharton, the Fortune Shanghai Conference or Davos, remained restricted to a relatively small number of knowledgeable people.

The joint authors of this most useful volume, Jeannie Yi and Shawn Ye, have special advantages. They share a bicultural background and are familiar with the business literature and issues in the West, as well as with the Chinese historical background, current developments and cultural nuances. Unlike many academic case studies, this volume is highly readable and unburdened by the overuse of technical jargon. It should, therefore, be enjoyable reading not only for specialists but also for the general public.

From a broad perspective, the volume throws light on a number of important issues about China's development path. The evolving role of an inefficient and close-to-bankrupt collective, sometimes wrongly identified as a "state," enterprise, into a robust transnational corporation with its own brand demonstrates that there are more pragmatic ways of transition than regime change, shock therapy or wholesale privatization, as has often been proposed by well-meaning outside observers. In spite of Zhang's bold and innovative style of management, one should not forget that he remains a loyal party secretary, and that his corporate culture is laced with military discipline as well as age-old paternalism. The story of Haier also hints at great promise for the continued robust growth of the Chinese economy in general, at least in the near future, even if the Haier experience may not be readily duplicated elsewhere, as admitted by Zhang himself. The advantages of the latecomer and the under-performer, as is the case with many Chinese enterprises, should not be lost sight of. Moreover, the correctness of China's decision to enter the World Trade Organization, notwithstanding the hysterical cries of "selling the country out," should be amply demonstrated by Haier's metamorphosis, not only in meeting domestic competition but also in challenging international corporations abroad, sometimes in cooperation with the competitors.

Looking into the future, five areas appear which could be especially fruitful. First, a Chinese version of the study is called for. Evidently, the dearth of detailed Chinese language enterprise case studies is even more marked, especially in relation to the mushrooming of Master of Business Administration (MBA) and executive (EMBA) programs in China. Many instructors are not experienced in preparing case studies or in conducting such studies in class. The use of non-Chinese company case studies for instructional purposes, such as those of Harvard, do not always serve the purpose, because of differences between institutional, legal, and cultural environments in China and elsewhere. In that connection, the present authors themselves should be ideal to undertake the task, especially since they are well placed not merely to translate their own work literally from English into Chinese, but also to use their discretion to modify and expand the case for Chinese readers. For example, many expressions may be more indigenous to the Chinese language than straightforward translations from English. Current developments can be added. Such a volume should also be of general interest. It may even inspire numerous struggling Chinese enterprises to ask the question, "If Haier can do it, why can't we?"

The second related area for further work is to examine the degree to which the Haier experience has been applicable in other Chinese enterprises, and the reasons why it has worked or not worked. This could be a good exercise for business school students, as well as for instructors.

The third related area is to examine the viability of certain Haier strategies in the long run and to take a look at experiences in other selected Chinese enterprises as well. For example, do mergers and acquisitions result in $1 + 1 > 2$ or < 2? Do diversifications into unfamiliar territories, from refrigerators, freezers, wine cellars, air conditioners, washing machines, microwave ovens, toasters, irons, TVs and DVD players to game machines, cell phones, travel services and banking and insurance, complement each other or distract from core competence? To what extent does the concentration of strategic decision-making in a single supreme leader and the attendant emphasis on worker discipline have to be modified when the enterprise becomes truly transnational and the workers place more emphasis on work-satisfaction than on simple productivity and pecuniary gain?

The fourth area is to respond to the rising skeptics elsewhere. This is particularly timely in view of the disclosure of wrongdoings and the unbelievability of corporate information in such blue-chip firms as Enron, Worldcom and Tyco International in the United States—where business practices have long been regarded as the world's management model. Even for such evidently exemplary corporations as General Electric, the disclosure of over four hundred million dollars in personal assets and more than $360,000 in monthly personal expenditures for its former CEO, as an unintended result of a divorce lawsuit, raises questions about adequate corporate transparency in executive perquisites and director independence. The need for timely and honest disclosure of corporate information goes beyond the interests of shareholders and extends to all constituencies. Consequently, it is not limited to financial items, but extends to non-financial information, such as corporate structure, the locus of decision-making, labor relations and health and environmental measures.

The fifth area is to make available to the interested reader detailed methodological discussions, even where they have not been included in the book, in order to emphasize readability. Such discussions may include interview methods, as well as accessibility to company personnel and accounts.

If the above follow-throughs are carried out, the impact of the recent study will extend far beyond a better understanding of a single Chinese corporate success story.

N. T. Wang, Ph.D.
Director
China-International Business Project
Columbia University

Haier

THE HAIER WAY

Map of China

Introduction:
A Defining Moment

All day, every day, people in China work at making things for Americans to buy, but one can hardly name a single product that has a "Made in China" sticker on it and is considered a high-quality product. The truth of the matter is that the words "Made in China" evoke other, unspoken words, like "cheap goods," "low quality," and "disposable." Many Chinese products are ones we come across every day in American discount stores, from popular One-Dollar Stores to mega-stores like Office Depot or Home Depot.

In industries such as the manufacture of toys, kitchenware and textiles, China leads the world in exports, sending $100 billion worth of goods to America alone in the year 2000, and filling to capacity the American home, from bathroom to kitchen closets.

However, the Chinese very rarely sell their homemade products under their own names. Instead, the products are sold under somebody else's name or with a foreign firm's brand affixed, like "Whirlpool" or "Kenmore." "Made in China" simply does not sell, with the exception of one brand—Tsingtao Beer—which was one of the first products to emerge from China after it reopened its doors to the West in the 1970s.

Americans love Tsingtao Beer. But don't they also love the user-friendly, smart-looking wine cellars that complement and chill Tsingtao Beer, a brand named "Haier?"

In truth, the famous Tsingtao Brewery and the factory that produces the unique Haier wine cellars and another ten thousand and more products, including quality home appliances and electronics featuring cutting-edge technology, are practically neighbors. They were born in the same country, the same province and the same city, a few miles apart, and within the reach of Americans after only fourteen hours of flight or two weeks by sea. The two products, beer and wine cellars, are shipped out of the same port.

This puts Haier (pronounced "higher") in the rarest of companies. It is one of just a small handful of mainland Chinese firms whose names are known outside their home market.

Somewhere in the aisles of the American wholesale store, "Sam's Club," amid the festivities of the past Christmas, we caught a glimpse of a country trying to come up with a brand name that would be as well-known as Tsingtao Beer. Among the General Electric and Whirlpool refrigerators and air conditioners quietly stood some of Haier's cool-looking coolers and slick Chest Freezers. We asked about its origin, and were told by a young salesperson, a student trying to make some fast cash during the Christmas rush, that Haier was a brand the store had recently started to carry.

"Maybe a German brand?" the salesperson offered.

The answer is partly true, and it illustrates one of the most unusual success stories of all time, one that has attracted the attention of the world, both in business circles and in the academic arena.

Only eighteen years ago, "Haier" did not exist. Its predecessor was Qingdao General Refrigerator Factory, which manufactured substandard refrigerators that were sold locally.

"The factory was suffering great losses. It seemed an impossible task to revive it," said Zhang Ruimin, who has been regarded as the Jack Welch of China. He is Chairman and CEO of the Haier Group, a 72 billion RMB or $8.7 billion producer and the largest appliance maker in China, with over 30,000 employees in China and thirteen other countries.

But back in 1984, the factory employed about 800 people, all crammed into a tiny, old building on a crowded street, and was on the verge of bankruptcy. There were a lot of refrigerator factories in China, but most of them were making poor-quality products. Qingdao General Refrigerator Factory wanted to make a difference.

Zhang's first step was to destroy all the inferior-quality refrigerators, and to introduce an advanced refrigerator production line from the German Liebherr Company, through a joint venture. In December 1991, Qingdao General Refrigerator Factory merged with two other companies and changed its name. After much consideration and several false starts, it finally settled on the Haier Group in 1992. The name represents both the German fine machinery and the Chinese ambition to create a brand of their own.

"Haier is a sea," wrote Zhang in the mission statement of the company. "Like a sea, it has no boundaries; it is a blue ambition." Haier wants to attract talent "from the five lakes and the four seas" to make Haier a success both in China and overseas.

This event marked the end of an era, and of the structure of a stagnant central-planning system that, for decades, had created no incentive for either state enterprise or the individual worker. At Haier, the unbreakable socialist Iron Rice Bowl was broken.

Subsequently, Haier pioneered an innovative road, a semi-Western model under a politically more tolerant and liberal-minded China. It strode from the verge of bankruptcy to the position of a global brand during the time of China's economic reform and the initiation of the market economy that allowed and encouraged the co-existence of a competitive, profit-driven collective ownership along with state and private ownership.

Eighteen years is a short time in a man's life or in the life of a corporation. To make such a giant leap to the plateau of significance and high visibility in such a brief period of time would demand huge efforts from any ambitious corporation. The past eighteen years has witnessed the development of Haier into a household name in China and a recognizable and respectable brand around the globe. Its success so far represents the drastic economic changes that China has gone through in recent decades. This change includes a change in management style as well as in the way in which Haier conducts its business.

On the domestic stage, Haier represents a new business model, challenged by China's constantly changing economic policies and conditions at the juncture of China's entry into the World Trade Organization. On the international scene and among multinational corporations, Haier is an international phenomenon that has succeeded in expanding and increasing its market share in the highly saturated global market. Their strategy of moving into more sophisticated and tougher markets, such as the U.S. and Europe, to sharpen their technical skills and research capability provides an alternative to the age-old tradition that was practiced in Asia for centuries—export cheap labor, export cheap material and export cheap products for profit.

Haier exports a brand name and sophisticated technology—a new business model respected by the world at large.

Today, Haier has eighteen design centers, ten industrial parks, 58,800 sales agents and 11,976 after-sales services in 160 countries and regions. Their products have greatly diversified, as their markets expanded from the single refrigerator in 1984 to the current situation, with eighty-six categories and 13,000 models of appliances, including white, black and brown household appliances such as refrigerators, freezers, air conditioners, washers and dryers, air purifiers, microwave ovens, electric irons, TVs, DVD players, computers, and mobile phones.

Haier became a case study at Harvard Business School and Zhang was invited to a seminar at Harvard Business School on March 25, 1998, to speak on the role that the Haier culture had played in the company's mergers and acquisitions.

In December 1999, the London-based *Financial Times* ranked Zhang among the World's Thirty Most Respected Business Leaders. With Jack Welch of GE topping the list, Zhang was placed at Number 26, just behind Rupert Murdoch of News Corporation (No. 23), but ahead of Michael Eisner of Disney (No. 29), and Jeff Bezos of Amazon.com (No. 30). The only other Asians on the list were Hiroshi Okuda of Toyota (No. 7) and Noboyuki Idei of Sony (No. 8).

The survey was conducted among 754 chief executives from seventy-five countries, and the core premise of the survey was to identify those business leaders most respected by their peers. All participating CEOs were asked, among other things, to nominate the three business leaders they most respected, and state the reasons for their choices.

Once the fieldwork was completed (in China, it was done by PricewaterhouseCoopers), the raw data were aggregated and weighted. The weighting was based on the GDP of the country of origin of each participating CEO. To qualify as a "world's most respected business leader," a minimum of five nominations were required. So the end product truly represented the global opinion of Chief Executive Officers.

On October 7, 2000, Zhang was invited by the International Institute for Management Development (IMD) in Lausanne, Switzerland, to the Symposium on Management Achievements of

Global IMD Schoolfellows, to which Zhang delivered an inspiring speech on Haier's creative management, including the market chain theory. Zhang was the first Asian to deliver a speech at IMD. On April 2 and 3, 2001, Zhang gave speeches at Columbia and Wharton Business Schools.

In the February 2001 issue of AM (*Appliance Manufacturer*), Haier secured ninth place on the publication's Top Ten Global Appliance Manufacturers list. Just as Electrolux (Frigidaire) of Sweden was slotted between Whirlpool and GE of the U.S. as the top three, Haier of China was sandwiched between Toshiba and Hitachi of Japan at the end of the list.

Zhang Ruimin was featured in the August 6, 2001 issue of *Forbes Global*, standing tall next to his jolly Haier boy—a character in the Chinese cartoon, "The Haier Brothers," owned by the Haier Group. In the same issue, Haier placed sixth on *Forbes'* list of the world's top ten makers of large kitchen appliances for 2000, achieving a total sales volume of 8.35 million units. With Whirlpool at the top of the list and GE in third, Haier was ahead of LG Electronics of South Korea, Matsushita (Panasonic) and Sharp of Japan.

But Zhang does not seem to be content with all this. His next goal for Haier is to make it a *Fortune* 500 company and to be among the top five appliance makers of white goods in the United States, which means that Haier would overcome rankings currently held by Whirlpool, GE, Maytag and Frigidaire.

Is all this possible? Zhang, at least, has good reason to believe so, given the fact that, in the space of eighteen years, he has turned the once-nearly-bankrupt company into a multi-billion dollar conglomerate and that he has led it from a seaport city in northeast China to the world capitalist strongholds of New York, London, Berlin and Paris.

1

Haier and Higher:
The Las Vegas and Broadway Stories

In an article on the August 6, 2001 issue of the *Forbes Global* magazine, Russell Flannery correctly points out: "Beyond its own standing and success, Haier is important because it offers an insight into the changes washing across the Chinese economy. Haier's arrival as a serious brand player in the global appliance business—it has plants in thirteen countries and sells its products in more than 160—signals that the initial phase of market economic reforms in China's once-closed economy are nearing an end. Winning domestic brands such as Haier and the computer maker, Legend, will increasingly turn outward for growth, as they face the prospect of more foreign competition on their own turf, following China's admission into the World Trade Organization."

Convention Center, Las Vegas
On the morning of January 9, 2002, we arrived at the Las Vegas Convention Center to check out for ourselves both the Haier Group and the Haier products, as they stood side by side with other world brand names at the 2002 International Consumer Electronics Show (CES). We wanted to see where Haier really belongs.

The CES show is the largest and the most important electronics trade show in the world, and is held every January in Las Vegas.

We passed through a long hallway filled with sight and sound, exhibitions of sophisticated cutting-edge technology and fantastic live shows put on by the most famous brands in the world of electronics. Actors and actresses impersonated Marilyn Monroe and Elvis Presley, and there were extravagant stage-shows by the mega-names: Canon, Panasonic, Sony and Samsung. We finally made it to the Haier exhibition booths in the far-left corner, toward the end of the hall, behind the gigantic center stage with the Microsoft exhibit.

Haier caught our attention with its splash of ocean blue and the large, quietly-daring slogan on one of the walls of the two-story booths: *Taking Your Viewing Experience To A Haier Level*. The use of the pun "higher/Haier" is unmistakable.

Haier is bold. Their strength is by no means just sight and sound; they are known to the world for their refrigerators. But who knows? Haier might be the next Sony or GE.

We saw a young Chinese technician with a Haier tag on his left arm working on a flat-screen TV. We had grown familiar with the Haier logo on Haier employees' uniforms: six lines and six columns of blue dots in a square format, with the first line having five dots preceded by a red square. For simplicity's sake, the publicized Haier logo is just the first line. We had been told, while we were touring Haier Industrial Park in Qingdao in December 2001, that the six dots represent ingenuity in getting things done smoothly and creatively—in Chinese popular culture, the Chinese numeral "6," *liu,* is a pun on smoothness and creativity, while the red square represents the firm's fundamental guiding principle.

The logo also has another meaning—the relationship between the satellite Haier facilities around the world (the dots) and the Haier headquarters (the square) in Qingdao, which is a square building with four red columns on the outside, as partly shown on the front cover of this book.

Inside the square building is a circular structure of twelve floors of offices, conference rooms and showrooms. The logo's symbolic meaning is evident: although situations might be different in different parts of the world, and things have to be done differently according to local customs, the guiding principle must not bend. Together, the Haier Building and its logo symbolize an ancient Chinese wisdom, a philosophy and a code of conduct of "thinking squarely; acting smoothly."

"This is the second time that Haier has exhibited at CES," a lady in a yellow dress told us. She was as busy as a bumblebee, arranging blue fliers around various large and small products. Her name was Joanna, and she was the publicist Haier had hired to help organize their part of the show in the American way. Chinese companies had learned painful lessons, doing things the Chinese way at American trade shows. Decorations like red balloons, golden wrappers, gaudy silk streamers and fireworks simply don't work.

Joanna told us, "Chinese names don't usually translate well. 'Haier' is an exception. It doesn't sound Chinese." With the taste and skill of an expensive interior decorator, she was putting the final touches to the little piles of fliers she had arranged in various shapes around the cell-phones, Game-Boys, mini-recorders and some futuristic-looking electronic gadgets that teenagers would favor.

"Last time, there was a Chinese company here, too. They hung up red flags and cute little black-and-white pandas, but that didn't work. I don't see them here today. Gone, I guess. Do it the American way. 'When in Rome, do as the Romans do.'"

Doing it the American way was the right approach. This was America. A Chinese product trying to break into the American market has to do it the American way. This is the only way an understanding and transparent relationship between product and customer can be established. The way the product is presented to the market says a lot about both the product and the corporation that manufactures it, just as the way a salesperson talks to a customer will infinitely affect the relationship not only between the store and the customer, but between the product and the customer. Apparently, this is exactly what Haier is doing, and they do it very well: localization in its smallest form.

"You have to localize," chimed in Rebecca Espinueva, a young MBA who is the Public Relations Manager for Haier America. "Look, I'm an American, although I have Filipino blood. I was born and bred in this country, and I know the way the American commercial world will respond to me. I also know what I should expect from my American boss. It minimizes cultural misunderstandings and gets the job done better and faster."

Her mobile phone rang. She made an "excuse me" sign with her finger, and answered it.

"Yes. I'm packing up, and I'll leave for the airport in half an hour's time." She then turned to us, "We have a household-appliances show this Sunday, and a kitchen-and-bath show in April, in Chicago. We are awfully busy. In the past, Chinese products were sold under somebody else's name. Now, they're sold under their own name.

Everyone has to work hard to make that happen. I mean *extremely* hard."

We could tell that everyone was working hard. At the exhibition booths, Haier marketing executives in black suits and red ties were rushing in and out, greeting customers.

Rebecca had finished her call and turned to us.

"I'll get our product designer for you. He is on his way to the airport with me. He has a few minutes to spare. He's our consultant. The moment he finishes his contract with another firm, he'll be working for us full-time. Everyone is new, you see. Everyone has put their houses on the market, to move up here and work for Haier."

We were left with the stainless flat-screen TV sets, TVs with built-in curtains, and anti-short-sightedness TV sets. Some chic Gameboys lay on a stainless-steel counter top and looped around the fingers and slender neck of a sculpture of a handsome Greek youth with a mystic expression of joy and sorrow. The multi-colored MP3 audio players with built-in microphones and a string of small accessory gadgets looked like expensive Gucci watches and jewels. All the TV stands were in bold colors, to complement the bold home designs of today's America. A couple of boldly colored, advanced-technology CD players reminded us of Chanel handbags in a Saks Fifth Avenue department store. They were very futuristic and high-tech-looking, in a display with larger, flat-screen television and HDTV sets along the walls.

The booths were impressive, large and airy and colored ocean-blue. The exhibit showed evidence of the American attention to detail, but the high conception of modesty and reserve was definitely Chinese. The entire exhibit was a proper introduction and presentation of products that were reaching out to the public through advertising and retailers and by word-of-mouth.

A Chinese man who had been standing nearby approached us and spoke to us in Chinese. "Among Mainland Chinese appliances, I like Haier products best." Then he changed to English. "Haier products are good. I know for sure."

He told us that he was with a trading company in New Jersey, but had a factory in Shanghai. In 2001, he had bought a Haier washer/dryer combo in China, which had done the work of two appliances in less than the space normally taken by one. It had run very well, washing and drying his clothes in one hour. He said it had made no noise.

He had recommended it to a friend who lived in Washington, D.C., who then ordered the same brand, via Haier's website, for his mother in Shanghai. Haier shipped the washer/dryer to his mother's home in Shanghai in less than three days.

"Free delivery and free installation!" He grinned, and raised his thumb.

When we saw a Chinese gentleman wearing a Haier badge bearing the name "Shariff Kan," we talked to him. He turned out to be the VP Merchandising for Haier America. Another man, wearing a black suit, walked up and introduced himself as "Charlie," Marketing Manager for the New York and New Jersey metro area. Charlie was a talkative person who had come on board just two months before, lured by Shariff Kan, whom he had known for years.

"So you are new. What makes you think you can be successful with Haier or Haier can be successful in America? There are already so many products," Jeannie asked.

"Let me tell you the secrets of how a business can be successful. I don't have an MBA and all that; what I say is based on my own experience. First of all, you must have a sophisticated product and product-line, which Haier does. Then you must have experienced marketing specialists, with know-how and successful track records in dealing with large clients in the North American markets, which Haier has—us. Thirdly, you must have faith in the company, and you must have a passion for the job. Fourthly, you must know your shortcomings and weaknesses. Haier is the new kid on the block...."

"...but because of the advantages we already have, we'll move in. We'll move in and stay there." Jeannie finished it up for him with their CEO's words.

Market first, profit second—this was Zhang's simple strategy, and it was working in the global market. Zhang had insisted on a longer-term approach. Market share and cash flow are far more important than a corporation's net profit at any given stage.

Can Haier manage to stay? This is a question everyone is asking today. And we had addressed this question to Zhang during our interview in his Qingdao headquarters.

Zhang had not been daunted by the question. He had answered it quite confidently, saying that he saw a bright future for Haier in the global market. We asked about the loyalty issue, with overseas employees—the problem of localization was the loyalty issue, wasn't it? How could he trust a multi-million-dollar business to a group of foreigners? Americans today simply don't believe in the word "loyalty." Would Haier employees be loyal?

Zhang said that he has left the business in America completely to the Americans. Almost all the top management members in his South Carolina factory and in Haier America Trading are natives of the United States. "We can talk about our culture, about the ways Chinese do things, but in the end, we have to respect Western ways in their market, or we will fail." This is Zhang's concept of localization.

"You may say what you want, but I tell you I like this firm. I like the name and I like the people." We had been joined by Jack, who had been hired by Haier three months before. Jack was in charge of parts and services. Like the others, he had worked for national wholesale chain stores. All his life, he had lived in Philadelphia. "But now my house is on the market, and I'm moving into New Jersey."

"Me, too." A tall, handsome man about forty-five years old came over. "I have just sold my house in California and moved to Morris Plains." He handed us his card; he was Gene Russell, Senior Vice President of Sales.

Moving all the way from California to New Jersey in order to work in New York? It sounded like moving from Beijing to New York. We were curious to know what had propelled him to make such a big career decision.

"Michael Jemal and Haier. You see, I've known Michael Jemal for about twenty years. A friend of mine who is also a close friend of Michael's told me about Haier and urged me to work for them. Later, Michael called and asked me to come to the East Coast.

"I was not ready. It was a major move and I had to be absolutely sure where I was moving. I have a wife and family, and I didn't want to move them here if the opportunity wasn't right. This is a new product, and Chinese products are famous for being 'here today and gone tomorrow.' But later, I became convinced that Haier is different. Haier is going to stay. Haier is the next big thing in the appliance industry."

"How do you know?"

"I know because I've heard Haier's success story and have seen the product line. I went to Qingdao, and the people and products convinced me. So, in three months, I sold my house and moved. Haier is going to be big."

"Your strategy is...."

"Get in, stay in and take over. You know why we love Wal-Mart?" Gene became excited. "The key to Wal-Mart's success is to make your business partners successful. Slashing your suppliers' prices only runs the business down. Haier is like Wal-Mart in many ways. They make their suppliers and employees and all the people involved in the business successful."

"I'll simply show my customer the total package of the products: the features, the values, the quality and the price. Sell value." Charlie stressed the last sentence.

We looked around us at the enthusiastic salespeople with strong, successful track records, and the passion and the faith they had for their company and their products. Why couldn't they be successful with Haier? As individuals, they all knew each other directly, like Charlie and Shariff, or indirectly, like Jack and Gene, and they formed a strong human chain, like one big family with one goal: to sell Haier products. They had one thing in common, as Charlie had best summarized: "Believe in the product. Believe in the company."

1356 Broadway, New York

Consulting the address on the invitation, at seven o'clock on March 4, 2002, we arrived at 1356 Broadway in midtown Manhattan. From two blocks away, we could see the ocean-blue light illuminating the eighty-year-old landmark building that once housed the headquarters of the Greenwich Savings Bank, and that had been purchased by Haier America in July of 2001. In front of the gate flew a blue Haier corporate flag and an American flag, under which stood two uniformed security guards. At the top of the building were the freshly painted words, "The Haier Building," with the Haier logo of five blue dots following a red square.

A TV production vehicle was parked in front of the gate. Well-dressed and graciously mannered men and women, some of them of Asian origin, streamed in through the brass doors. Quite a few pedestrians stopped in front of the building, though New Yorkers are usually not curious about anything. One of them, a young man with long hair, inquired of the security guard, "What's going on?"

"Haier's grand opening."

In English, the word "Haier" sounded cool, though unfamiliar. The young man repeated the word, and peeped inside. Since Haier had purchased the building, it had attracted quite a bit of media attention. The *New York Times*, the *Wall Street Journal* and the *Financial Times* had all run stories about the purchase.

Built in 1922, the property covers approximately 47,000 square feet of usable space and about 370 linear feet of frontage on Broadway, Sixth Avenue and 36th Street. Prior to the Haier America purchase, the building's occupants had been banks—Greenwich Savings, Metropolitan, Crossland, Republic National, and HSBC. With foot-traffic of over 100 million people per year, the building is close to all major subways, PATH trains, and NJ Transit. In 1992, the Landmarks Preservation Commission of New York City designated the building a landmark.

In July 2001, New York-based Insignia/ESG brokered the sale of 1356 Broadway to Haier America for $14 million. The seller was Himmel & Meringoff Properties Inc. It took Haier America more than six months to renovate the building and put a new face on it. Everyone had been anxiously waiting to see how it would turn out: Haier had planned to make it both a grand showroom and a banquet hall, just like the Trump Tower on Fifth Avenue, serving both as a high-end apartment house and a public entertainment center, with a lower level of waterfalls, restaurants and cafés.

Haier's grand opening was like a housewarming party. Haier employees, friends, business partners and people in the same trade—buyers and suppliers—and people in the media or with the press were invited. There were about five hundred people showing up that evening. Inside the building, the warm glow immediately made us feel relaxed, while the American flag and the Haier flag made us feel at home. At the entrance, by the reception desk, was a large

Chinese national flag. After checking in, we were given an American-flag pin.

We walked into the 15,000 square-foot elliptical main hall that offered six stories of unobstructed column-free space with a glass mosaic dome above. The space was unparalleled in its drama and ability to inspire every person who stepped into its rotunda for the first time. We were immediately greeted by a large ice-sculpture of the word "Haier" in the center of the hall. For a moment we stood in front of the ice sculpture and looked through the transparent ice into the fabulous reception hall, with fresh, lovely, yellow morning glories and yellow orchids on each table and serving station. In the midst of bottles of sparkling wine and crystal wineglasses—there were several bar stations around the circular building—were the fabulous Haier wine cellars that had been enjoying considerable popularity in the North American market.

There were eight service stations serving all types of food, authentic and beautifully prepared: Chinese *dim sums*, Japanese sushi, American steak, Mexican spicy rolls, Italian pasta, French lamb chops and a variety of soups. All of this was complemented by waiters in a human chain about the room, with champagne and traditional cocktails.

We looked around just in time to catch sight of a tall, handsome American bringing a bamboo steamer full of dumplings. It was quite a sight, for people were used to seeing Chinese come out with bamboo steamers, not tall, handsome Americans. Certainly, times had changed. It was a moment in Haier history: Haier, from Red China, had made a home at the center of Western capitalism.

Michael Jemal, President and CEO of Haier America, made it official at the reception when he said, "Welcome to Haier's new home."

By the podium, Jemal, whose family was also present, was talking quietly to a happy Zhang Ruimin, Chairman and CEO of the Haier Group, headquartered in China's eastern port city of Qingdao.

Zhang had made the trip to New York with sixty other people from Qingdao, a city of over 6.8 million population, and around the world—Haier Europe, Haier Middle East, and Haier Southeast. He would reward Haier overseas distributors and sales managers for the team spirit that had made Haier a success around the globe.

The dignitaries from Haier Qingdao included Zhang, Wu Kesong, Vice Chairman of the Haier Group, and Chai Yongsen, Executive Vice President of the Haier Group. Frans Jamry, President and CEO of Haier Europe, also joined Zhang and others in the ribbon-cutting that opened the celebration.

Among the distinguished guests were China's Ambassador to the United Nations, Wang Yingfan, and the Chinese Consul General to New York, Zhang Hongxi, both of whom were proud of having a Chinese company like Haier selling its own brand name products in America.

Kevin Alexander, VP of Global Sourcing for Wal-Mart Corp., was pleased to meet Zhang Ruimin and shared his joy at Haier's growth in the U.S. market. Wal-Mart now carries an array of Haier products, ranging from refrigerators, wine cellars and freezers to air conditioners and washing machines. Other guests included NATM buying-group Executive Director Bill Trawick and representatives of the member dealers ABC Warehouse and Nebraska Furniture Mart.

Professor N. T. Wang of Columbia University was one of the guests from academia. A Ph.D. from Harvard, Professor Wang's teaching and research interests are in international business, economic development and multinational corporations. He is currently the director of the China-International Business Project at Columbia University and a Fellow of the International Academy of Management. Previously, he had served with the United Nations as Director of Information in the Analysis Division of the United Nations Center on Transnational Corporations and as head of technical assistance on missions to developing countries. He has been an honorary or visiting professor at universities in mainland China, Taiwan and Hong Kong. A recipient of the New York Governor's Outstanding Asian American Award, he has published a number of books on Chinese business. In April 2001, he invited Zhang Ruimin to Columbia to talk about Chinese business and his company.

Dr. Marshall Meyer of the Wharton School at the University of Pennsylvania was also present. A professor of management and sociology who is also an ambitious researcher into the nature of state-owned companies in China, Dr. Meyer had been to China numerous times and had talked to senior Chinese managers at more than twenty firms. When Zhang Ruimin delivered a speech at Wharton in April 2001, Dr. Meyer was drawn to both Zhang and Haier, which led him to make another tour of China. In July 2001, he went to Haier headquarters in Qingdao, where he stayed for three days, to see the company for himself, and had talks with Zhang and with Yang Mianmian, President of the Haier Group, about Haier's organizational structure.

The grand opening was the second time we were meeting Zhang, the first having been in late December of 2001 at Haier headquarters when we flew from New York to Qingdao for an interview with him and President Yang Mianmian. At the opening, Zhang was more exuberant and radiant, and we talked in a more leisurely manner after all the hubbub was over. Our conversation began, naturally, with the building.

We asked him how he would compare this New York landmark building with the Haier headquarters building in Qingdao. Zhang was quick to point out that both buildings have square structures and round pillars, which underlines the Haier concept of "thinking squarely, acting smoothly."

Eighteen years of "thinking squarely, acting smoothly" had resulted in securing this outstanding opportunity for a visionary new owner. The new location at 1356 Broadway offered the Chinese appliance giant the opportunity to boost dramatically its image and exposure.

Haier embraced the opportunity, and made the building a highly visible flagship showplace and a key component of the company's success. It would have been understandable if Zhang had allowed his happiness to show, but he was surprisingly calm and low key. When asked what was on his mind at such a moment, he spoke in his usual slow and pronounced tone.

"Of course, tonight is a milestone in Haier's overseas expansion, but Haier people do not have the habit of gloating over our footprints, even though they were beautiful or even splendid. They belong to the past. Now we have achieved another goal. For years, we have maintained this mentality of constantly bettering ourselves by jumping at every opportunity offered us. Otherwise, it wouldn't have been possible for us to stand in this building tonight."

That is probably an honest assessment. Maybe they do not even have time to look back at those footprints. Since 1999, Haier's globalization engine has been running at high speed, and the momentum they've gained will not allow them to slow down even a little. In late 1998, based on demographics, geopolitics and economics, Zhang divided his world map into ten targeted markets: Southeast Asia, South Asia, North America, Central America, the European Union, the Middle East, the Confederation of Independent Countries, the South African countries, the North African countries, and East Asia (including China and Japan). He envisioned having a head office in each of the ten markets to coordinate localized design, production and distribution in the area. By the end of 2001, Haier had basically completed its global expansion plan in the targeted markets, with two industrial parks (one in the United States and another in Pakistan), thirteen factories, eight design centers and fifty-six trading companies.

Early on opening day, Zhang presided over the second annual conference of Haier overseas distributors/managers, held at the Hyatt Hotel in New York (the first had taken place a year earlier in Qingdao). More than sixty representatives of Haier's overseas distributors/managers from Asia, Europe, the Middle East and North and Central Americas met and compared notes about selling Haier products to customers of different nationalities and cultures. Attending the grand opening in the evening was not the last event for them, for the next day they were going to fly to South Carolina to visit the Haier Camden manufacturing facility there.

"We cannot stop. We must keep going," said Zhang. "No matter how grandly and solidly we have built, we cannot stop to turn around and take another look at the path we have traveled. We must keep moving forward. There's still a lot to be done."

While most people were watching the performance of the Chinese acrobats, we found a chance to talk to Chai Yongsen, the Haier Group's Executive Vice President in charge of Overseas Operations. In the Haier hierarchy, that is the third most important executive position, next to Zhang, the CEO, and Yang, the President. We had missed the chance to meet him the last time in Qingdao, but he told us that he knew that we had been there. His business card was bilingual, with the Chinese version listing two of his positions:

Executive Vice President of the Haier Group and Head of the Overseas Promotion Division, while the English version simply gave the first title. We asked him some questions about Haier's overseas operations and got short, but to-the-point, answers. A quiet, down-to-earth man was our impression of this potentially even more powerful Haier executive.

We made our rounds of the showrooms located along the sides of the building, divided by categories. The products that commanded the most space were refrigerators and wine cellars, followed by home-comfort products (air conditioners and dehumidifiers), laundry products, electronics and small appliances such as microwave ovens, convection ovens, irons and toasters. Except for some large-size and compact refrigerators that had been manufactured in Camden, South Carolina, most of these stylish, quality products were made in China and shipped across the oceans.

Michael Jemal told us that this array of Haier products was sold nationwide in America in most major chains, such as Wal-Mart, Lowe's, Best Buy, Home Depot, Office Depot, Target, Fortunoff, Menards, Bed Bath & Beyond, BJ's, Fry's, ABC, and BrandsMart. He expected the list to continue to grow.

That evening, Jemal was the star who was too busy for us to land even a five minute interview, but he agreed to set aside two hours for us to do a lengthy one, which later became three long interviews, an exchange of email and telephone conversations, most of which we have incorporated into this book.

Three months after the gala party at the Haier Building, we learned that the Real Estate Board of New York's award for the Most Creative Retail Deal of the Year 2001 had been given to the three executives at Insignia/ESG who had brokered the sale of 1356 Broadway from Himmel & Meringoff to Haier America. The sale showed how an eighty-year-old, Greek-revival, landmark bank could be transformed into a flagship for the sale of high-quality home appliances, as well as corporate headquarters for a Chinese manufacturer.

2

A Brand Is Born:
The Sledgehammer and Beyond

People in China first learned about Haier in 1985, when the company received national media attention over the destruction of inferior-quality refrigerators—seventy-six in total—at a time when refrigerators were in high demand, and were sold at prices higher than today's. That event put Haier into the national spotlight, and their moves were closely monitored thereafter by both the Chinese business world and consumers.

In the years to come, along with quality products, came quality people. In turn, the quality people produced quality products. By 1998, Haier had surged far ahead of its competitors in almost all home appliance sectors, from refrigerators and air conditioners to washers and dryers. Their products were sold in all major cities in China and abroad, and were preferred by consumers because of their excellent quality and the superb service, both before and after sale. Their major products—refrigerators, freezers, air conditioners and washing machines—have taken over about thirty percent of the Chinese market. Their revenues have been increasing by an average of seventy-eight percent for seventeen consecutive years.

Haier had its origin in 1955, when a group of people formed a handicraft-producers' cooperative, a collective enterprise according to the Chinese industrial classification. A collective enterprise differs from a state-run enterprise in that the assets and profits of the former are owned by all the members of the company, while the assets and profits of the latter are owned by the state. Before the Chinese government initiated private ownership in the 1980s, there had been only two types of business ownership in China: state enterprises and collective enterprises. A collective enterprise was regarded as inferior to a state enterprise in size, cash reserves and social prestige.

In 1990, there were about 500,000 such collectives in China, which employed a workforce of over thirty million people.

In 1958, the handicraft-producers' cooperative changed its name to "Qingdao Electric Machinery Factory," and began to make motors, fans and other electric products. During the Cultural Revolution (1966-76), the name was changed to "East Wind Electric Machinery Factory." In 1979, the company merged with a small machinery factory, was renamed "Qingdao Home Appliance Factory" and began to turn out no-frills washing machines in the same year.

From 1979 to 1983, the factory produced about 58,000 washing machines under the White Heron brand, but, because of their poor quality and unattractive appearance, the machines did not sell well. In January 1984, the company started making refrigerators, and its name was changed to "Qingdao General Refrigerator Factory."

But things did not improve much. By the end of 1984, the company had incurred a debt of 1.47 million RMB, and was on the verge of bankruptcy. In December 1984, Zhang Ruimin was appointed director of the Qingdao General Refrigerator Factory. He decided to leave the unprofitable washing machine market altogether, and focus exclusively on the more promising refrigerator market.

Under Zhang's directorship, the company's fortunes changed. In 1991, it merged with the Qingdao Freezer Factory and the Qingdao Air Conditioner Factory to form the Haier Group, which later, through a number of mergers and acquisitions, became the largest household appliance maker in China.

At the heart of Haier's history, according to Zhang Ruimin, is creativity—the ability to think outside the box—but behind its success lies a strong brand name supported by quality products and unrivalled services.

"We had a three-step goal, each step taking about seven years," said Zhang in April 2001, at the Wharton School of the University of Pennsylvania, one of the most prestigious business institutes in the United States. He was addressing a group at the East-West Dialogue of the Wharton Global Chinese Business Initiative. "The first was to establish a brand name. It was something new in China to have quality design in appliances. In 1984, there were three hundred refrigerator factories, most of them making poor products. We wanted to distinguish ourselves, and eventually we did."

Shortly after taking over the Qingdao General Refrigerator Factory, Zhang became aware that Chinese consumers would not be satisfied with the poor-quality products his company was making. With domestic and foreign competitors looming large, if the company did not have quality products, it would be doomed to lose its market share, and eventually be driven out of business.

The problem at the time was that workers in his company, like many elsewhere, did not share his view about quality products, and were resistant to rules and regulations that aimed at implementing change. Zhang had to be resolute in his determination. In the spring of 1985, his chance came.

One day in April, a consumer sent a letter to the factory complaining about the defects of the refrigerator he had bought: it wouldn't chill his food. Zhang decided to check the matter out. He went to the warehouse and found seventy-six defective "Auspicious Snow" refrigerators produced by the factory.

Past practice would have been either to give the defective refrigerators to employees who had made special contributions to the factory, as a reward, or to use them as "sweeteners" to open the doors of some important people in the network, such as officials of the Bureau of Commerce or the Energy and Water Department. But Zhang made a different decision this time: to destroy the poor-quality refrigerators so that factory employees would learn a lesson about quality.

He called a meeting of the eight hundred employees and lined up the seventy-six defective refrigerators. After the defects were pointed out and acknowledged, he asked the ones responsible for the defects to come forward. Saying that defective products are junk products, he ordered the employees to smash the refrigerators with a sledgehammer.

The workers were shocked by Zhang's demand, and nobody followed his order. Zhang raised the sledgehammer and swung the first blow.

During our visit to Haier in December 2001, we asked our guide, Mr. Xie Jingchang, a senior staff member of Haier's Enterprise Culture Center in charge of lecturing on the company's history, if he had been present when Zhang gave the order to smash the defective refrigerators. He said that not only had he been present, but that he remembered the day very well.

What he had experienced that day was as disturbing and exciting as it was for anyone else who witnessed the event.

"I remember that day as if it were only yesterday." Mr. Xie looked at the photo of the large sledgehammer, wrapped gracefully in a red ribbon, which we had taken at the Haier Museum of Science and Technology the day before and had developed in a one-hour photo shop. Seeing is believing. The sledgehammer was certainly large and heavy enough to destroy a refrigerator.

"That was April of 1985. I had been transferred from the countryside back to the city in 1980, after being a peasant for over a dozen years. For five years, I had worked in the factory, and we produced only single-tank washers. We were doing terribly, and the factory could hardly pay our salaries. In January 1984, the factory changed its name to 'Qingdao General Refrigerator Factory,' and we changed our product line, as well, to refrigerators. That year, we changed directors three times. Each director left after a couple of months. They didn't believe this factory had any hope.

"You may not know that the factory was very old, and the doors and windows were broken. People had taken down the window-frames and wooden doors to make fires on winter days, and most of us had nothing to do in the summer but wander to the nearby mortuary to watch dead bodies being cremated."

The day before, we had gone to the old Haier plant, the "Qingdao General Refrigerator Factory," to take a look. It was quite small, jammed into an ordinary, crowded Chinese alley, and the roof-tiles were half-gone. We had learned that the workers had been so undisciplined that they frequently urinated on the floor. That is why one of the first factory rules Zhang made was "Do not pee on the workshop floor."

It is hard for today's young people, sitting in the factory shuttle-bus, going from one stop to another, to imagine the situation at that time. Today's Haier Industrial Park is more like the Harvard Yard. But we can imagine it. We had family members working in factories like that—old machinery, out-of-date equipment, poor management and inadequately trained workers.

Such was the case everywhere in China, from Qingdao to Beijing and Shanghai. Nothing was unusual. We had worked in such factories in our home towns. Before going to university in 1978, Shawn had worked as a drilling-machine operator in a switch factory in Hangzhou, Zhejiang Province, where working conditions were not much better than in Zhang's refrigerator factory.

"The factory was doing very poorly," said Mr. Xie. "In 1984, even after three leaders, the factory was going from bad to worse, until it was 1.47 million in debt. And our assets were less than our debts. There was nothing to do but knit or gossip. There was no money to be paid to the workers, and the factory had been borrowing money from nearby villages that had become better off during the early open-door years.

"After Zhang was transferred by the Qingdao Municipal Government's Household Appliance Division to become the director of our factory, part of his job was also to borrow money from the peasants. Another part of his job was to turn the business around. He decided he would have to change the way the factory was functioning."

The situation was a bit like that at Chrysler in the late 1970s, when Lee Iacocca, the world's greatest business-turn-around specialist who had rescued Chrysler, took the job of CEO. His first reaction to the automobile manufacturing plant was that it was a sinking ship, and the first thing he decided to do was set up rules and regulations. The similarity between Iacocca and Zhang was apparent: both were boarding sinking ships, and both needed to save the ship in order to save themselves.

In his autobiography, Iacocca recalled his first day in office. "On November 2, 1978, the *Detroit Free Press* had two headlines: 'Chrysler Losses Are Worst Ever,' and 'Lee Iacocca Joins Chrysler.' Great timing! The day I came aboard, the company announced a third-quarter loss of almost $160 million, the worst deficit in its history. 'Oh, Well,' I thought, 'from here things can only get better.'" (Iacocca 1984, 151)

Zhang faced a similar situation. By the time he was sent to the factory, three directors had tried and left, and the factory was suffering the greatest losses in its history. Both Iacocca and Zhang did two things: they set up regulations and enforced discipline. "Right away, I knew the place was in a state of anarchy. Chrysler needed a dose of order and discipline—and quick." (Ibid., 152)

For the next year, what Iacocca went through mirrored what Zhang would have to go through in order to rescue and turn around the business of the factory. This included raising the quality of the employees, raising the consciousness of the employees and improving understanding and cooperation between departments, because every member of the team had to understand what his job was and exactly how it fitted in with every other job.

If the Chrysler workers' main problem was lack of discipline and order, the workers at Qingdao General Refrigerator Factory, besides the above two problems, had no incentive at all to work harder and do better. This problem was worse because it was an inherited problem that came along with the experience of the Communist system over the previous thirty-some years.

"Zhang saw two bad things that had been hampering the factory: inferior-quality products and too large an inventory. You may not know that the way of the government in factories was to have reservoirs," Xie continued. "Reservoirs hold a lot of inventory, in the hope that, someday, someone will want it.

"In those days, there was no competition, and there was no issue of demand and supply. The refrigerators stood in a line in a department store. If a customer could afford one, then he'd take one home. At that time, Chinese products were categorized into three grades: top grade, second grade and third grade. No matter what, these products would be shipped out of the factory and sold in the department stores. Zhang said that our idea was to have a river, with goods flowing out, and very little inventory. "

But in order to get his river, Zhang had to find funding outside the traditional government system. And in order to get that funding, he would have to prove that his factory could sell refrigerators, not one or two in a day, but hundreds.

The only way he could make that happen was to start making better refrigerators. As the deputy manager in charge of quality control at his old job in the Municipal Home Appliances Division, Zhang was very sensitive to the harm done by a poor product: there were no places or spare parts to repair it. Combining high quality and customer service was the main priority in order for the factory to get out of debt. But there seemed to be little incentive on the part of his workers to do so, because they were accustomed to doing otherwise.

We continued our conversation with Xie, and asked if he had been shocked by Zhang's order to smash the products of the company.

"Of course, I was; my mouth hung open! Then tears started to run down my cheeks, too." Xie pondered. "Each refrigerator was worth 1,000 RMB, more than my salary for two whole years. Some older workers began to beg Zhang to stop. Seventy-six refrigerators would be enough money to pay the workers three months' salary.

"I also begged to take one of them home, and the factory could deduct the money from my monthly salary. But Zhang insisted. He said this was the only way we could take the lesson to heart and get better."

Afterward, Zhang and Deputy Director and Chief Engineer Yang Mianmian, today President of the Haier Group, whom Zhang had brought along from the municipal government to the Qingdao General Refrigerator Factory in 1984, blamed themselves, in front of the workers, and shouldered the responsibility. They said that there were irresponsible employees because there were irresponsible leaders like them, for which both Zhang and Yang Mianmian asked to be fined three months salaries. Then the employees understood Zhang's intention: without responsible leaders, there would be no responsible employees, and no quality products.

Mr. Xie showed us a tape of that dramatic scene. On the screen, we saw a worker swing the huge sledgehammer, striking a refrigerator again and again. Tears fell from his eyes, and from the eyes of other workers standing by.

The news got to the national level that night through the media. Some people, including some of Zhang's bosses, were very unhappy about Zhang. Some people cursed him for "wasting the government's money."

Zhang stood his ground. After this incident, Zhang also fired a worker found stealing for a second time after being warned previously, another unprecedented move. Zhang's purpose was to warn the others—he meant business, and he was serious about doing things differently.

When the dust from smashing refrigerators had settled, Zhang hedged his bets with a joint venture with the German appliance maker Liebherr Group to produce quality refrigerators.

Established in 1949 and headquartered in Strasse, Germany, Liebherr is a group of companies with operations in Europe, America, Asia, Africa and Australia. The company's 2001 sales were 4.13 billion Euro, and the number of employees by the end of 2001 was 20,600.

Liebherr technology is firmly established in the fields of building construction and civil engineering, though it also offers comprehensive product lines in a number of other areas, such as shipping, container and cargo board cranes for freight handling, machine tools, material flow, handling and assembly systems and aerospace and transport technologies. In addition, Liebherr has a range of refrigerators, freezers and wine cellars for household use.

A common feature of the Liebherr refrigeration products is their low specific energy consumption, with about half of their models having the A-rating that puts them in the top class for energy efficiency. A further forty percent or so belongs to efficiency-class B. (According to official German standards, decreasing efficiency is valued in ratings from A to G.)

We asked Xie why Haier hadn't formed a joint venture with the Japanese. At that time, in 1984 and 1985, Japanese products were quite hot on the Chinese market, and a Japanese refrigerator product line was introduced into China.

"Qingdao had a stronger relationship with Germany, and we had always thought the Germans had better workmanship. Look at their cars," Mr. Xie explained.

"As you may know, Qingdao was under German occupation between 1897 and 1914. Between 1914 and 1922, Qingdao was under Japanese control. Germany was superior in manufacturing. They've made Mercedes and BMWs. So Haier formed a joint venture with the Germans to learn their technology. Now *we* export to *them*." Mr. Xie sounded proud.

But at that time, it was not easy for the company, a small collective enterprise, to get funding for such a joint-venture program. The first thing that Zhang needed to do was get his application for foreign currency approved by government agencies at several levels.

One story had Zhang and his colleagues standing outside in the snow, waiting earnestly, because an official in a Beijing Government office had told them to do so—the guy simply didn't want to do anything for the factory, and was annoyed at being asked. A few hours later, when he happened to look out and see the factory people standing in the snow, waiting for his response, the man was moved. He signed the authorization for the factory to apply for a certain amount of foreign currency to set up a joint venture with Liebherr.

Quality, Quality, Quality
In order to build a brand, for seven years, from 1984 to 1991, Zhang concentrated on just one product—refrigerators. He set higher standards for the company than were required by the industry. For example, the required standard for scratch-visibility on the surface of a refrigerator was 1.5 meters, but Haier's standard became 0.5 meter. While the industry noise tolerance was 52 dB, Haier's was 50 dB.

Zhang was constantly preaching to his employees the idea that it is the company's objective and responsibility to make perfect products in the first place, with "zero tolerance of error" in mind. While most companies concentrated on an "after production" check in their quality control, Haier focused almost exclusively on "during production" processes.

To implement his "zero tolerance of error" concept, Zhang used the Six Sigma methodology he had learned from his U.S. counterparts.

Six Sigma is a data-driven management system aiming at near-perfect performance. The lower-case form of the Greek letter "sigma" (σ) stands for the standard deviation from the mean of a statistical sample. The Six Sigma concept was developed at Motorola in the 1980s and made famous by GE's CEO Jack Welch. To achieve Six Sigma, a process must produce not more than 3.4 defects per million opportunities. A Six Sigma probability is then a very low probability of defect.

Zhang's primary purpose in using the Six Sigma approach was to instill in his employees' minds a consensus about the importance of product quality, which would pave the way for building a brand name for the Haier products.

In 1985, Haier put onto the market its first generation of refrigerators, the Qindao-Liebherr Refrigerator, which swept China's market with its four-star quality. The following year, China's refrigerator market exploded with phenomenal demand and soaring prices. All other refrigerator makers were churning out their products like short-order cooks turning out hotcakes. Department store buyers lined up before refrigerator makers with cash or checks in their hands, and any refrigerator was bought and shipped off the moment it came off the production line.

Faced with such exploding demand, Haier stayed cool. Zhang knew that Haier was not ready for mass production because of its inadequate equipment, management and technology. If they made too much too fast, their product quality would suffer, and their reputation would be tarnished. Zhang decided to shy away from the market frenzy and stay with his brand name building.

Zhang's goal was to win the gold medal at China's national refrigerator quality competition, the highest level of refrigerator-quality certification in China, and the most authoritative.

In 1988, Haier won that honor with its Qindao-Liebherr refrigerator, defeating more than one hundred competitors. Zhang had reached his first goal.

By 1990, Haier had won a number of top domestic product-quality awards and certifications for its refrigerators, and firmly established its Qindao-Liebherr refrigerator as a strong brand name in China.

Since 1991, Haier has diversified its product lines to include washing machines, freezers, air conditioners, microwave ovens, TVs, computers and even mobile phones. They are all produced under the "Haier" brand, and recognized by Chinese consumers as quality products, like their refrigerator cousin.

The Story of Wei Xiaoer
In August 1997, thirty-three-year-old Wei Xiaoer was sent to Japan to study bathroom-equipment technology. During her stay, she found that the Japanese had a thirty to sixty percent rejection rate among their products in the mold-testing period, and a two percent rejection rate in the normal production period.

"Why can't you raise your pass rate to one hundred percent?" she asked.

"One hundred percent?" The Japanese mold designer was surprised. "Do you think that is possible?"

During the conversation, Wei realized that the Japanese had a serious misconception about quality control. They were trying to minimize the rejection rate, while Wei's goal was to reach perfection. She was determined to do better than the Japanese.

Sixth months after she got back to China, Wei received her Japanese "teacher" in Qingdao. She had by then been made Director of Haier's Bathroom Equipment Factory. Looking at the clean-as-a-mirror production site and one-hundred-percent pass rate, the Japanese mold designer was very impressed.

"Our production site has always been dirty and untidy. We have been trying very hard to solve the problem, but with no success. How did you do that? In addition, it is only natural for us to have a two-percent rejection rate and five-percent substandard products. We have never imagined a one-hundred-percent pass rate. How did you attain all this?" the Japanese asked with sincere admiration.

"With heart," was Wei's simple answer, which surprised her Japanese "teacher" even more. The answer sounded simple, but, for Wei, it had meant a long journey.

When she had come back from Japan, Wei had worked hard toward the one-hundred-percent pass rate for her products. From time to time, she had been troubled by a few tiny spots on the surfaces of the products they were producing. She had looked into the problem and decided that the spotting was caused by waste coming off the production line.

It took her some time to find a way to solve the problem. One night, she happened to watch her daughter sharpen a pencil with a pencil-sharpener. The lead powder that came off the sharpener all dropped into a small box, where it was contained. Wei suddenly was inspired, and, quickly, she began to draw some designs. What came out the next day was a box used specifically to catch production waste. All the waste from the production line dropped automatically into this waste box, keeping the workplace clean and tidy. Never again were there black spots on product surfaces.

On another occasion, Wei chanced to see a piece of hair on the raw material to be used for the mold-testing the next day. Alert to the possibility that hair like this might cause quality problems, she required that all operators wear white uniforms and keep their hair tucked up under caps.

With such strong awareness of quality, Wei was able to achieve a one-hundred-percent pass rate for all the products made in her factory, during both the mold-testing period and the normal production period.

From Liebherr to Haier

When the Qingdao General Refrigerator Factory, the predecessor of the Haier Group, signed the joint-venture contract with the German Liebherr company in 1985, the contract terms specified that the trademark for the product must be Liebherr. But the German company allowed its Chinese partner to use "Qindao," an older name for Qingdao, to indicate its Chinese location. In Chinese, "Qindao" means "zither island," because the shape of the island looks like a zither, while "Qingdao" means "green island." Therefore, the earlier products of the joint venture had "Qindao-Liebherr" as their brand. The German name in the brand certainly helped boost the image of the product at a time when Chinese consumers believed that a foreign brand carried a lot of prestige.

The joint-venture contract also specified that, beginning in 1992, the brand name could be changed to "Qindao Haier." In December 1991, Qingdao General Refrigerator Factory merged with a freezer company and an air conditioner company to form the "Qingdao Qindao Haier Group," in order to match more closely the brand name "Qindao Haier."

"Haier" is a variation of the second part of the German word "Liebherr," both in spelling and pronunciation. In Chinese, it means "sea." Coincidentally, the Chinese pronunciation of Haier is also a pun on the Haier logo, which is composed of two children, one Chinese boy and one Western boy. In Chinese, "child" is pronounced *"hai er."*

In December 1992, Zhang and other company leaders decided to change the company name to "Haier Group," in order that it be simpler and more user-friendly on the one hand, and to complete the process of the company's independence as a major Chinese appliance maker, on the other. Accordingly, the brand name was changed to "Haier," which they believed was a very good name for both Chinese and international customers, with the implication of Haier products flying "higher and higher."

This three-stage name change reflects the predicament as well as the smart strategy of the Chinese company in its brand-making. By entering into a joint venture, Zhang was "borrowing somebody else's hen to lay eggs for him," so to speak. He had to do that in order to build up his company's image and win the confidence of his customers.

David Baldacci, a descendent of Italian immigrants to the United States, and author of the best-selling novel, *Absolute Power*, once told a very interesting story about how his novels got to be translated and published in Italy. Shortly after his novel had hit the *New York Times* bestseller list, he was approached by an Italian publisher who was interested in translating and publishing his novel in Italy. But the publisher told him that, if he wanted to sell his Italian version in quantity, he must change his last name to something "American," because readers in Italy would not be crazy about a translated book with an author who had an Italian last name. Poor David thought for a moment and decided to change his last name to "Ford." The publisher was right, and *Absolute Power* by David Ford sold like hotcakes in Italy.

For the second novel in Italian translation, David Ford talked the publisher into agreeing to add his last name, "Baldacci," as a middle name. That book, by David Baldacci Ford, also sold very well because readers understood that he was the author of *Absolute Power*.

Starting with the third book, Mr. Baldacci insisted on dropping "Ford" and his name has been David Baldacci in Italy ever since.

Just as David Baldacci has had nothing to do with "Ford" since the third book, Haier has had nothing to do with "Liebherr" since the name change.

Haier-Merloni Joint Venture
In order to prepare themselves to enter international markets, Haier had, over time, obtained or passed some crucial European and American certifications for its products, which included the UL certification in the United States, EEV and CSA in Canada, VDE,

GS and TUV in Germany, and the International ISO 9001, among others.

In April 1993, Haier signed a joint venture contract with the Italian company Merloni Elettrodomestici, the third largest appliance maker in Europe, to form "Haier-Merloni Washing Machine (Qingdao) Ltd.," which would primarily manufacture front-loading washing machines for the Chinese market. The registered capital for the whole joint venture was 24 million U.S. dollars. Haier invested 39,840,000 RMB (4.8 million U.S. dollars) and held twenty percent of the stock in the joint venture. A year later, the joint venture turned out its first Margherita model washing machine, which ranked among the top ten washing machines for 1995.

Merloni Elettrodomestici had its origin in 1930, when Aristide Merloni founded Industrie Merloni in Albacina, a small village within the municipality of Fabriano in central Italy. The family-owned business was initially focused on weighing scales, and subsequently diversified into liquid-gas cylinders and hot-water heaters. In 1960, the "Ariston" brand was created, and the company began to produce consumer goods, such as cook-stoves.

In 1975, from the Household Appliance Division of Industrie Merloni grew what is today a multinational in the household appliance industry, "Merloni Elettrodomestici." The company has since been headed by Vittorio Merloni, the son of Aristide Merloni.

The new company produced a complete range of appliances under the Ariston brand, and soon became a market leader in Italy. In the 1980s, Merloni Elettrodomestici widened its product lines and developed a network of subsidiaries throughout Europe. It grabbed important market shares in France and Great Britain, and established itself in other principal markets.

In 1987, the company went public, and its shares were traded on the Milan Stock Exchange. In the same year, it acquired Indesit, a well-known European brand, and two years later, Scholtes, a French brand. As part of an effort toward product personalization, "Margherita" is the first washing machine model with the name of a woman.

Since the 1990s, the company has adopted a multi-brand strategy throughout Europe. As one of the main European appliance producers, it produced millions of household appliances in many European countries.

In 1997, the process of establishing a new management structure was completed. Andrea Guerra was nominated as the Chief Executive Officer of the company, the first ever from outside the Merloni family. At the end of 1999, Merloni Elettrodomestici became the first in the world to launch digital appliances onto the market that were capable of connecting to the Internet.

After the acquisition of Stinol in 2000, which enabled Merloni to achieve leadership in the former Soviet Union countries, the company made its fourteenth acquisition at the end of 2001, taking over from Marconi fifty percent of GDA (Hotpoint), the largest domestic appliances manufacturer in Great Britain. With this act, Merloni Elettrodomestici assumed third position in Europe, holding a fourteen-percent market share. In 2001, the company's revenues were 1.97 billion Euro, with an operating profit of 139 million Euro and a net profit of 74 million Euro. The company now has twenty-one subsidiaries around the world and employs about 20,000 people.

Merloni's joint venture with Haier not only enabled Haier to absorb another advanced European technology, in addition to that of the German Liebherr, but also strengthened Haier's position on its road to diversification. The washing machine experience was helpful to Haier in later mergers and acquisitions, especially in the case of acquiring the Red Star Electric Appliance Company in 1995. The Haier-Merloni cooperation went quite smoothly, and, in September 1998, both parties agreed to invest more money to make top-loading washing machines.

Sincere and Forever
One of the major means of domestic promotion for Haier is television advertising. Haier has spent millions to purchase the best time slots on major Chinese TV channels, such as China Central TV, where Haier bought slots right before and after the evening news. Even after more than eighteen years, Chinese viewers still remember quite well Haier's early, engaging TV ads, with the two little Haier brothers calling to each other about the value of their Qindao-Liebherr refrigerators, inspiring the viewer to buy.

Haier's goal was to produce a kind of Pavlovian response to their products: the moment you think of Haier, you picture quality products which you can trust and want to buy, much the same way people think of Sony or GE.

One of the ways to achieve that goal was to use the attractive slogan or tag line "Sincere and Forever" to go with the advertisements. For Zhang, it is more important to build emotional bonds in advertising than to make physical claims for certain products.

"When customers buy Haier products, what do they care more for?" he asked. "Not a particular washing machine, but appropriately clean clothes; not a particular refrigerator, but fresh food. That is to say, they are not buying physical products, but the functions of those products. Therefore, their demand is endless. We have to meet such insatiable demands, and that is why we promote our 'Sincere and Forever' motto to our customers."

One of the new brand concepts in recent years is to expand brand relevance and brand resonance, which are two measures of brand strength that are much more valuable than mere brand awareness can ever be. In *A New Brand World*, Scott Bedbury points out: "One of the most rewarding strategies in achieving this goal has been mass customization, the process of creating a broader array of 'niche' products that emanate from [the] central brand position like spokes on a wheel."

According to Philip Kotler in his *Marketing Management*, there are four strategies companies can use in branding their products: individual names, as followed by General Mills for its "Bisquick," "Gold Medal," "Betty Crocker" etc.; blanket family names, as adopted by Heinz and General Electric; separate family names for all products, as in the case of Sears ("Kenmore" for appliances, "Craftsman" for tools, and "Homart" for major home installations); and a company trade-name combined with individual product names, as practiced by Kellogg ("Kellogg's Rice Krispies," "Kellogg's Raisin Bran," and "Kellogg's Corn Flakes"). (Kotler 2000, 412-13)

Like Heinz and GE, Haier adopted blanket family names under the Haier umbrella. Since Haier already had a very good reputation for its refrigerators, adopting this strategy had the advantage of easy brand-recognition for its new products, reducing or eliminating the need for heavy advertising expenditures.

Zhang has a very simple, but vivid, explanation of what a brand name is: "A brand name is what I can sell while others cannot; it is what I can sell more of while others sell less; and it is what I can sell at a premium while others sell at a discount."

After years of tireless effort, Haier has made tremendous accomplishment in its brand building. In the annual "Most Valued Chinese Brands" survey conducted by the Beijing Brand Evaluation Corp., the Haier brand was estimated to be worth 43.6 billion RMB in 2001, the number one brand in China's appliance industry and the second national brand, after Red Pagoda Mountain (*Hongtashan*) cigarettes, which was valued at 46 billion RMB. The third national brand was Changhong TV, with a value of 26.1 billion RMB.

In a June 2002 poll on the top ten brand names (both Chinese and foreign), conducted by the Red Pagoda Mountain Group and the *Beijing Youth* newspaper, the top three were Haier, Coca-Cola, and Red Pagoda Mountain, followed by Legend (Chinese computers), Wuliangye (Chinese liquor), Nokia, Changhong (Chinese TV), McDonald's, Tongrentang (Chinese traditional medicines), and Erduosi (Chinese cashmere clothes). Polled were over 5,000 people across China's major cities, with 61.4% of the participants aged between twenty and twenty-nine.

In December 2002, the annual "Most Valued Chinese Brands" survey announced that the Haier brand in 2002 was valued at 48.9 billion RMB, the number one national brand in China. Red Pagoda Mountain (*Hongtashan*), which had been the number one national brand for seven consecutive years since 1995, slid into a number two position, with the same 2001 value of 46 billion RMB. Changhong TV remained the third in the race, with a slightly increased value of 26.6 billion RMB.

3

Taylor Would Admire It:
The OEC Management Model

In Communist China there has been a tradition of learning from good examples. During the Cultural Revolution, Mao called on all Chinese workers to learn from Daqing, an oil field in the northeast of China that exemplified Mao's ideal of self-reliance; he called on all the peasants to learn from Dazhai, a small production brigade in the mountainous area of Shanxi Province that distinguished itself by turning barren mountains into crop fields; and he called on the whole nation to learn from the People's Liberation Army (PLA) for being loyal to him and the Communist Party. Hundreds of millions of people from across the country visited Daqing and Dazhai and various PLA barracks, hoping to turn their experiences into successes of their own. Though nobody is learning from these three models anymore, the idea and practice of learning from someone or something good have not died out entirely. With Haier in the national limelight and being recognized as a model enterprise in China, people visit the company in droves, every year, especially from the manufacturing sector.

Since 1996, about 20,000 people per month have visited the Haier Group facilities. They have found that Haier has a management model called OEC, which has been crucial to Haier's success, and which basically says that each employee should finish the assignment of the day, and add a little more to what has been done the previous day.

That did not seem very difficult to do and many visitors wanted to try it, too. There have been many who have walked away with Haier's OEC model written on a piece of paper or in notebooks. They have tried it in their own companies, but almost all have ended by giving up, complaining that their employees found it too hard to go by the strict rules and regulations, not to mention the tedious procedures the employees are required to perform every day. Some companies have tried for only a few weeks before giving up, the longest lasting for a few months.

Soon, there was a general consensus that Haier and the OEC model were inimitable.

Maybe these people were right, because Rome was not built in a day. One thing Haier and its CEO Zhang Ruimin are proud of is Haier's corporate or enterprise culture, which is behind the company's OEC model. It is that part of Haier's management that is not easily learned or imitated.

What is the OEC model, anyway?

By Haier's definition, "O" stands for "Overall," "E" stands for "Everyone," "Everything" and "Every Day," and "C" stands for "Control" and "Clear." OEC management aims at overall control of everything that every employee does every day. The basic requirement is that every employee finish his or her assignment every day, with a little increase (1%) over what was done the previous day.

OEC management is composed of three parts: target, control system and incentive mechanism.

Target:
1. Each assignment or job is specific and measurable. For instance, for a refrigerator quality check, Haier divided the 156 procedures into 545 items, including checking each screw on the door-handle.
2. Each job is assigned to a particular employee, with a clear understanding of the job's item manager, the targeted employee, the targeted employee's partner, and the quality-check person. Its purpose is to assign to every job a person responsible for it. For example, if there are 1964 pieces of glass in a warehouse, each piece is associated with the name of an employee who is supposed to be responsible for taking care of it.

Control:
This is a two-fold process. First, "Get today's things done today." Employees are not supposed to postpone jobs or assignments till

the next day. Secondly, "Higher than yesterday," which means constantly improving on-the-job efficiency. Employees are supposed to increase their job efficiency by one percent each day. After seventy days, they can double their job efficiency.

There are two ways to conduct the control process: self-check by each employee on a daily basis and a check by management on a regular or spot-check basis. In the latter case, managers not only check their own areas of responsibility, but also the work of those employees reporting directly to them.

The key to the control system is the recheck or follow-up check. An assignment is not completed if it hasn't been checked and rechecked. During the recheck, whenever managers find problems, they can correct them on the spot. Haier requires managers to make inspection tours every other hour, and fill in any problems and their solutions to the problems on an OEC form. If managers do not find any problem within a certain period of time, the job quota will be increased.

Incentive:

Haier's incentive policies are "openness" and "fairness." By using the "3E" card, the management calculates each employee's daily wage in a clearly understood way, so that each employee knows how much he or she makes on a particular day, and why. Haier adopts a "payment by points" method for production workers, which values a job at a certain number of points. If an employee earns more points, he or she makes a higher wage and bonus.

Haier also uses quality-check coupons to supplement its incentive mechanism. Each Haier employee has a quality-check coupon handbook, which contains red and yellow coupons, the former for rewards and the latter for penalties. The handbook lists all the product defects or quality problems the company has detected, and specifies clearly the value of checking for each defect, which includes a self-check, a cross-check and a managerial check. If an employee has failed to self-check a defect which has subsequently been found by his colleague during a cross-check or by his manager during a managerial check, he loses the red coupon and gets a yellow coupon. The number of red and yellow coupons an employee gets at the end of the day will be counted toward his or her wage and bonus on that day.

Three Accounts and Three Forms

Based on the above framing structure, Haier sets up three accounts and three forms to implement its OEC management at all levels, in order to arrive at overall control. The three accounts are the corporate management account, the division management account and the employee's personal management account.

The corporate management account dictates the company's goal over its fiscal year, and its implementation. The account specifies the company's projected values, advance targets, job deadlines, divisions or factories responsible for the jobs, quality criteria and check mechanism and so on. The account is issued by the corporate president who will oversee its implementation.

The division management account basically follows the same pattern as the corporate account, subdividing jobs and responsibilities to departments or factories. The account is issued by division heads or factory directors to functional departments.

The employee's personal management account consists of detailed classifications of job items, evaluation criteria, values, a daily progress report, check results, etc. All employees are required to fill out this form on a daily basis.

Three Forms

These are the OEC form, the "3E" card and the on-the-spot form.

The OEC form is made up of two parts. One is a large, public form with seven items on it: quality, technology, equipment, material consumption, production plan, production propriety, and labor discipline. It is placed on each production site and completed by managers, who check it every two hours.

The following are details of the seven OEC items:

1. Quality: check whether or not one has reached the required product-quality standard during the current day. If there are quality problems, determine the cause and who is responsible for the problem areas, whether that is the worker him- or herself or a colleague. Workers also have to check the red or yellow coupons and record them on the form.
2. Technology: check the quality of the first product of the day, as compared to later products.

3. Equipment: check the maintenance of the equipment used, including its status, condition and the person responsible.
4. Material consumption: check the cause and responsibility for material consumption, in terms of quality, equipment, raw material, energy and employee competence level.
5. Production plan: check production progress and the factors that influence progress.
6. Production propriety: check production safety, quantitative management, and workplace conditions.
7. Labor discipline: check how well the rules and regulations governing work are observed.

These seven items are called "area OEC check points," and are basically carried out by production workers under their supervisors and managers. The main purposes are to ensure that, for a particular working day, all areas of production are covered, all problems are identified and solved and the employee's compensation is determined.

The "3E" card is a work-record card for each employee. "3E" stands for Everyone, Everything and Every Day. Haier deconstructs the above seven items, and puts actual, measurable values to each of them. All employees are required to fill in a card themselves so that they can easily calculate how much they can make that day. The card is subject to check by supervisors and managers and is submitted to management at the end of the month for payment.

The formula for calculation is: wages = points x point-value x quantity + awards - penalty.

In this way, each employee knows exactly how much he or she makes and why, leaving no room for ambiguity and favoritism.

In addition to area OEC management, there is also functional OEC management meant for functional departments. This is a two-part control process: production-site control and functional control.

There are nine elements in production-site control, called "5W3H1S," which are:

1. WHAT: What has gone wrong?
2. WHERE: Where is the problem?
3. WHEN: When did it happen?

4.   WHO: Who is responsible for the problem?
5.   WHY: Why did it happen?
6.   HOW MANY: How many problems like this have happened?
7.   HOW MUCH: How much cost has been incurred?
8.   HOW: How can the problem be solved?
9.   Safety: Are there any safety issues?

As for functional control, staff members in the functional departments check the work within their responsibilities and record the results on their OEC forms. The purposes of functional control are to detect problems, find out ways for improvement and calculate salaries based on recorded performance.

OEC at Work
To implement OEC management, Haier divides it into three stages and nine steps.

Stage One is made up of the first three steps:

1.   A daily briefing before work starts. Every employee is clear about what he or she is going to do.
2.   Operational routines based on job requirements. Production workers operate with the seven OEC criteria while functionaries follow the "5W3H1S" rules to check and control.
3.   Complete the production site OEC form. Supervisors and functionaries make inspection tours every two hours around the production site, detecting and solving any problems before recording them on the site OEC form.

Stage Two, after-work control, involves five steps:

4.   Self-check: all site workers check their own work, item by item, to see if it complies with the OEC criteria. Production workers fill out their "3E" cards and submit them to the supervisors, while functionaries fill out their OEC forms and hand them over to the department chief.
5.   Supervisory check: the supervisor of the work team or group examines the "3E" cards submitted, and makes sure that the

contents are correct and accurate, before reporting to the workshop manager.

6. Managerial check: the workshop manager checks the submitted "3E" cards based on his knowledge of the work teams or groups of that day. After returning the "3E" cards to the work teams or groups, the manager fills in his own OEC form and submits it to the factory director.

7. Director's check: the factory director reviews the OEC forms submitted by the workshop managers and records the results in the factory OEC account. He or she also files a progress report of that day to the Assistant Division General Manager. At the same time, all functionary heads review their staff's OEC forms and file a comprehensive report to the Deputy Division General Manager regarding problems detected, solutions offered, problems unsolved and solutions suggested.

8. Division managerial check: the Deputy Division General Manager reviews the submitted reports, suggests solutions and gives feedback to the functionary heads before reporting to the Division General Manager.

Stage Three is about working toward perfecting structural management:

9. A coordinated effort is made among the functionary departments and all other departments and divisions involved to discuss and analyze the problems found through the OEC process, and work together to hammer out new management ideas that will help perfect the company's management system.

How OEC Management Has Worked for Haier
After years of practice, Haier finds that its OEC management has worked very well for the company. It has effected changes or improvements in four areas:

Improvement in Precision Management:
Since OEC management aims at achieving a zero error rate through precise and meticulous routine work, it is capable of detecting almost all, if not all, problems during production, greatly minimizing any possible monetary loss on the part of the company. Rarely has an

error or a defect escaped the watchful eye of this multi-level control system.

Improvement in the Control Process:
OEC management has improved the control process at three levels. First, self-control by the employees gets better. All production workers are keenly aware that what they do will impact the next step in production, and that the quality of their work is closely linked to their pay. It is to their interest and benefit not to pass on any defective piece to the next person down the production line. Secondly, cross-control between employees of the two production procedures is strengthened. With the implementation of the quality coupon book, those employees who can detect errors in products handed over from the previous procedure will be rewarded with a red coupon, and the one responsible for a defect will get a punitive yellow coupon. This mechanism causes employees in both production procedures to pay great attention to product quality. Thirdly, special or managerial control is enhanced. With functionaries checking the production sites every other hour, all production lines are under effective and dynamic control by management. The most important effect of this control is to ensure that any potential errors are eliminated during the production process, rather than after they come off the production line.

Improvement in the Incentive Mechanism:
Under OEC management, the most important way for Haier employees to be rewarded or promoted is through excellent work, not favoritism or nepotism. Haier employees fall into three categories: model, or fixed-term workers; qualified, or contract workers; and probationary, or temporary workers. There are huge differences among the three categories in terms of wages, benefits, insurance coverage, housing and retirement plans. If a probationary worker distinguishes him- or herself, he or she can be upgraded to "qualified worker." By the same token, if a qualified worker does an excellent job, he or she will be upgraded to a fixed-term position.

Promotion is also based on performance and not on seniority. It is not uncommon in Haier to have factory directors or department heads in their early or mid-twenties.

Improvement in the Quality of Employees in General:
Haier considers this the most important achievement of OEC management, because it has been inculcated into the minds of Haier employees, to whom it becomes second nature. It forms the basis of the Haier corporate or enterprise culture that is hard for outsiders to imitate.

The Need for OEC

When Haier started its joint venture with the German company to make Qindao-Liebherr refrigerators in 1985, Zhang Ruimin knew that he must establish an effective management system to run his company. Since the Cultural Revolution, Chinese workers had not been used to strict rules and discipline in workplaces, and it came as no surprise that the first rules Zhang Ruimin posted on the company wall, when he was appointed director of the company, included such outrageous items as "Do not pee on the workshop floor," and "Pilfering is prohibited."

"You can take a look at people at traffic lights. When the red light is on, people simply turn a blind eye and cross the street anyway. If they do not mind the possible danger of crossing on red lights, how do you expect them to be bound by your rules?" Zhang once said ruefully to a Japanese joint venture partner who insisted on enforcing their time-honored management style in the joint venture.

Zhang was, of course, correct. Three months later, the Japanese admitted to Zhang that their management system was not working, and requested that Zhang use his instead.

"If you train a Japanese to clean the table six times a day, he will definitely do as instructed. But a Chinese will clean the table six times for the first few days, then he will feel that five or four times a day will do, and eventually he will completely give up cleaning the table." Zhang knew his employees so well that, to start with, he knew he must have a tough management system to help him get things done properly.

Zhang was keenly aware that one of the problems with Chinese workers is not paying enough attention to detail. Too many small errors added together would be big enough to ruin the whole product. Zhang decided to start from scratch by orchestrating OEC management, which aimed at preventing and solving any potential product quality problem before it went to market.

Zhang was an admirer of the American management maverick Frederick Winslow Taylor (1856-1915), from whose *Principles of Scientific Management* he drew inspiration for constructing his OEC management. Zhang had basically borrowed all four elements which constitute the essence of Taylor's scientific management: the development of standardization of methods; the careful selection and training of personnel; extensive supervision by management and payment of bonuses, and an equal division of the work and responsibility between the workman and management.

Like Taylor, Zhang believed that scientific management is achieved primarily by imposing order and discipline, especially for the production workers.

We felt the effect of that part of Haier's workplace management in December 2001, when we visited Haier's air conditioner manufacturing facility in the newly developed Haier High Tech Industrial Park at Yellow Island, about fifty miles from Haier headquarters in Qingdao. The workshop floors were clean, and uniformed workers wearing photo ID badges operated quietly and in an orderly fashion at the assembly lines.

We noticed a huge slogan hanging right under the roof that read, in both Chinese and English, "The Secret of Management Is Location, Location, Location." The English translation may not be very accurate, but the idea was that all problems should be detected and solved on the product site.

On a large bulletin board, we saw two OEC area forms with evaluation items waiting to be filled in. On another board, there were two notices, one red and another white, posted side by side. The red one contained praise, and the white one, criticism. The praise was for members of Assembly Line Number One, for good performance in the previous month with no defective products and a number of small innovations implemented. The compliment was for the whole team, and its team leader Wang Luping was awarded ten *yuan*—the basic unit of *Renminbi* (RMB), the Chinese "People's Currency," similar to the U.S. dollar or the Japanese yen)—as a "positive incentive."

The white criticism was for members of Assembly Line Number Three, for poor performance in the previous month because of excessive material consumption, loose discipline and, overall, the lowest rating among all the assembly lines. All members of the team were criticized, and the team leader Wang Xinrong was fined ten *yuan* as a "negative incentive."

On the factory floor, we saw the much-talked-about and somewhat contentious "6S" footprints. This is a pair of big footprints carved on the factory floor in front of a poster bearing six words, all beginning with "s." At the beginning of each workday, team leaders stand there, briefing their members. At the end of the workday, some employees will be singled out to stand on the footprints, criticizing themselves for making some mistakes or errors during work. This practice may be inimical to the Westerners for its negative or even humiliating connotation, but it is a mixture of many things in the Asian, especially Chinese, history, culture and business management concepts. One source can be traced back to Confucius who said, "I daily examine myself on three points." Another is found in the popular practice of "criticism and self-criticism" during the Cultural Revolution, when people openly criticized others as well as themselves, although in most cases falsely, for not doing the "right thing." In the West, especially in America, when one admits some wrongdoing (not in the legal sense), that person is usually penalized for what has been done. The normal consequence is demotion or resignation. But in China, when one admits some wrongdoing (again, not in the legal sense), that person is regarded as having the "right attitude" in the face of mistakes or criticism. Usually, there is no penalty for the people involved. In some cases, people who have made self-criticism may even get promoted because they are viewed as honest and trustworthy. Depending on the circumstance, some Chinese find it offensive and humiliating to admit wrongdoing and make self-criticism in public, while others find the practice acceptable, or at least bearable.

This practice at Haier originated during a visit by Zhang Ruimin to some Japanese companies, where he was attracted by the clean, orderly workplace environment brought about by the "5S" Japanese management concept. The "5S" were five Japanese words beginning with the "s" sound, which stressed the values of the company: *seiri*, preparation; *sieton*, putting things in order; *seusi,* sweeping and polishing; *seiketsu,* keeping clean; and *shitsuke,* discipline. Zhang imported this Japanese management system created by the noted Japanese management expert Masaaki Imai, and added one more "s"—"safety"—to make it "6S."

Behind the concept of "5S" is Imai's management theory of *"kaizen,"* which is a Japanese word meaning "gradual, orderly, and continuous improvement." The *kaizen* business strategy involves everyone in an organization working together to make improvements, usually without large capital investments.

According to Imai, *kaizen* is a culture of sustained, continuous improvement focusing on eliminating waste in all systems and processes of an organization. The *kaizen* strategy begins and ends with people. With *kaizen*, an involved leadership guides people to continuously improve their ability to meet expectations of high quality, low cost and on-time delivery. *Kaizen* transforms companies into "Superior Global Competitors."

Masaaki Imai first advanced his *kaizen* theory in his book *KAIZEN, the Key to Japan's Competitive Success*, in the mid-1980s. He expanded this idea in late 1990s in *Gemba Kaizen: A Commonsense, Low-Cost Approach to Management,* a sequel to the first book. *Gemba* is a Japanese word meaning "real place."

In the book, Imai emphasizes how to maximize the results of *kaizen* by applying it to *gemba*—business processes involved in the manufacture of products and the rendering of services, areas of business where the "real action" takes place.

Imai's *kaizen* concepts have been well received by many companies both inside and outside Japan, which has encouraged him to set up a Kaizen Institute to promote his management ideas worldwide. Haier's OEC management has obviously drawn much from Imai's models. At the Haier air conditioner production *gemba*, we got a strong impression of the order and discipline that Zhang has been emphasizing from the time he took over the factory's management.

Zhang must be familiar with the popular western "Theory X and Theory Y," advanced by the MIT professor Douglas McGregor in his monumental book *The Human Side of Enterprise*, published in

1960, in which he advanced Theory X and Theory Y to discuss managerial behaviors based on two opposing working attitudes.

According to McGregor, believers in Theory X tend to think that people do not really want to work. They are seen as lazy, incapable and opportunistic. Because of this, management must structure work and energize the workers. Tasks have to be well specified and work rules and discipline strictly enforced. On the other hand, believers in Theory Y tend to think that people are by nature motivated to work. They are seen as energetic, capable and honest. Therefore, no strict work rules or discipline are necessary.

Zhang undoubtedly believes there is a grain of truth in Theory X, given the history and background of the Chinese workforce. He has talked much about the basis on which his OEC management is established: the ball-on-a-slope hypothesis. The hypothesis basically says that the position of the company in the market is like that of a ball on a slope, which faces the pressures of the inertia of employees from within and market competitors from without. If there is no force to keep its position on the slope, the ball is doomed to roll down. That force is achieved by implementing an appropriate management system. OEC management is part of that system, characterized by enforcing firm work rules and discipline.

At Haier, new employees receive a month's military training before being put to work. Thirty days of intensive drilling and camp life will definitely give the new employees a sense of rule by discipline. Haier is like the military in other ways, as well; they do not accept any excuses for mistakes or oversights. In the fall of 1998, Zhang and some corporate executives flew to the city of Xi'an to inspect Haier's marketing arm there. On the bus from the airport to the city, the general manager of the Xi'an branch spoke eloquently about Haier products in the Xi'an market, and answered questions about them to everyone's satisfaction. But when asked some other questions about Haier not directly related to the Xi'an market, the general manager stumbled, and gave a number of excuses for his lack of knowledge.

Zhang interrupted the general manager with a story about West Point, where new cadets are permitted only four answers to any question they are asked: "Yes, Sir," "No Sir," "No excuse, Sir," and, "I don't know, Sir."

"If the cadet says 'I don't know, Sir,' he knows the next thing he must do is get to know that thing," Zhang added.

The general manager flushed at Zhang's indirect criticism, and learned a lesson about discipline.

But, on a deeper level, Zhang is in favor of Theory Y, which views people in a much more positive way. They are seen as intrinsically motivated, willing to work and basically honest. To Zhang, the ultimate goal of management is to change from supervision to self-management, a healthy concept in which employees feel that work becomes second nature. Zhang has taken steps to arrive at that goal.

Self-actualization

Although Haier's management is effective because of a firm hand, Zhang knows quite well that the lasting success of a company depends not so much on a strict management system as on a high level of employee participation in the management system itself. Consciously and subconsciously, he used Maslow's need-satisfaction model of motivation to develop his management style.

Abraham Maslow was a remarkable psychologist who, in 1954, published *Motivation and Personality*, a book that would influence not only psychology, but also business management, for many years to come. At the heart of Maslow's theory was the "hierarchy of human needs," which is characterized by five levels of motivation: physiological needs, safety needs, social needs, self-esteem needs, and self-actualization. Maslow holds that, once basic needs such as food and shelter are met, people are capable of growing and reaching unprecedented levels of achievement and satisfaction. At the top of Maslow's needs-pyramid is the desire to reach self-fulfillment, or in Maslow's word, "to become everything that one is capable of becoming." Just as a musician feels self-actualized when making music, and an artist when painting, a worker reaches self-actualization through work which he believes to be his second nature.

The first step Haier made toward the self-actualization of its employees was to create a friendly working environment in which employees feel they can display the best of their abilities and explore their potential to the fullest. It is also important to let employees feel their work is important, and be proud of being part of the company's management process.

The embryo of Haier's self-management lies in group- or team-briefings before work. In late 1990, the refrigerator factory started briefing its workers about production problems such as quality, progress, maintenance, discipline and material consumption. One of the purposes was to let workers know what was going on in the company and the group so that employees felt a sense of importance because things like these had been the concern of managers.

The next step was to form "self-management teams" aimed at loosening supervisory control and increasing the self-governing power of the workers. Workers started to communicate in a more positive way, exchanging more ideas, critiquing each other's job performance and learning from each other. Feeling that what they were doing was important to the company, they had a stronger sense of responsibility.

With decreased control from above, the burden of self-control increased among the workers. They had learned to generate the comments and criticisms which had previously come from management. That way, they were, in fact, shouldering part of the managerial responsibility and carrying some of the managerial pressures.

A case in point can be found in the Number Two Refrigerator Factory. When the team responsible for door-sealing became one of the "self-management teams" in 1993, their daily production increased to 1,200 units from 800 without adding a single hand. The dynamic was self-pressure among the group members, who worked at various tasks. Surprisingly, instead of complaining about the increased work-load, everybody in the group was happy, for they felt they had the opportunity to explore their potential to a greater degree.

Another example was the "twenty-five-minute team leader," popular with some teams or groups. In 1991, Liang Jun, team leader of the general assembly line in the Number Two Refrigerator Factory, initiated this practice. Every day, he yielded twenty-five minutes of his authority to one of his group members, ten minutes in the morning and fifteen in the afternoon, letting that member take full responsibility as team leader to keep the workplace tidy and clean, make routine inspections of the assembly line, help those who needed help of any sort, get supplies from the warehouse, exchange operational skills with other assembly lines and so on.

This practice proved to be productive. The interim team leaders acted as if they were in charge, and felt good about taking that role. They also learned a lot from the position, for they had to think and act like leaders. The biggest benefit was that, after playing the role, everybody in the group really cared about the image of the whole group, and would work hard to maintain and boost the image of the group. Therefore, a better working relationship and coordination among group members ensued.

Before the practice was invented, only the team leader had been familiar with all twelve job procedures on the assembly line. Now, many more members could do all of the jobs, making substitution easier, among other things.

Building a Strong Enterprise Culture

Based on the momentum of "self-management" and the "twenty-five-minute team leader," Haier's top management was well on its way to building a strong enterprise culture for long-term success in the market.

Corporate or enterprise culture is generally thought of as the deep-rooted, but often unconscious, beliefs, values and norms shared by the members of an organization. It guides how they think, act and feel. In *Corporate Culture and Performance*, John Kotter and James Heskett, of Harvard Business School, pointed out that corporate culture can have a significant impact on long-term financial performance, and that such a culture probably will become an even more important factor in determining corporate success or failure in the future.

Enterprise culture is both visible and invisible. Things like architecture, organizational processes and structures, symbols and celebrations, commonly used language and company slogans are examples of the former, while basic assumptions that guide members of the organization in their thinking and action are invisible.

It is the invisible that is more important and enduring. This concept coincides with a saying of the ancient Chinese philosopher Lao Tzu, which Zhang Ruimin quotes frequently in his speeches:

"All things under Heaven come into being from the visible,

And all beings come into existence from the invisible."

Zhang once offered his comments on the Haier enterprise culture. "The soul of the growth of an enterprise lies in its culture, and at the heart of the enterprise culture are its values. Haier's enterprise culture can be viewed as having three layers. On the outside is the material culture, seen as the company's growth speed, its products and services. Further inside is Haier's management system. At the core are the Haier values, the spiritual culture, so to speak. Most visitors to Haier were interested in Haier's management system, which was what they wanted to take away from here. Actually, it is the values that are more important. What kind of values a company has dictates the kind of system culture and management it has, which in turn decides its material culture."

Some Identifying Features of Haier's Enterprise Culture

A Sense of Pride and Honor

Haier's top management understands that, in a knowledge economy, employees are a company's single most valuable asset. It is of utmost importance to make all employees feel happy and motivated at work and proud of being Haier employees. From our visit to the company, we could tell that people at Haier, from assembly line workers to managers at all levels, take great pride in working at Haier, much like a student who feels proud of studying at a prestigious university. Since Haier has been so exposed to the national limelight, the company name carries a lot of prestige, not only in Qingdao, but also in almost all parts of China. Haier employees pride themselves on the products they make, and are accorded respect when they interact with customers and suppliers, and even on the street, where people can identify them.

One story tells that the police stopped a taxi, after ten o'clock in the evening, to check the ID of the passenger who was a Haier employee in Hefei, Anhui Province. It so happened that the Haier employee had forgotten to carry his ID with him. While he was riffling through his wallet, trying to find some other ID, the policeman saluted him and said, "No need to show me your ID. I know you work for Haier because I saw your Haier brochure in your portfolio. Sorry to have inconvenienced you."

Another story shows how Haier is regarded as a reliable source of help. In July 1997, Granny Li of Qingdao bought a Haier air conditioner. A few weeks later, her husband tripped over something and fell when he was moving the gas tank in the kitchen, breaking his leg. Granny Li was at a loss because she was unable to help, and their children were away from home. All of a sudden, she remembered the card the Haier salesperson had left her when she purchased the air conditioner. On the card were written the words, "Please call if there is any problem. We will be happy to help."

She dialed the number on the card, and a Haier service vehicle arrived in front of their building shortly afterward. Two Haier employees rushed to the fourth floor, where the old couple lived, and carried Grandpa Li down to the vehicle, which drove him to a nearby hospital. Granny Li was so grateful that she kept saying that they would thank the two Haier employees in person when her husband got better.

The next story was more deeply emotional. Wang Juncheng, an assembly line worker at Haier's Number One Refrigerator Factory, died of cancer at the age of twenty-two. On her death-bed, she asked her family to let her have a last look at the place where she had worked for three years. Her parents could not refuse her last wish, and her funeral procession stopped in front of the factory for fifteen minutes.

An Emphasis on Creativity and Innovation
The buzz-word at Haier is "creativity," and it rings from CEO to assembly line worker to sales representative. Haier encourages creative thinking and technological innovation at all levels. Workplace operators often come up with small innovations to improve the efficiency of certain equipment, and, in many cases, the innovations will be named after the innovators. When we were visiting the Haier air conditioner division, we asked for a list of such innovations adopted in the previous month. A quick look at the list reveals that in November 2001, there was a total of twenty-six innovations adopted by the division, ranging from improved paint-spray procedures inside the casing to relocating power outlets for welders.

One innovator suggested putting an identifying colored tube on each of the six wires of a testing machine so as to avoid mismatches. The innovator, Song Shangchao, won fifth prize. Another innovation, or a suggestion to be more exact, involved setting aside a place for storing used foam in the lab. Li Xiuju, the originator, won sixth prize.

One of the interesting innovation stories at Haier is that of the creation of the "Little Prodigy" washing machine. For quite some time, Haier salespeople had been puzzled by the paradox that washing machine sales from June to August were the lowest in the year, when people were thought to use their washing machines the most. Haier market researchers discovered later that people in such cities as Shanghai were reluctant to use the standard five-kilogram washing machine in the summer because they did not have heavy enough loads of clothes to warrant the use of a large machine. Electricity bills were a big concern for them. But they would be happy to use a type of washing machine that was much smaller and more energy saving. Haier decided to meet that challenge and put the lightweight, all-purpose Little Prodigy washing machine onto the market in 1996. The product was enthusiastically received for its shape, size and color. It was popular not only with individual customers, but also with a lot of hotels. One five-star hotel ordered 1,000 and another three-star hotel in Beijing ordered more than 4,000. In forty-five days, Haier received over 100,000 orders for Little Prodigy.

At Haier, we heard a story that bordered on incredibility. In 1996, a farmer in Sichuan Province wrote Haier to complain that the water-hose of his washing machine had often been clogged. When servicing the machine, the Haier repairman found that the farmer had been using the machine to wash sweet potatoes. A little shocked by the customer's "innovative" use of the machine, the repairman installed a larger hose for him, anyway. Apologetically, the farmer said that if there had been washing machines for sweet potatoes, he wouldn't have used the Haier machine for that purpose. This incident alerted Haier, and inquiry revealed that there were quite a lot of people in Sichuan Province who had been using washing machines to wash sweet potatoes in the winter and clothes in the summer.

Zhang, the CEO, made the decision to create a special kind of washing machine that, in addition to normal clothes-washing functions, could also wash sweet potatoes, fruits and even shells. The first ten thousand such machines were sold out almost overnight. Of course, the demand for such machines was not very high, but the decision to meet the special needs of some customers shows Haier's willingness and ability to adapt to change.

Company-wide, Haier has a Central Research and Development Institute that undertakes such advanced projects as all-weather simulator (for new product adaptability testing), digital TV, Internet-ready refrigerators, CAD-CAM software, mobile phones, anti-virus plastic materials and so on. Haier spends about 6% of its total revenues on its R&D, as compared to an average 0.39% at other large- and middle-sized companies in China.

One thing that Haier management cannot emphasize enough is that technological innovation must go in tandem with the market. Technological innovation, if not turned into actual sales, does not mean anything for Haier. This approach to technological innovation is in itself creative thinking, at least in China, where the majority of scientific and technological innovations find no material outlet.

Seeking Excellence and Doing One's Best

At Haier, everyone is expected to do his or her very best to reach the highest level of professional competence. The equipment at the Number One Refrigerator Factory was old, producing a maximum of six hundred refrigerators a day. Determined to explore potential production to the fullest, the factory director, Li Kejin, and his workers spent a whole year figuring out ways to reduce each procedure by twelve seconds, and, eventually, were able to increase the output to eight hundred per day.

A more typical example is found in Tang Haibei, a young engineer and Assistant Director of the Number Two Refrigerator Factory, who did his best to save the company a great deal of production time. In 1995 the factory had been working for some time, under the direction of a German engineer, to transform its production lines from making refrigerators using freon to freon-free refrigerators. Before the new lines could be put to use, the German engineer wanted to shut down the whole factory for two weeks to test the new equipment, as was the general practice in Germany.

That bothered Tang very much, because shutting down the whole factory that long would have cost the company too much. He volunteered to conduct and finish the test in three days. The German engineer could not believe his ears, for that was something he had never heard of. Tang, of course, faced extreme difficulties in this undertaking, for he not only had time against him, but also had to overcome the complexities of technologies which included mechanics, electronics and chemical engineering. With determination and devotion, Tang beat all the odds against him and made the change in three days.

The German engineer was moved, and so was the Haier CEO, Zhang Ruimin, who wrote an article in the company newspaper, *Haier News,* praising Tang's selfless contribution and tireless pursuit of excellence as "the spirit of the enterprise."

Everybody Is Somebody

In China, people with ability waiting to be promoted by their bosses or superiors are compared to good horses waiting to be picked by a horse expert known as "Bo Le." But at Haier, good "horses" are promoted not by being handpicked by bosses who like them, but through horse races in which the winners take all. As a result, able young people in their twenties or thirties are promoted to factory director, department manager or even division head.

Haier's rules for "horse racing" are openness and fairness, giving everybody the same chance in competition. In October 1992, the then Qingdao General Refrigerator Factory undertook a big change in the company's promotion system by openly selecting cadres through examinations which were open to all employees, regardless of their current status and positions. At that time in China, this was a very new thing. A lot of people had strong doubts about the initiative, especially the part about breaking the boundaries between operational workers and company cadres such as directors and managers. Traditionally, there was a big gap between workers and cadres in terms of status and benefits. "A worker for a day is a worker for life."

To test the waters, 102 workers applied for the 242 positions posted. The competition turned out to be a success. Of the 102 workers who applied and took the examinations, 31 passed them and were subsequently promoted to appropriate supervisory and managerial positions.

Ren Xiaoquan had been hired by Haier from the countryside, as a contract worker in the refrigerator factory. A young man with a lot of ideas and a pair of able hands, he frequently came up with some good suggestions and small technical innovations, which resulted in a forty-five percent reduction in use of excessive material for the refrigerator cover. He was soon promoted to team leader. Within a month of his promotion, he increased his team's daily production by 120 units, which led to his further promotion to workshop supervisor.

The average age of Haier employees is thirty-two, while the average age for Haier managers is twenty-six. From time to time, the fact that some Haier executives are so young poses problems for their business partners at the negotiating table, and sometimes to the employees reporting to them.

Ma Jian was twenty-six when he became manager of the quality department at Haier's refrigerator division. He was negotiating with a Japanese delegation headed by a fifty-year-old senior manager from the manufacturing department of the Japanese company, regarding compensation for the compressors Haier had imported from them. In the beginning, the Japanese manager did not regard Ma as an equal who could make final decisions, and therefore he did not take him seriously. During negotiations, the Japanese manager began to realize that Ma was not only a well-informed technocrat, but also an experienced and tough negotiator. In the end, he agreed entirely to Ma's suggestions on compressor improvement, and paid Haier the $186,000 compensation Ma had asked for.

Sincere and Forever

At Haier, customer satisfaction is achieved at any cost. Their motto, "Sincere and Forever," has become everyone's investment in the company. Haier has abundant stories to tell about employees who went the extra mile to serve customers. The most talked-about is the story of Mao Zongliang, a Haier maintenance person in the city of Guangzhou, in China's south. In July 1995, a customer in Caozhou, a neighboring city, ordered a Haier "Margherita" washing machine, and the delivery date was set for the morning of July 8.

Early in the morning of July 7, Mao rented a truck and drove off to deliver the machine to the customer.

At about two o'clock in the afternoon, the truck was impounded by law-enforcement officers because of insufficient paperwork. It was only halfway to its destination, and Mao and his washing machine were stuck in a place where no service or help could be found.

He stopped more than a dozen trucks on the highway, but none of the drivers was willing to help. After about an hour's futile effort, Mao decided to carry the one-hundred-forty-pound machine to the nearest town about two miles away.

To common wisdom, it was a "Mission Impossible," given the weight, the heat and the distance. Despite that and curious stares from people who passed by, wondering what was happening to the man under the machine, Mao finally inched into the town two hours later, and called the sales company for a pickup truck.

It wasn't until eight o'clock that evening that help finally came. By then Mao had missed two meals and was completely exhausted. When they arrived at Caozhou, it was already midnight. The next morning, the installation technician was relieved when he saw Mao arrive at the customer's home with the machine.

The customer was beyond words when he learned the story. He later wrote to Haier, praising the company's commitment to customer satisfaction. Although some wondered if it was worthwhile for Mao to stress himself doing what he did, Mao simply said that he did not want the customer to think ill of the company because of his mistake.

A customer wrote a letter to Haier Customer Service to report that his freezer compartment had been running without stopping for a long time, but, out of carelessness, he left out his street address, giving only the city name, Fushan, a Qingdao suburb. The Customer Service Center figured that they could not wait till they found out the exact address of the customer and decided to dispatch a service-man immediately to look for the customer. With the incomplete letter and his tool kit, the serviceman went into the numerous streets and alleys in search of the customer. At dusk, he finally located the customer, with help from the local police, and fixed the problem.

Wang Qin works in Beijing, and his hometown is a small village in Shanxi Province. He bought a Haier TV in Beijing and took it to his Shanxi home. He was a little troubled by the picture, which he thought was not as clear as what he had seen in Beijing.

He made a call to Haier's Beijing TV sales office, which was relayed to Haier's Shanxi branch office in Taiyuan within half an hour. Mr. Xu was immediately sent from Taiyuan to the customer's home. His arrival in the village after over ten hours' long-distance bus travel gave the customer a pleasant surprise.

Xu checked the TV with the testing equipment he had brought with him, and found that it worked fine. He suspected that the poor image was due to poor signal strength, so he visited several of the customer's neighbors. Their experience confirmed his belief.

It turned out that they were all watching the village's closed-circuit TV channel, which was sending a weak signal. That night, Xu helped the village fix the closed-circuit TV system, and the next day the whole village was enjoying better pictures.

People at Haier believe that, although it looks as if the things that happened in Caozhou, Fushan and Shanxi were not worth the company's time and money, it is their sincerity in serving the customer wholeheartedly, at any time and at any cost, that counts.

In *Management Challenges for the 21st Century*, Peter Drucker, one of the most influential American management philosophers of the twentieth century, believes that, just as traditional management was instrumental in increasing productivity in manual work, modern management must be transformed to play a similar part in increasing productivity in "knowledge work," the biggest management challenge of the new century.

There is little doubt that Haier has inherited much from the Taylor management system, but it has picked up where Taylorism left off. Haier's notion and recognition that people are the most important asset of the company, in their contribution to the company's growth, can never be underestimated. OEC management, under the banner of an excellence-driven enterprise culture, will go a long way toward permitting a company the size of Haier to be successful in the future.

We would like to apply a *yin-yang* analogy to the situation. If we say the Haier enterprise culture is the *yin*, then the Haier OEC management is the *yang*. It appears that the best formula for success, if there is one, is to strike a balance between the *yin* and the *yang*.

4

Revitalizing the "Stunned Fish": Mergers and Acquisitions

March 25, 1998, Harvard Business School

The beautiful, lush Harvard University campus is located on the south bank of the quietly flowing Charles River in Cambridge, Massachusetts. Beyond the huge university cathedral is the business school.

In a spacious classroom, Professor Lynn Sharp Paine was having an open discussion on China's economic situation, and the topic was how a Chinese firm called Haier had revived a bankrupt company it had acquired.

A member of Phi Beta Kappa and a graduate *summa cum laude* of Smith College, Professor Paine holds a Doctorate in Moral Philosophy from Oxford University and a law degree from Harvard Law School. She has practiced law in Boston and has taught at Harvard since 1991. Her focus has been new phenomena in business practice in the global era. Subjects such as business ethics, leadership, management across cultures and organizational integrity have special appeal for her. She believes that a successful business must possess a successful culture, one that can be duplicated and transferred.

In 1998, intrigued by Haier's internationally renowned success in China, Professor Paine turned her attention to the company's 1995 acquisition of the Qingdao Red Star Electric Appliance Company, one of the most important of Haier's mergers and acquisitions. In three months, without putting up a penny, Haier had turned Red Star around from money-losing to profit-generating.

Paine and her colleagues looked into Haier's structure and came to the conclusion that it was Haier's enterprise culture that had revived the "stunned fish"—companies with good products, facilities, equipment or distribution channels (things that are often referred to as "hardware" in China), but with poor management (known as "software").

Unlike the Sloan School of Management at MIT, which relies on empirical data to formulate a more scientific approach to problems, Harvard Business School trains its students by using real-life cases, or case studies, to sharpen the students' senses and to inspire practical skills in solving real-life problems that pester corporations. What had attracted Professor Paine's attention to Haier was what she called its "movable enterprise culture," which was able to affect other sleeping corporations and bring them back to a waking state. Professor Paine found the revival of the Qingdao Red Star Electric Appliance Company particularly illuminating.

Haier's earliest mergers and acquisitions began in 1988, when it bought a small electroplating company in Qingdao, which was later turned into a microwave company. In 1991, having established itself as a national brand in the refrigerator market, the ambitious Qingdao General Refrigerator Factory started its second phase of strategic development—diversification into other fields of the home appliances industry. With its jaws wide open, the company was on constant watch for prey—those "stunned fish." Two such "fish" were the Qingdao Air Conditioner Factory and the Qingdao Freezer Factory, both in financial trouble, with dwindling sales and under fierce competition.

After the acquisitions, Zhang introduced a new product line to the air conditioner company by making split-unit air conditioners that could be used in multiple rooms. That innovative design created a new spectrum for China's air conditioner market, and the company prospered with rising sales. The freezer company was a tougher case, because its workforce basically had no idea what a quality product was, or why they needed one. Zhang had to change the employees' minds before he could change the quality of the products.

Shortly after these two major acquisitions, Zhang decided to make an organizational overhaul. In December 1991, the Qingdao General Refrigerator Factory was renamed "Qingdao Qindao Haier Group." A year later, in December 1992, the name was changed to "Haier Group," which has been used ever since.

The newly formed Haier Group had three major profit centers—refrigerators, air conditioners and freezers—along with a number of functional departments such as marketing, technology management and quality control. With Zhang as President and Yang Mianmian as Vice President, the company moved more aggressively to achieve a higher goal.

One major move took place in 1992. In April of that year, two months after the then paramount Chinese leader Deng Xiaoping's reform-oriented speech to encourage China's businesses, an inspired Zhang decided to take a big risk. Having obtained approval for the purchase of land from the government and the promise of a loan of 1.6 billion RMB from the bank, he bought a large piece of land, 800 *mu* or about 5,000 acres in size (1 *mu* equals 6.7 acres), on the east side of Qingdao. The purchased land was meant as the future site for Haier's industrial park, where the corporate headquarters and sixty-six of its factories and subsidiaries were to be housed. However, within thirty days of the purchase, the central government tightened credit in order to halt real estate speculation, and all loans were frozen.

The actual amount of the loan to Haier, by 1993, was only 240 million RMB. On the day when the bank closed the door on Haier's real-estate deal, Zhang lost sleep for the second time since he had taken the job in 1984 (the first having been in 1989, when China's refrigerator market faced oversupply, and he was battling within himself as to whether he should increase the price of their products, rather than dropping the price, as common wisdom dictated). With no other choice, Haier decided to take chances with the stock market. In November 1993, Haier went public in Shanghai Stock Exchange Market. Luckily, they raised 300 million RMB with their IPO.

The money from the IPO helped Haier mitigate the impact caused by its real-estate crisis. In May 1995, the Haier Industrial Park was completed and became the new home for the company's headquarters and all its factories and subsidiaries. Although, by 1996, the whole investment for the industrial park—money borrowed from the bank, Haier's own money and the money from the stock market—had been paid off, Zhang retained a nervous memory of the event. He recalled, "It was the first time Haier had done such a risky thing. If we had not been successful with our IPO, Haier would have disappeared. We'd never done anything like this and that should be the only time we do it."

Despite the real-estate problem, Haier was moving forward at an amazing speed. By 1995, Haier had been known as one of the largest Chinese manufacturers of household appliances. It ranked 107th among China's top 500 companies, with revenues hitting 4.33 billion RMB. It was against this backdrop that the Red Star Electric Appliance Company acquisition came onto center stage.

Red Star Electric Appliance Company

Red Star, like Haier's predecessor, the Qingdao General Refrigerator Factory, was also a "collective enterprise," for it was owned collectively by all the employees of the company.

Red Star had been one of the top three washing machine manufacturers in China, making turbo-washing machines at 700,000 units a year. In its heyday, the company was very proud of its Red Star brand. In 1994, the company had 3,240 employees, with reported revenues of 500 million RMB. But that was not the whole story. Since 1991, the company had been in serious trouble due to poor management. First, its founder was put into prison for embezzlement, leaving the rest of the management team in a disturbed state. Then, the long-existing quality problem had shown its worst impact, with overflowing inventories sitting in the company's warehouses. Plus, there had been huge uncollected bills and outstanding accounts receivable. By 1995, Red Star had incurred a heavy debt of 132 million RMB, which left the company's cash reserves at just 20 RMB, less than three U.S. dollars at the then exchange rate. With the company virtually gone bankrupt and the morale of its employees at an all-time low, the Qingdao municipal government officials were extremely concerned about Red Star's future. The last thing they wanted to see was unemployed workers taking to the street, disturbing order and stability.

The municipal government decided that the best way to cure the Red Star headache once and for all was to let some company in the city take over Red Star entirely. The ideal candidate for such a takeover was, of course, Haier. In June 1995, an arrangement was made between the municipal government officials and Haier executives to talk about the matter.

Now, Zhang had to decide what to do with Red Star.

In June of 1995, Haier was still hurting from the real-estate deal, and Zhang, having overworked himself for the previous two years, was suffering poor health and had to be hospitalized. On the hospital bed, he was fighting his own "to be or not to be" battle over the Red Star Electric Appliance Company acquisition. It was not something he had done before, and the assets were not there to do it lightly.

The mathematics of the acquisition was simple: If Haier took over Red Star, it could certainly enlarge Haier's market share in the washing machine market and allow Haier to grow much bigger overnight. Moreover, Haier didn't have to pay anything for the acquisition because the municipal government had decided to give Red Star to Haier completely "free of charge." In addition, Haier would keep all Red Star's advanced equipment that could be moved to the newly completed Industrial Park.

The downside of the deal was that the municipal government told Haier to pay off Red Star's debt of 132 million RMB—a number equaling Haier's total profit in 1993—and keep its employees.

Haier, heavily in debt itself, shuddered at the prospect of another huge debt, while employees at Red Star expressed deep resentment and hostility toward the people from Haier, even during the initial stages of negotiations. An acquisition of such magnitude and nature would be a huge gamble that might simply crush Zhang and Haier, if things didn't work out.

The biggest challenge was that, in order to make this acquisition work, Zhang had to change the minds of the people at Red Star before he could change the quality of the product. Red Star's products had been deteriorating, and there was a huge inventory of 110,000 unsalable units that had defects of all kinds. And he had to change the Red Star company culture, which did not value product quality, before he could turn the business around.

Having been there and done that, Zhang only knew too well what he was facing, and the fruits he could reap. Being extremely sensitive to the Chinese political and economic climate, Zhang had recognized the destiny of Chinese companies long before most Chinese business leaders, including his own colleagues. They had to diversify to survive, and employees had to cope with new situations or end up on the street. He decided to take the chance.

In July 1995, the Red Star Electric Appliance Company, along with five other companies that were affiliated with it, was "completely given or allocated" to Haier by the Qingdao municipal government, without costing the company a single penny. Considering the nature of the government intervention in the matter, the acquisition process was relatively smooth. In order to reduce the emotional impact of the transfer on the Red Star employees, Haier decided to keep the company name for a while before officially changing it to "Haier Washing Machine Company" (HWMC). A bigger challenge, though, for Zhang Ruimin and his management colleagues, was how to turn the company around, and how to revitalize this giant "stunned fish" in the best possible way and in the shortest possible time.

The Harvard Business School case study "The Haier Group (B)," included in this book as Appendix E, focuses primarily on the situation after Haier's acquisition of Red Star and how Haier used its enterprise culture to turn the company around. There are three related Harvard Business School case studies on the Haier Group. While case study (A) gives some general introduction to the Haier Group and the background of the Red Star acquisition, case study (C) picks up where (B) left off, with the Fan Ping episode.

Fan Ping was a quality inspector who failed to detect some improperly inserted switches and plugs. Following the rule, she was fined fifty *yuan*, and life went on. But the new management at Red Star wanted to hold Fan's supervisor responsible for her oversight.

That posed a question for Haier management as to what share of responsibility management should shoulder if an operator or a staff member made a mistake that deserved to be penalized.

Starting July 12, 1995, the *Haier News* carried a number of articles and editorials on the Fan Ping episode, discussing whether or not Fan Ping's supervisors should also be held responsible for Fan's error. The July 12 editorial argued that Fan Ping was only a rank-and-file employee, and that simply penalizing her alone did not address the real challenge, that is, to reach the Haier goal of zero defects in the whole product process, from design through production to after-sale service. The editorial maintained that Fan's supervisors should shoulder their share of the responsibility in the matter.

The *Haier News* reporter also interviewed Mr. Xu Xuezheng, Fan Ping's supervisor, who, under the pressure of newspaper exposure and peer reaction, admitted that the managers of the quality-control group should be responsible for Fan's mistake. He then wrote a self-criticism to the effect that he understood the importance of taking responsibility as a manager for the mistakes his subordinates had made, and that he had learned a lesson in that regard. He subsequently fined himself 300 *yuan*.

Chai Yongsen, the central figure in the Red Star overhaul, was the General Manager appointed by the Group to head the newly acquired washing machine company, and soon found the boomerang he had thrown out flying back to hit him. He had set deadlines for Red Star employees to fix the defective washing machines the company had accumulated over the years. When the deadlines were missed, due to inertia and a lack of sense of responsibility, Chai decided to fine himself 500 *yuan*, to set a precedent with regard to the management responsibility he was promoting. Chai's move shocked the Red Star employees, especially the managers, who began to be awakened to management responsibility.

Chai's next step was to post a weekly list of ten good and bad managers, called the red list (*hong bang*) and the yellow list (*huang bang*), in Chinese, openly evaluating the performances of middle-level managers. The lists were so shocking to some managers on the yellow list that the first few lists were torn down. Chai kept posting, and people at Red Star gradually grew accustomed to the lists, just as other Haier employees, especially managers, had become accustomed to open criticism in the *Haier News*. Eventually, ten managers fined themselves for not fully living up to their responsibilities. A lot of problems carried over from the previous management, such as quality and service, were tackled seriously or solved.

Chai arranged for all Red Star employees to visit other Haier facilities, such as refrigerator factories, to impress them with the clean working environments and disciplined workforces there. Shortly after these visits, the old Red Star began to put on a new face, with clean factory floors and clear responsibilities for both front-line production workers and managers.

Reorganization was also underway. Chai disbanded the thirty-four Red Star management offices and replaced them with five functional departments—Sales, Finance, Production, Technology and Quality, and General Management—and one R&D institute. Managers were chosen according to their abilities and job performance, rather than by seniority or nepotism. More than fifty people with college educations and strong technical backgrounds were hired for the Sales Department alone, which resulted in increased sales.

Technology was also improved with help from the Haier-Merloni washing machine joint venture, which Haier had established in 1993 with the Italian appliance maker. Two models soon rolled off the Red Star production lines: the fully automatic Little Prodigy, and the bubble-style, double-basket Magic Bubble, both of which were well received in the market.

Three months after the acquisition, the new Red Star showed significant financial change. By the end of September 1995, the company had generated a profit of 20,000 RMB. In October and November, the numbers were 76,000 and 100,000 RMB, respectively. The biggest jump came in December, when the profit figure hit 1.5 million RMB.

In 1996, the company passed the ISO 9001 certification, and was ranked as the number one washing machine manufacturer in China, in terms of brand name recognition and export volumes. It was around the end of 1996 that the company was officially renamed the "Haier Washing Machine Company (HWMC)."

In 1997, the Haier washing machine division turned out a total of one million units, and HWMC sales went up to 1.2 billion RMB.

The successful turn-around of Red Star has become a classic case in China's business mergers and acquisitions. The biggest change, however, at least to Zhang and Haier top management, was that former employees of Red Star had taken on a new attitude toward the company and the job they were doing. The Haier enterprise culture, which Zhang had been cultivating, had finally found its home in the minds of the HWMC employees.

Xiao Min, a former Red Star worker, became emotional when he tried to describe the change. "Before the merger, I wouldn't have cared a bit if a co-worker had caught fire, as long as I was unaffected, because everybody was just thinking about himself. Now, if I see something that is detrimental to the company, I want to intervene, because I consider Haier my family, and I have complete confidence in this family."

Yellow Mountain Television Company

If the acquisition of Red Star was basically smooth and peaceful, that of the Yellow Mountain Television Company was nothing but strenuous and eventful.

Haier had been planning to enter China's TV market for quite some time. In September 1997, it set up a search group headed by Yu Zida, Deputy General Manager of the Haier Group's Electronics Division, to look for possible candidates. The "stunned fish," this time, included the Yellow Mountain Television Company, a leading electronics producer in Hefei, capital of Anhui Province. Founded in the early 1950s, Yellow Mountain Television was a state-owned enterprise with over 2,700 employees at the end of 1997. That year, it produced 47,000 TV sets, and its gross sales amounted to ninety million RMB. A year before, the company had imported a big-screen TV assembly line from Japan, but it had never been put to use because of management problems.

Even with government funding and advanced technology, the company's books had always been in the red because of poor management. It had been a burden on the city government of Hefei. Officials of the municipality had tried different means of bringing the company back on track, such as appointing new top managers, providing low-interest loans for the company to purchase advanced equipment from foreign countries and even encouraging the company to file for bankruptcy in the mid 1990s. The bankruptcy filing resulted in the discharge of its two-hundred-million RMB debt, but nothing really helped.

By the end of 1997, the company had again incurred about fifty million RMB in debt. The employees of the company were very unhappy about the state of affairs, as well.

Despite the fact that the company was owned by the state, the government had stopped subsidizing salaries and medical insurance, under new policies brought about by enterprise reform in the 1980s. Since it was not profitable, the company had to borrow money from the bank to pay its employees. Making an average 300 RMB (equivalent to $36) a month with no bonuses or medical insurance, the workers felt they needed something to cheer them up.

When the Hefei municipal government learned that Haier was considering buying the company, its new mayor, Mr. Che, could hardly wait to make the deal happen.

We must keep in mind that this happened at a crucial moment when the Chinese government was trying desperately to rescue money-losing state enterprises that had long been a burden. It was a time of desperation for the state, and a time of expansion or death for corporations. Between 1996 and 1998, drastic changes in China's economic policy had sent millions of state employees out into the street. (In Jeannie's family, five out of seven cousins who had worked for state-owned companies in Sichuan Province were laid off, or *xiagang*. Shawn's sister, who had worked in a chemical fiber company in Zhejiang Province, was given the option of early retirement.)

During the painful economic-reform period from 1995 to 1999, proposals for further reducing the extent of state ownership continued. State ownership would be limited to "non-competitive" sectors, such as financial services, oil and gas, aviation, railways, telecommunications, and large chemical and steel plants. Meanwhile, with Hong Kong (1997) and Macao (1998) returning to China and an incredible amount of foreign investment pouring in from Taiwan, Singapore, America and Europe, China awoke with a jolt to the call of the world. To survive, China had to undergo radical economic reform by dropping state burdens—the money-losing state enterprises. From rich coastal cities to poverty-stricken mountainous areas and the western frontier, on all fronts and in all areas, China was trying hard to speed up the brutal but necessary change.

Slogans such as "Patriotism is measured by the amount of taxes paid" were hung everywhere—at airports, in train stations and in people's squares. To become strong, to be respected as an influential player in the international arena, China had to get to its feet financially by any means, including allocating state-owned companies to other successful companies, be they state- or privately owned.

Zhang's ingenuity and incredible luck had led him to sense the coming change, and he grabbed at the opportunity before other companies could fully understand what was going on. Zhang was in the right place at the right time. He seized the moment to expand his business.

In November 1997, a delegation composed of decision-making people from the Yellow Mountain Television Company and from the city government of Hefei came for talks with Zhang Ruimin at Haier headquarters in Qingdao.

Zhang pondered the pros and cons of the possible Yellow Mountain acquisition. The down side was that Hefei is far from Qingdao, which meant that close monitoring by headquarters would be a problem. A thornier issue was that Yellow Mountain was a state-owned company, and that could cause some problems for Haier in implementing management styles such as OEC. On the up side, the company had good products and advanced technology, and its fifty-million RMB debt was relatively low, compared to other companies under consideration. A bonus was that the city government officials were open-minded, which could be helpful in times of difficulty.

After four days of negotiation, Haier reached an agreement with the Hefei government on the terms of acquisition: Yellow Mountain Television was going to be given to Haier, along with its debt. As in the case of Red Star, Haier did not have to pay a single cent for the acquisition. In return, Haier would have to keep all the Yellow Mountain employees and make 400,000 TV sets in 1998. The deal was cut. Starting from January 1, 1998, Yellow Mountain became part of the Haier Group, and was renamed "Haier Hefei Electronics."

The first thing Haier did after the acquisition was appoint Sun Qunli as General Manager of the newly formed company. A graduate of Xi'an Communication University in the late 1980s, majoring in refrigeration, Sun had spent most of his years at Haier working in the field of air conditioners. From 1994 to 1996, he had served as General Manager in a Haier-Mitsubishi air conditioner joint venture. In September 1997, he was appointed head of the electronics sub-division of the Group. Later that year, he was sent to Hangzhou, capital of Zhejiang Province, to form a joint venture—the Haier-Hangzhou Electric Company Ltd.—with the West Lake Electronics Group, to make TV sets. That assignment had given him some experience in the TV industry before his Hefei mission.

Haier headquarters sent Sun two associates to form a management trio in Hefei: Xu Guangyi and Fu Zongxin, the former as Executive General Manager in charge of operations and the latter as the company's chief accountant.

Under Sun's initiative, Haier Hefei began a structural overhaul aimed at streamlining the company's existing management team. At the time, the company had about 150 people holding managerial positions. Sun considered this excessive for a company with a workforce of fewer than 2,000 people. (Like most other companies in China, Haier Hefei was responsible for the pensions and medical insurance of its 845 retirees.)

Sun decided that he could only keep thirty-eight managers in their positions, based on his criteria of leadership ability, physical ability and age. It was a tough process to go through, but Sun finally completed his selection without meeting too much opposition.

Sun also reshuffled the workforce by clearly redefining job categories for both management and front-line workers, and by linking positions to corresponding pay schedules. Discarding the old wage system, under which the government had decided the pay standard, Sun introduced an approach in which a group of ten employees, randomly selected by the company's top management, established a pay schedule for each position. He rotated the members of the ten-person group every month to give more people a chance to be involved in the decision-making process.

In addition, Sun encouraged employees to apply for good or important positions by taking part in examinations, so as to eliminate *guanxi*, the Chinese word for nepotism or preferential treatment.

The third major change was aimed at production lines. Sun ordered the regrouping of twelve assembly plants into four, for better efficiency. He also introduced some new assembly lines, including twenty-nine-inch- and thirty-four-inch-screen lines, to increase the company's competitiveness in the market. Customers were opting more and more for bigger-screen TV sets.

To instill in the employees the idea of quality products, Sun began to enforce strict quality-control methods by emphasizing zero tolerance for defects. That was a tough sell to a workforce who had previously thought that a four-percent defect rate would not matter much.

Sun's weapon was OEC management, which had worked well in other acquired companies. Every day, each worker was given a detailed form to fill in, regarding quality, production procedures, equipment maintenance, material consumption, work objectives, workplace cleanliness, discipline and safety. The form would be checked and graded by a supervisor and posted on the wall, so that every worker would know how well or poorly he or she had been doing. Monthly salaries would then be decided, based on each employee's performance at work.

A supplement to the OEC practice were the "6S" footprints. Every day, all Haier Hefei employees, like their colleagues elsewhere, would line up in front of a big pair of footprints on the workshop floor, to be briefed by their supervisors on the work of the day. Good work was praised and poor performance was criticized. Very often, employees who had not done a good job would be singled out to stand on the footprints and make self-criticism, a practice not liked by many people.

Changes were also made to the company's strategic planning, financial control, research and development and marketing strategies. The company was back on track rather quickly. There were signs of improvement in the company's books. In March 1998, the company broke even. In April, there was some profit, though the output for the month was a bit lower than the previous month. In May, the company produced a total of 21,304 TV sets, way up from the 3,350 units in the same period the year before the acquisition. By the end of May, with an accumulated output of 86,051 units, Haier Hefei's TV market share rose to eighth in the country.

To Sun, it seemed that the company was moving in the right direction, except for a few glitches in the employees' adjustment to the OEC and "6S" footprints practices. He was ready to proceed to the next step: formalizing the management-labor relationship by asking all employees to sign an Employment Contract, a standard practice for all Haier companies across the board.

The main clauses of the Employment Contract included the following:

- The duration of employment is usually one year, renewable based on job performance.

- No second job is allowed outside of Haier employment. Once found out, an employee with a second job can be asked to resign or be fired.
- Wages are determined by the employer, based on the employee's employment status—whether he or she is an outstanding, a qualified, or a probationary employee.
- The employee's benefits, health insurance and other work-related compensations are subject to change commensurate with the employee's status. (This has been the case since Haier adopted the policy of "dynamic switching among the three statuses," which means that a qualified worker can be downgraded to a probationary employee if he or she severely violates company rules and regulations or has done something which management deems detrimental to the company.)
- If an employee breaks the contract by resigning before the contract term expires, he or she will have to reimburse the employer's expenditure for training received.
- Violations of the contract on the part of the employee will be punished. Serious violators are subject to government regulatory penalties.

On May 30, 1998, Sun distributed the contract to all employees in the company, with a cover memo explaining that this was a formality of the Haier Group. He expected the signing to go smoothly. On that same day, the entire top management of the company went to Haier headquarters in Qingdao for a prescheduled meeting on product development.

Now, the vague concern that had been in the back of Zhang Ruimin's mind when he was weighing the pros and cons of the Yellow Mountain acquisition became a real nightmare. Distributing the contract was like throwing drops of water into a pan full of hot oil; it caused a great stir and commotion among the employees.

Until recently, all of Haier Hefei workers had been employees of a state-owned enterprise protected by "iron rice bowls," which meant a job position that could not be lost, no matter what. Their first reaction to the one-year employment term was that their job security was threatened. Besides, they had never heard of such strenuous terms of employment, with what they regarded as too many restrictive clauses on their employment.

A petition was drafted by some workers on June 2, 1998, to boycott the signing of the employment contract and to demand supplemental pay and a change in the company's management style. The main points of the petition were:

- that Haier revoke the signing of the employment contract, which they regarded as "illegal," to honor their years of service in the company, including both the years before the acquisition and the months under Haier management.

- that employees immediately sign a labor-protection contract with the Labor Bureau of Hefei city, to assure their legal rights.

- a demand for overtime pay and a guarantee of employees' legal income.

- that Haier stop "the worst employee of the month" practice, which they regarded as a humiliation. They compared the practice to what people were forced to do during the Cultural Revolution—criticizing themselves and being criticized by others.

- that employees be allowed to select their own employee representatives, who would participate in discussion and approval of major company-wide decisions

The organizers of the petition launched a door-to-door campaign to solicit signatures, and handed out leaflets to other employees at the company gates to win more support. On the afternoon of June 2, more than two hundred Haier Hefei employees took to the streets and handed their petition to municipal government officials. The officials talked with the representatives of the striking workers and listened to their grievances.

After he flew back to Hefei, Sun met with officials from the city government. A man of mild temperament, he decided to handle the situation gently. He drafted a response to the petition and posted it on the company bulletin board with the following major points:

- Haier would invalidate the employment contract. The company would draft a future employment contract based on provincial and municipal employment laws and regulations, and would discuss it with employee representatives before putting it into effect. The company would also honor an employee's years of service prior to the Haier takeover.

- Overtime pay would be available on the day of Haier Hefei's semi-annual celebration, which meant at the end of June.
- The company would continue the "best employee of the month" practice, while the "worst employee of the month" practice would be postponed until everyone understood the rationale for it.
- The employee representatives would be elected after the company completed its organizational restructuring. Major decisions would be made available to the employee representatives for approval.

Sun's conciliatory tactics did not work. When the strikers saw the responses, they became even more agitated. They rallied again to demand the elimination of Haier management and the abolition of the Haier culture. They specifically called for the dismissal of a manager in charge of a component assembly line who had been strictly implementing Haier practices.

With the situation becoming out of hand, Sun called Yu Zida, his immediate boss at Qingdao headquarters, for help. Yu, in turn, reported the situation to his immediate boss, Liang Haishan, who was the head of the air conditioner and electronics division. The two men compared notes briefly before taking the matter to Zhang Ruimin and Yang Mianmian, then Group President and Vice President.

Zhang and Yang listened carefully to Yu's report and felt that Haier had not done anything wrong. After weighing the legal and financial ramifications of the situation, Zhang came up with his decision.

"Shut down operations immediately!"

Zhang reasoned that this was not simply a matter of an employment contract, but a matter of two different value systems at war. He believed in the Haier way of management and its enterprise culture, and he wanted employees at Haier Hefei to share his beliefs. To him, there would be no point in keeping the company within the Haier family if it grew independent of the Haier culture.

Whether Haier would pull out completely from Hefei depended on the degree of support Haier could get from the city government. If the city government were against Haier, Haier would pull out.

Zhang's sentiments were shared by Yang, who also wanted Yu to discover the leaders of the strike and their motives. Yang believed that Sun was being too soft in yielding to the petitioners. Before sending him to Hefei, she advised Yu to let everybody at Haier Hefei know that the company had achieved a lot within five months of the takeover, and it would be up to them to decide what the future would hold for them.

It was after nine o'clock in the evening of June 4 when Yu arrived at Hefei. He immediately drove to the city government with Sun and Xu, the Executive General Manager who had been assaulted by the strikers, to hold talks with the Vice Mayor and other government officials.

Sun had reported to Yu that the behind-the-scenes organizer of the strike was Du Wenbin, a former sales manager who had been under investigation because of a large number of uncollected accounts. Sun also told Yu that many of the two hundred strikers were troublemakers and malcontents. Six of them had thrown bottles at Xu and beaten him, a clear violation of the criminal code. There were others who were moonlighters, unhappy with the "no-second job" clause in the contract.

Yu instructed Sun to post on the bulletin board a list of government-audited accounts disclosing the names of people with outstanding balances. With Du Wenbin topping the list, Yu wanted people to decide if it was wrong for Sun to audit him.

During the talk, Yu clearly spelled out Haier's intention of shutting down the operation if the situation did not change. Then he touched on the legal aspects of the strike. He had learned that the strikers had not requested a permit from the city authorities, a requirement for such an act under Chinese law. Those who had beaten Mr. Xu were in violation of the law, and should be punished by the law. Yu specifically requested the detention of the law-breakers. He also indicated that, if Haier could not get support from the city government, they would have to pull out completely.

The city officials were now in a dilemma. They wanted to protect their citizens, and they did not want Haier to shut down operations, let alone pull out. They told Yu that those who had assaulted Xu were not criminals and should not be detained. If they were detained, that might drive more of the sympathetic workers to join the strike. They also expressed the fear that shutting down operations might fuel the unrest. But the last thing they wanted to see was the complete pull-out of Haier, which would cause the city to lose face, on the one hand, and discourage future investors, on the other.

They proposed that Haier Hefei continue its operations while discussing with the workers matters such as the Haier culture.

But Yu was tough and unyielding. He insisted on stopping operations effective June 6, and on punishing those who, he thought, had broken the law. Early in the morning of June 5, Hefei government officials retreated from their previous position. They decided to lend full support to Haier, and let the case be handled the Haier way.

As was customary in China in handling matters involving large numbers of people, Yu knew he must first muster the support of the cadres by persuading them to reach a common view of the matter. A meeting was called on the morning of June 5 for the company's managers to discuss the matter. Yu handed them some discussion questions he had prepared, which included "Why didn't the people go through normal channels to report their grievances?" "What did you do at the time of the strike? Were you for, against, or neutral to the strike?" and "Why did some of your subordinates go on strike?"

As expected, the consensus that managers had reached was pretty much what Yu wanted to hear. They generally agreed that it was illegal to go on strike without a permit, and that some people had manipulated the whole thing, in an effort to return to the old system. They further concluded that the majority of the strikers had joined the strike without knowing the true intentions of the organizers.

That afternoon, the city government and its Party Committee sent a high-ranking official to the company to address the managers and all the Party members in the company. He spoke openly in favor of Haier, and urged the Party members to examine their own roles in the incident.

The same afternoon, Yu posted an announcement on the company bulletin board to the effect that, because of the strike and the cloudy situation in its wake, product quality could not be guaranteed. Therefore, starting the next day, the company would cease operations in order to hold a voluntary discussion about the strike, hoping to reach a consensus on the matter. The company would not resume operations unless a consensus was reached.

Though the discussion was supposed to be voluntary, the next day, more than thirteen hundred employees showed up, including all the strikers. Divided into small groups, they were handed discussion questions such as, "Should Haier Hefei stop or continue operations? Can our production quality be guaranteed under the current situation?" "How should we continue operations? Is it necessary to implement strict rules?" "What caused the current abnormal situation, and why?" and "What should we do to those who have caused harm to the company?"

The discussion lasted the whole day. Yu, Sun and other top managers attended the discussions of many groups. Yu's boss, Liang Haishan, came from Qingdao to attend. During the discussions, employees generally spoke in Haier's favor and some praised Haier's management practices. All strikers made self-criticisms, both orally and in writing. The six strikers who had physically assaulted Haier managers were detained for a few days by law enforcement. Du Wenbin, the strike organizer, resigned, after returning his kickbacks.

On Monday, June 8, the company resumed operations, and all went back to normal. Production rose steadily, after that, to 21,862 units in June, 28,487 in August and 55,216 in October. By the end of October 1998, Haier ranked fourth in China's TV market, with a 9.8% market share.

In retrospect, the first week of June 1998 could be regarded as the bleakest week in the short history of Haier. Sun admitted that he had been a bit carried away by what the company had achieved in the first five months after the acquisition, and that he had not been sensitive enough to the local environment and the company's old culture. Zhang Ruimin also pointed out, later, that Sun had taken Haier's management practices so much for granted that he had not properly explained them to the Hefei employees before handing out the employment contract. Zhang regarded the incident as a good indicator that Haier culture could not easily be duplicated.

In March 2000, Haier was facing another problem in Hefei. Having walked out of the shadow of the strike, Haier Hefei was ready to move on to the next phase of growth—building an Industrial

Park. The challenge, this time, was to relocate the villagers near the factory to make room for the construction of the Industrial Park. At the time, over one hundred fifty peasant families were refusing to leave their home sites, no matter what.

Chen Yuming, an editor who was with Zhang Ruimin on the Haier helicopter to Haier Hefei Industrial Park for its grand opening, wrote in the *Haier Magazine*: "As we were admiring the chopper, Zhang said that Haier One, which Haier had bought for three million U.S. dollars, served one purpose: to fly the two '*laos*'—*lao wai* and *lao xiang*, foreigners and peasants."

When foreigners came for a visit to Haier, they could see in one day all five Haier Industrial Parks in Qingdao. Whenever Haier products were going to move into a new market—Chinese suburban areas and the countryside—Haier's helicopter would be the first to do the marketing: it would circle overhead to let the peasants know.

Zhang then talked about the Haier Hefei Industrial Park, which also occupied 800 *mu* (about 5,000 acres) of land. Back in March, the peasants had refused any suggestion of relocation. What the Haier officials had done was to invite the village head, the Party Secretary and other village leaders to Haier headquarters in Qingdao, and let the Haier facilities impress them. Zhang Yingniang, the village Party Secretary, later recalled the tour and its significance. He said that, after visiting Haier Headquarters, the Haier Museum of Science and Technology and the Haier Industrial Park, they were so impressed by Haier's accomplishments that they felt that it would be a shame for them to stand in the way of Haier's further expansion.

Upon returning to Hefei, they immediately called a mass meeting, at which two relocating teams were formed—one measuring the land for fields and the other measuring the land where the houses sat. In ten days, one hundred fifty-eight families were relocated to other parts of the city. During the ten busy days, there was one day of hard rain, but that didn't stop the peasants. Except for the old window frames, which the peasants were allowed to take with them, everything was leveled to the ground, including the two-story houses of the village head and the Party Secretary.

On March 28, construction of the Industrial Park was begun. Party Secretary Zhang asked everyone involved in the relocation to learn from Haier and to learn from Zhang Ruimin, who, during the pioneering stage of Haier, had been supported by money from peasants. "Why shouldn't we support him today? You see, a village looks to other villages, a family looks to other families, people look to the cadres and the cadres look to the party leaders."

With the full support and cooperation of the village leaders, Haier Hefei Industrial Park was completed by the end of 2000. Four new plants had been built, which considerably increased Haier Hefei's productivity and competitiveness in China's TV market.

As has been said, Haier undertook a total of eighteen mergers and acquisitions between 1991 and 1998. Of these eighteen cases, the Red Star and the Hefei cases fell closest to the "catching the stunned fish" scenario, with Haier taking over entire companies and making them wholly-owned subsidiaries. A number of other cases, however, can be better described as joint operations or strategic partnerships in which Haier controls the majority of the stock.

An early example of this type of operation can be found in the case of the Wuhan Freezer Company of Hubei Province. In December 1995, Haier purchased sixty percent of the company's stock, becoming its largest owner.

The Wuhan purchase was Haier's first expansion outside the Qingdao area. This model was duplicated in March 1997, when Haier invested in the ailing Shunde Washing Machine Factory in Guangdong Province, to form Shunde-Haier Electric Ltd., producing washing machines. This was a low-cost expansion, because, though Haier controlled sixty percent of the stock in the joint venture, it did not have to put in much investment capital. Haier's stock was in the form of loans from the local government, which provided generous investment incentives to Haier, including loans, taxes and land use.

Another such instance is the joint venture between Haier and West Lake Electronics, one of the most technologically advanced TV-makers in China. In June 1997, a joint-venture contract was signed between the Qingdao Haier Air Conditioner Company, Ltd. and the West Lake Electronics' Xisha Electric Company, Ltd. to produce large-screen televisions. The total registered capital of the joint venture was 5.6 million RMB, with Haier investing 3.36 million and taking up sixty percent of the stock, and West Lake throwing in 2.24 million and keeping the remaining forty percent. The first product of the joint venture was the Pathfinder, a large-screen digital TV set, which was an immediate success in the Chinese TV market.

In reviewing the business expansions that had taken place in the previous twenty years in the United States, Zhang pointed out that they had taken three forms: large fish (companies with large capital) eating smaller fish, such as GE acquiring other smaller firms; fast fish (companies with advanced technology) eating slow fish, such as Microsoft buying other firms; and sharks eating other sharks, such as the merger of Boeing and McDonell Douglas or the merger of Citibank and Salomon Smith Barney.

But on Chinese soil, it was almost impossible for such mergers to take place, because, in the economic situation of China in the 1990s, a live fish would not allow any other fish to swallow it, while eating dead fish would only cause a stomachache. In the end, there was only one type of fish that could be eaten—the "stunned fish."

Back to the Harvard MBA class discussion on the Haier acquisition of Red Star. The discussion topics covered Haier's management style, its market orientation, and the corporate culture that combines Eastern and Western philosophies. Some students figured that Haier had learned from Japan, and stressed efficiency in their production area, while others assumed that Haier had learned from Jack Welch, and had introduced GE's quality-control system and Six Sigma into their precision quality-control system. One maintained that Haier was a product of China's economic readiness to revive after thirty-five years of slumbering, and that Haier had been propelled by the market economy of supply and demand. A few reasoned that Haier had learned from their German teachers to be technically competitive in their craftsmanship. There were also those who argued that, having learned something from each of its predecessors at the right time and at the right place, Haier was simply a product of its time.

At this point, Professor Paine made an unexpected announcement to the class.

"We're very fortunate to have Mr. Zhang, the Haier CEO, here today, to answer your questions."

Zhang had been sitting quietly among the students, listening to their discussion of his company's mergers and acquisitions. He had arrived in Boston the night before, and was tired and still troubled by jetlag. The Harvard trip had boosted his confidence in what the company had been doing regarding its management. In the past, Zhang had not thought too much about his management style, in any theoretical terms, or its bearing on management studies.

"We never thought that we would become a case to be studied by people in other countries. We have used what we thought would work for us. That was it. The trip to Harvard made me realize all the more that if the result is good, the method will be recognized, sooner or later. Ours is a result-based management style."

A student raised a question: "What is the most profound influence Mao Zedong had on you?"

Zhang recalled later that this question was so unexpected that it triggered a spontaneous answer that was equally unexpected: "Be practical and realistic," a quotation from Mao. Zhang reasoned that, at Haier, they knew the situation they were in and *had* to be practical and realistic. Only that way would they be able to find the correct solution to problems. Zhang felt that was what Mao Zedong had taught him, and that the answer really expressed what he had been feeling all along.

5

Foreign Concepts and Chinese Soil: GE, Sony and Haier

People in the home-appliance business often call Zhang Ruimin the "Jack Welch of China." If we think about that and what it implies, the comparison may not seem too far-fetched. First and foremost, both men are excellent business leaders who have helped generate a tremendous amount of wealth for their companies and for their investors. In the process of doing so, their companies have invented a great many products, with customers' specifications in mind, and have revolutionized the concept of modern business management. They have exalted the role of leadership and changed the landscape of the global market in their own ways, managing across cultures and manufacturing across boundaries. As leaders, they both take charge of their own energy, and then help orchestrate the energy of those around them. Passion is the key-word both men use to link employee capability, employee productivity, employee commitment and employee loyalty.

Service-driven and result-driven, the two men had been burdened with responsibilities and pressures rarely experienced and endured by CEOs of large corporations before them. Since GE has played a very important role in Haier's development, and continues to influence its business direction, in this chapter we'll take a closer look at General Electric by drawing a comparison between GE and Haier in product diversification, globalization, leadership and management practices.

While stressing the influence of GE, we must not forget Sony's impact on Haier in two important aspects: determination to make a brand name and diversification into other businesses, especially into life insurance services.

GE and Haier

Jack Welch and Zhang Ruimin are two extraordinary business-builders of the twentieth century, who have, in different ways, created legends in their own worlds. In the process of doing so, they have realized their identities as diligent thinkers. This is probably the most important point of comparison. Both men are blessed with clear vision and the ability to transform vision into reality. Armed with technical know-how, they have turned corporations from money-losing to fantastically profit-making, in Zhang's case, and from traditional domestic manufacturing to a diversified global company with a market capitalization of $450 billion, in Welch's case. In both cases, numbers mean a great deal, because change in quantity eventually leads to change in quality, in almost every aspect of business, from product to personnel to management, and from employee to customer to market.

GE's market value moved from number eleven in 1981, when Welch became the company's CEO, to number one in 2001, when Welch retired. Likewise, Haier's revenues grew at an average rate of seventy-eight percent for seventeen years, going from 3.48 million RMB ($1.25 million) in 1984, when Zhang took charge of the company, to 60.2 billion RMB ($7.3 billion) in 2001.

In his forty years of service at GE, the first twenty as an employee and the second as its CEO, Welch changed GE's business practice by diversifying and globalizing. GE under Welch was the world's most profitable and most valuable company, and the rewards to investors were huge—a 1,155% increase in the value of its shares from 1982 to 1997. In the summer of 1997, GE became the first corporation to be valued at more than $200 billion, up from $57 billion a decade earlier. By July 1998, its shares had risen to a total of $450 billion.

In terms of the dollar amount, Haier is the "new kid on the block." Yet Haier's vigorous growth and way of doing business mirror those of General Electric, a successful business based on technological and scientific inventions. Both companies are famous for their strategies. For instance, during the Asian financial crisis of 1997-98, neither GE nor Haier was daunted, because they had expanded their businesses by taking advantage of the discount available everywhere in the Asian countries.

Zhang was most impressed by what Jack Welch had done during the Asian economic crisis. "GE's highest gain came at a time when the whole world was not selling in 1997 and 1998," he remarked, at an interview with us in late 2001. We could see in his eyes a genuine admiration for GE and its helmsman. Zhang knows that being able to claim a market in peace is like being able to take a city in war. It requires a clear understanding of the world economy and a cross-cultural strategy in the global market.

Jack Welch understood his environment and the world situation before he contrived such a global market strategy.

Reflecting on globalization, Welch said, "Half a century of wars, fear and huge defense-spending burdens is over. And the opportunities of an increasingly peaceful world await us. Russia, Eastern Europe and China have gone from military targets to market opportunities, overnight. Peace is breaking out all over the world. Borders and markets are opening up, creating vast opportunities for fast, creative, competitive companies." (Lowe 1998, 54)

In the early 1980s, some people had called GE a mature business with limited future growth, just as people believed that Haier had hit its ceiling when the Chinese market was hit with oversupply in 1998-99, but both Welch and Zhang looked at their markets differently. In a letter in the *Haier News*, Zhang addressed the concerns of the Chinese market about oversupply by quoting a well-known story circulating among the Chinese salespeople. The story goes like this:

Two salespeople are sent to the remote countryside to open a new market selling shoes. When the first salesperson goes there and sees the people work in the fields with bare feet and is told that people are not accustomed to wearing shoes, he is very disappointed. He calls his manager, asking him to forget about opening a shoe market here. "People don't wear shoes here. Period!"

The second salesperson is dispatched, and he sees the same situation and is told the same story—people are not accustomed to wearing shoes. He is so overjoyed at the prospect of having such a great frontier market all to himself that he calls his manager, telling him that he's not coming home because he's going to teach people here to wear shoes—to protect their feet!

The moral of the story is that a market is a matter of attitude. "What business could be mature when you have economies with more than two billion people in India, China, and Southeast Asia?" Welch argued. (Lowe 1998, 54)

Zhang saw vast opportunities in the global market after 1998, just as Welch did in America at the end of the Cold War. Zhang moved into the United States with the ideas of "Market first, profit second," and "Difficult things first, easier steps later."

If GE was facing one problem in getting into the Asian market, which was how to educate Asians to buy and use quality American products, Haier had to face at least two. Chinese products had no credibility in the West, and the cost of running a business in the United States was simply too high to be feasible—it had crushed many foreign businessmen's dreams and wallets, Asians included. Yet, if Haier didn't take this step, what, then, was its alternative?

In 1998 and 1999, deflation and unemployment in China had become so bad that everywhere there were signs begging customers to buy goods from companies, with banners saying things like "suicidal sale." Businesses were looking for the minimum return on their principal, and letting go of profit, if there was any. In theory, deflation was recognized as a complex macroeconomic problem. But the simplest cause of this problem in the Chinese market in 1998 and 1999 was the oversupply of a wide range of industrial and consumer goods and the loss of jobs at the same time.

From one perspective, the problem was related to China's economic cycle. In particular, many of the industrial prices that were falling fastest were the same ones that had earlier been driven up by the boom of the early 1990s. Electronic products, household appliances and the whole line of Haier products were terribly affected, although Haier was the least affected, due to high-quality products and excellent customer services. They were willing to go the extra mile to satisfy either the most difficult or the least significant customers in remote areas.

"No matter how small they are," said Zhang, "they are ours to keep."

Price slumps were also related to the attitudes of Chinese consumers, particularly their propensity to save rather than spend.

Bank savings, which grew by nearly twenty percent in the first half of 1999, stood at a record high by September of the same year.

A series of interest-rate cuts, which took the one-year bank deposit rate down to 2.25% by September 1999 (it had been 13% in 1995), failed to boost consumer spending. Fear of unemployment was perhaps the biggest damper on consumption. State-owned enterprises laid off an estimated six million workers during 1998, and a further seven million in 1999. Some of the most painful cuts took place in the labor-intensive coal and textile sectors.

Going global seemed the best solution for Haier, which had by now grown big and fast.

Both GE and Haier, forced by their disappointing domestic markets, took the big risk and went global. Among all the factors that could decide the outcome of a business—cultural differences, language differences, tax laws, international business conduct and laws—they put customers' needs above everything else.

Their strategies are simple: get to the market. In doing so, they both have reversed traditional business practices. Welch was going to manage markets, not factories; Zhang would go after markets first, profits second.

How to achieve that? Both companies regard satisfying customers as their ultimate goal and the measure of their success. When the customers are won over, the market will follow; so will the factories and the profit.

On globalization, Welch said, "Our dream for the 1990s is a boundaryless company, a company where we knock down the walls that separate us from each other on the inside, and from our key constituencies on the outside." (Lowe 1998, 147)

The strategy GE used is "Smart Bombing," the process of overseas marketing in which GE studies each country separately, in detail, and then arranges a mix of products, brands, manufacturing facilities and marketing and retail strategies to maximize performance in each. Welch's views on China and cultural differences bore great similarity to those of Zhang in his view of America: they discount cultural differences by learning from the locals.

Haier's international expansion aims at coordinating local design, production, distribution and after-sale services by employing local people. Wherever Haier products are sold, the company tries to hire local employees and managers. It is more costly to do business this way than it would be to send Haier's own Chinese employees, but the localization strategy has proven to be so effective that Haier deems it worthwhile to continue the practice over the long run.

Secondly, GE and Haier both derived huge success from the strengths of their highly prized technology and inventions. They both stressed the importance of new technology and diversification of products to capture the consumer market, big and small. Each year, both corporations spent a lot of money on research projects, GE at its many cutting-edge labs and Haier at its Central Research Institute in Qingdao.

The result was that "GE gave Americans products as diverse as the first talking motion picture, the first jet engine, the first synthetic diamond and the first children's Silly Putty. GE products were fixtures in nearly every sphere of American life: in the home, in the factory, in space, aboard trains, planes and ships, in communications, in sports arenas, even in the Panama Canal." (O'Boyle 1998, 12)

Zhang has done exactly the same, participating in Chinese family life by providing home comforts such as refrigerators, air conditioners, washers and dryers, TV sets, razors, vacuum cleaners, toaster ovens, microwaves, food processors, mobile phones, computers and ten thousand other products for convenience and comfort. The Haier Central Research Institute, established in 1998, has engaged in design, research and testing. It has twelve high-technology research divisions and advanced labs, forging cooperation with world-famous companies, research institutes and universities to develop new technology. It has forty-eight unified development centers, ten overseas information stations and six design centers to develop the newest products using the most advanced technology in pioneering sectors.

However, education of customers was the core of marketing. The Chinese were not used to high-tech electronic products. Until a decade ago, most Chinese were still struggling to put food into their stomachs, a piece of clothing on their backs and tiles over their heads.

Two other significant and costly projects illustrate Zhang's commitment to Haier and the society benefiting from Haier technology: the establishment of Haier University and the Haier Museum of Science and Technology.

Haier University is a training center for Haier employees and Haier clients. The Haier Museum of Science and Technology is geared toward the general education of the public, to foster awareness of the existence of technology and its function in our lives. We took a trip to the museum while we were in Qingdao, and were very impressed by its appearance. It was really very extraordinary for a Chinese company to purchase a large piece of land in the High-Tech Zone in Qingdao to house a museum which retraces every significant moment in the history of science and technology, from the first telephone to the most advanced computerized home kitchen and bath systems.

Thirdly, both Jack Welch and Zhang Ruimin are strong leaders. Welch devoted a whole chapter in *Jack: Straight from the Gut,* his memoir published in 2001, to his remodeling of GE's management-training center, Crotonville, in upstate New York. In the past, Crotonville had been more like a Camelot, a showplace for GE top managers to get together, where GE trained them to do their jobs the GE way.

The moment Welch got the CEO's job, he decided to change the center. "I wanted to change everything: the students, the faculty, the content and the physical appearance of the facilities. I wanted it focused on leadership development, not specific functional training. I wanted it to be the place to reach the hearts and minds of the company's best people—the inspirational glue that held things together as we changed." (Welch 2001, 171)

This inspirational glue, according to Welch, is the best of the people who have the following four Es: "Very high energy levels, the ability to energize others around common goals, the edge to make tough yes-and-no decisions, and finally, the ability to consistently execute and deliver on their promises… In my mind, the four Es are connected by one P—passion." (Welch 2001, 158-59) Based on case studies at other companies and on on-the-job "action learning," Welch made his point even clearer by drawing a graph of the "vitality curve" of a business in the following way: the top 20% (leaders), the vital 70% (performing employees), and the bottom 10% (non-performing).

Zhang Ruimin's idea of leadership is almost exactly Welch's definition. In a talk he had with the managers at Red Star Electric Appliance Company, after the merger, he made crystal clear his three rules for measuring leadership. One of them is the concept of 80/20, which means that twenty percent of the leaders are responsible for eighty percent of the job. The power given to the manager is not to be abused, but to be exercised properly toward the common goal of the business. The manager's job is to lead the other eighty percent of the employees to carry out their work diligently. This concept forms a "two-leg" policy, according to which Haier's managers and employees work and walk together. If the manager is the right leg, the employee is the left one. The manager must lead by example, while the employee must follow and excel.

The salvage of the Red Star Electric Appliance Company, the first important merger and acquisition Haier accomplished, with a dozen more to follow in the next three years, is the best example of how leaders could be "shocked" and "stunned" into action, and be retrained, no matter how "sleepy" they had become in the old, comfortable and messy Chinese business world.

After Welch, Crotonville became a "boiling pot" of learning, as well as GE's most important factory. Haier University and the Haier Enterprise Culture Center also play an extremely important role in training leaders who can make business more productive, with a concept that will change the organization forever, at both business and operational levels.

Built in 1999 and located within the company's Industrial Park in Qingdao, Haier University is an imitation, in architectural style, of China's most respected Beijing University, which is famous for its revolutionary role in the history of modern China since the Opium Wars.

According to Zhang, innovation is the key element in Haier's leadership spirit, which is further tempered and forged at Haier University, in the down-to-earth manner expounded in the Haier University principle, "Be realistic, be pioneering, and be realistic."

Every culture has its language, and Zhang's Haier is no different. Many business catchwords, phrases and acronyms originated by Haier employees through cartoon characters or articles are made popular by the *Haier News* and Haier's annual reports. One of them is "Haier Speed." Haier Speed is Haier's approach to developing and bringing new products onto the market at the fastest possible speed.

For instance, a Haier distributor in Europe wanted Haier to manufacture five sample products in three months' time. According to international standards, to manufacture such products would take six months. But Haier got the work done in one and a half months. When he saw the quality of the samples, the distributor was so impressed that he purchased a large quantity.

Such speed not only helps Haier create and occupy markets, it helps Haier's partners, in this case the distributor, become successful as well. That is precisely the secret of the success of Wal-Mart. The ability to get things done fast and well has become critical in today's highly developed market, where information flows around the world at the touch of a finger.

Microsoft, which has invented so many new high-tech products and changed today's world by changing the old ways things had been done, constantly reminds its employees of the importance of speed:

"In three years every product my company makes will be obsolete. The only question is whether we'll make them obsolete or somebody else will. In the next ten years, if Microsoft remains a leader, we'll have had to weather at least three major crises. That's why we've always got to do better. Ask anybody who's ever worked at Microsoft and they'll tell you that if there's one cultural quality we have, it's that we always see ourselves as an underdog. I see us as an underdog today, just as I've seen us as an underdog every day for the last twenty years. If we don't maintain that perspective, some competitor will eat our lunch. I insist that we stay on top of news, as well as pursue longer-term developments on the research front, and that we use 'bad news' to drive us to put innovative new features into our products. One day somebody will catch us napping. One day an eager upstart will put Microsoft out of business. I just hope it's fifty years from now, not two or five." (Gates 1999, 182)

To solve the problem, Bill Gates' Microsoft has designed a working strategy of "market first, fix product problems second." Each firm has its own strategy that works for it, but high speed and great innovation are two key elements which no successful corporation can do without.

That is true of Zhang's Haier, too. Haier speed appears everywhere and is in everyone's face in Haier parks, factories, museums, the university and at headquarters. Haier speed must go hand in hand with innovation. Innovation includes the technology, operations, management and leadership on which Haier has always focused.

Fourthly, in the process of building and expanding, both GE and Haier have built sophisticated and inspiring management systems that, to some extent, have changed the workers' mindset to the point where self-initiation becomes the core of management. Jack Welch's championing of initiatives like Six Sigma, globalization and e-business has helped define the modern corporation. At the same time, he's a gutsy boss who has forged a unique philosophy and an operating system that relies on a "boundaryless" sharing of ideas, an intense focus on people and an informal give-and-take style that makes bureaucracy the enemy.

First among all of his successful experiences with management is MBO—"Management by Objectives." This was developed by Peter Drucker and GE. Under MBO, each manager is responsible for a profit center, and is expected to achieve his or her goal. In GE's case, the goal is seven percent return on sales and twenty percent return on investment. This management style has worked well for GE and many other corporations in the United States.

The objective, or bottom-line, approach and the result-oriented approach, although they help a firm grow, carry a fatal flaw: the tendency of managers to "harvest" a business by depleting its long-term objectives for short-term gain. In contemporary America, lawsuits over such events are commonplace. This business practice causes the demise of loyalty and the need for constant morale-building. History shows that the tyranny of numbers will sooner or later lead to cannibalism. This social Darwinism in business practice has been a thorn in the side of large corporations all over the world, including GE, and has gotten GE into various lawsuits, as well as, in certain extreme cases, provoking a social outcry.

Kidder Peabody is one such extreme case. Because of over-trading and disregarding the rules of securities book-keeping, GE's Kidder Peabody securities firm lost one billion dollars before the remains were sold to Paine Webber in 1994. The Securities and

Exchange Commission subsequently sanctioned three of Kidder's former senior bond executives, one for books-and-records violations and the other two for failing to supervise adequately. These included Michael Carpenter, head of Kidder, who had reported directly to Jack Welch.

"His way of doing business carries with it a heavy penalty, not necessarily for him or stock-holders, but for the people who do his bidding and for government and society, which must often clean up his mess," observes Thomas O'Boyle in his book *At Any Cost.* O'Boyle mentions several GE cases, including the ill-fated rotary compressor, a refinement of the mass-produced home refrigerator which GE invented in the 1920s. Welch had championed the project as a "quantum" technological leap.

Due to pressure to get it to market quickly, the machine was not adequately tested. In the end, GE had to replace defective compressors in millions of refrigerators. In 1988, it took $450 million to offset its cost. About five hundred people had lost employment by the time the plant closed its doors for good in 1993, which almost cost GE its refrigerator business.

In 1992, GE's Aircraft Engine division pleaded guilty to stealing $42 million from Uncle Sam and diverting the money to Israel to encourage orders for jet engines. GE was involved in more instances of Pentagon fraud (before it sold its arms business in 1993) than any other military contractor, with fifteen criminal convictions and civil judgments between 1985 and 1992.

To replace the lost investment, General Electric has paid a heavy price, at the cost of both employees and the company's reputation. Some people observe that, more than any other large corporation in America, GE has assumed the personality of its general.

"People at GE don't go off to work every morning. They go off to war," says one former GE executive. The constant pressure to "go get the numbers" has led inevitably to this Darwinian mentality.

While it is true that the business world is like the world of war, where people fight for markets and profits, it is also true that the business world is a world of peace, where people co-exist to share markets and profits. Is it possible to strike a balance between the two worlds? Having studied Haier and Zhang's management, we believe that the bottom-line approach to business is not the only approach. Even if this is perceived as the only approach, it can be linked with charity of heart and an understanding of human nature.

Zhang is reflective when he points out that it's not necessarily the case that the problem is with bureaucracy—Jack Welch tends to blame his employees for business failures, and tackles his problems by "downsizing" or "rationalization"—letting people go—which earned him the nickname "Neutron Jack."

Zhang tackled the issue differently. He believes that, when people stop producing and the numbers are no longer acceptable, the problem lies deeper in human nature. To Zhang's mind, the human tendency is to fall, just like a ball on a slope. Zhang's ball-on-a-slope theory has helped Haier managers and employees to deal with the issue in a positive way: to bring everyone to a higher level by pulling and pushing them upward. A focus on the employee is as important as a focus on the market.

In Zhang's world, keeping shareholders happy is not in conflict with keeping employees happy. Given his Asian background and his understanding of the Confucian thought of "ruling with a charitable heart," in a culture that is defined by a web of relationships, he has made himself drastically different from Jack Welch and other CEOs who have made themselves rich through incredibly high salaries and stock options of millions of their corporate shares. Zhang has adopted a scientifically more advanced Western management style, along with the Chinese concept of benevolence. As a result, this more humane management method helps warm people's hearts and uplift their minds, as defined by Confucian doctrine.

On the one hand, Zhang is no different from Jack Welch and all other CEOs in the West, whose full-time job is to please investors by building profitable businesses, by always "beating the Street by one penny." On the other, Zhang is able to balance the interests of investors and employees with regard to the pursuit of profit. In addition to applying the Confucian ideas of benevolence and charity in business practices, Zhang can appeal to his employees' sense of patriotism, a Chinese leader's most sought-after weapon against competition, in business or in politics. One of the scenes at many Haier facilities is the poster that bears the word "patriotism" along with other Haier mottoes. To some Haier outsiders, this seems a bit too high-sounding in a quasi market economy in today's China, but it reflects the mentality of Haier, or Zhang, for that matter, who wishes to ultimately dedicate his diligent work to the country of his birth.

Zhang Ruimin and Jack Welch

Zhang has long been an open admirer of Jack Welch, from whom he has drawn business inspiration and learned many good management secrets. The following is an excerpt from an interview with Zhang Ruimin by a China Central TV (CCTV) reporter on January 4, 2001:

Reporter: Someone has made an analogy about a Chinese boy and a foreign boy. The Chinese boy is Zhang Ruimin, representing China's entrepreneurs. Who do you think is the boy standing beside you?

Zhang: I would say it is Jack Welch of GE, who has done an excellent job. For twenty years, he has made a huge business empire grow at very high speed, even under the new economy, which is really remarkable.

Reporter: How long have you been studying him?

Zhang: For sixteen years, starting from Haier's pioneering years. I have been studying Jack Welch of GE and Konosuke Matsushita of Japan. There is also Sony's Morita.

Reporter: As business leaders, when will the two boys stand side by side?

Zhang: In terms of size, Haier cannot beat GE. There is a huge difference. But when it comes to the spirit of creativity, I think we are absolutely on a par with them. We are certainly on the same footing, in that regard.

Reporter: I notice that you have been talking about foreign countries a lot, especially the U.S. My question is, how much of you is China and how much of you is America?

Zhang: When we look at business development, many management theories originated in the U.S. and many top-notch companies are American. There is no denying that America is the strongest economy in the world. As an entrepreneur, first of all I should learn from them. They have a lot of valuable experiences. Of course they also have failures, which we should guard against. Now that Harvard has written cases on Haier, why shouldn't we learn some good things from America?

Reporter: From the Haier brochures, I have read praises about you, such as "Zhang Ruimin is the high mountain; Zhang Ruimin is the big sea." But, in Microsoft, people will not compare Bill Gates to the high mountain and the big sea.

Zhang: It is not a bad thing that employees have complete trust in their leader. I think this is very necessary. When employees need you to lead, they must have such sentiments. If a business leader cannot achieve that, he should not be in the company. You must have such charisma; you must have such ability, so everybody thinks what you do is right.

Reporter: Is there any need to learn from foreign countries in this regard?

Zhang: It is the same story in other countries, only in different ways. In General Electric, for example, everybody regards Jack Welch as god and everybody treats him as god.

Reporter: But there are people who are very concerned about such personal worship. Are you concerned?

Zhang: I think there is no personal worship in this era of the market economy; there is only market acceptance. As long as you are accepted by the market, it doesn't matter whether you call it worship or a cult. But if you are too carried away by yourself and abandoned by the market, who will worship you? The market is the only test stone.

(Excerpted from *Haier Magazine*, No. 2, 2001, p.24)

But we have also observed that, on other occasions, Zhang seemed to be very concerned about his godlike image in the eyes of his employees.

"Now the problem is that people have put too much trust in me. Let's say there is a pit ahead of Haier. If I jump in, others will follow. That is very dangerous."

This may more truly reflect the mind of the Haier CEO.

Sony and Haier

Japan was bombed during the Second World War, lost the war and was left in disgrace. China was no better off, though it was one of the winners of the war. The Chinese were treated rudely and without respect by the Western powers. The need to stand up to the Western powers became deeply rooted in the consciousness of the Chinese.

In this sense, China and Japan share the same mentality. It is no coincidence that Zhang Ruimin and Akio Morita, one of the two founding fathers of Sony Corporation (the other being Masaru Ibuka), had similar experiences in their efforts to seek out western technology and markets, and that they reacted in the same way to similar provocation. As a result, two brand names were born, Sony and Haier. The story has to begin with Ibuka.

According to John Nathan, author of *Sony: The Private Life*, Masaru Ibuka's lifelong passion was technology. During the Second World War he served as an engineer in the Japanese military and was most fascinated by American technology, though the Americans were the enemy who had dropped atomic bombs on Hiroshima and Nagasaki.

When the war ended, he was overjoyed because he could finally take on some real work, not just produce weapons for the military. He believed that developing real products would allow Japan to catch up and even move ahead of American technology. In May 1946, Ibuka founded a small electronics company called "Tokyo Tsushin Kogyo" (Tokyo Telecommunications Engineering Corporation) with a small group of associates. He was soon joined by Akio Morita, who had been his military buddy. Thirteen years younger than Ibuka, Morita had a different mission in the company. As Executive Vice President, his job was to find markets, domestic and overseas. On his first trip to the United States in 1953, Akio was overwhelmed by what he saw: big cars, wide roads, soaring buildings, all signs of a robust economy. He doubted that a small Japanese company had any chance at all of surviving in this giant country that already had everything. Then he proceeded to Germany, which, like Japan, had gone through the disastrous war, and was in postwar recovery. He wanted to see if there was any chance there.

He visited Volkswagen, Mercedes and Siemens, and was disheartened by the robust economic health he had experienced in these companies. Then came the turning-point. At a restaurant in Dusseldorf, a waiter served him a dish of ice cream garnished with a tiny parasol, and commented obligingly that the paper bauble was made in his country.

"Morita never forgot his chagrin at that moment, as he reflected that the world's consumers associated 'made in Japan' with trinkets and cheap imitations." (Nathan 1999, 52) Morita saved the paper bauble for forty years.

After that trip, Morita spoke incessantly about the importance of building an international brand, and proposed to find a name for a company that could be pronounced and recognized outside Japan. He knew that a Japanese name would not sell. Finally, from a combination of the Latin word "*sonus*," meaning sound or sonic, and the English word "sonny," Ibuka and Morita created the name "Sony," to show that the company was made up of a small group of dedicated young people who had the energy and passion for unlimited creation.

At the time, the name "Sony" was considered by many Japanese to be quite strange, but it was easy to pronounce and read in any language. In 1955, they registered Sony as an official trademark of the company with the intention of establishing the name as a global brand.

The name sounded good, but meant nothing to the commercial world. The breakthrough came when Morita refused to sell Sony-made radios under the "Bulova" name.

In New York City, Morita was marketing a radio made by his tiny company back in Japan. A purchasing agent for the Bulova watch company saw it, and told Morita that he would take one hundred thousand units, provided that he could sell the radios under the Bulova name. "I'm sure you understand," he told Morita. "Nobody has heard of Sony."

One hundred thousand units was a huge order, worth more than the total capitalization of the company at the time. But profit wasn't the only issue to Morita; what mattered to him was establishing the Sony name around the world. He sent a cable back to Tokyo, explaining his intention to decline. Ibuka wired back immediately: the board disagreed with Morita. The company could not afford to reject the order, and Morita was to accept Bulova's terms. After one week of cabling back and forth, Morita was still unable to persuade the Sony board. Out of frustration, he made the decision to decline the offer on his own authority as Sony's Executive Vice President.

Years later, Morita and the whole world agreed that turning Bulova down was the best business decision of his career.

Between 1955 and 1960, Morita returned to New York several times a year, working extremely hard selling Sony products on the streets. Eventually, he opened the market for Sony in the United States through a small transistor radio, the TR-63. On February 20, 1960, Morita established the Sony Corporation of America.

Zhang's experience paralleled that of Morita. One day, during his German trip in early 1985, after the business talks, their German business partner took the visitors to a restaurant to celebrate. There were fireworks that night. One of the German hosts remarked that the fireworks were made in China, and commented that the Chinese were good at that. The host might not have meant anything more than a compliment, or perhaps he was simply stating a fact, but Zhang was perplexed and stunned. He felt a pain in the chest, hardly believing that, to the Western eye, the best thing China could show the world was still something that had been made a thousand years before. He vowed to make the best products and show them to the world someday.

There was another similarity between Sony and Haier, or rather between Morita and Zhang. When Haier was facing the worst nightmare in its history in 1993, when the promised loan of 1.6 billion RMB was stopped by the bank after the first 240 million RMB had come in, and Whirlpool offered to buy out Haier and use the company as its major supplier, Zhang adamantly refused, just as Morita had refused Bulova. As a result, both men got themselves into the most difficult situations in their lives, and suffered tremendous consequences: Morita had to sell products on the New York streets for five more years before he could see any results, while Zhang had to face the thousands of Haier employees who needed jobs to survive the financial nightmare.

For the following two years, Zhang worked with his employees on the construction side to speed up the construction of the industrial park. By sheer willpower, the Haier Industrial Park was finished far ahead of time.

A closer comparison reveals that there are striking similarities between Sony and Haier in two important aspects of their business development: brand name building and diversification.

By 1958, Sony had gained recognition for its Sony brand goods. The design of Sony's new products often emphasizes originality and uniqueness, as in the cases of the Walkman, Profeel and Handycam lines. Sony's strategy for building its brand image was to market its products as the "World's First," "World's Smallest," "World's Biggest," or "World's Best" products.

Haier has also experienced several stages of name change (see Chapter 2 for details). Like Sony, Haier has been working hard, since 1984, to promote its corporate identity and the image the Haier brand conveys to the public. By emphasizing product quality and after-sale services in a country where most appliance makers did not care much about them, Haier quickly established itself as a strong brand name. Zhang often stresses to Haier employees the notion that "The brand is the company."

To guarantee that the Haier brand is worthy of consumer trust, Haier will not put the Haier brand on its products until they pass quality standards at five levels. When new companies join the Haier Group through mergers and acquisitions, they keep their original brands until Haier determines that the products meet the Haier brand-certification criteria.

Both Sony and Haier have expanded their brand names from domestic to overseas, though Haier has a long way to go to catch up with Sony in brand recognition around the globe.

Sony began to diversify into fields other than electronics in 1961, when it founded Sony Enterprise Co. Ltd. to manage the Sony Building in the Ginza. Over the next several years, Sony Enterprise added Sony Plaza, a retail chain to market imported goods, the French restaurant *Maxim's de Paris*, Sony Travel Service, an insurance agency, and other services.

Most of Sony's diversification into new areas of business was through joint ventures with foreign companies. In March 1965, Sony started a joint venture with a U.S. company called Tektronix, Inc. to make oscilloscope, a measuring instrument, in Japan. Within ten years, production and sales of their oscilloscope led the industry.

The company later expanded into new fields, including other electronic measuring instruments, graphic displays, broadcasting equipment and optical devices.

The next joint venture was formed in 1975 with Union Carbide Corp. (UCC), another U.S. company, to produce batteries. UCC, which manufactured and marketed batteries under the Eveready brand name, was the largest producer of batteries in the world. With Sony-Eveready as the name of the joint venture, Sony not only had its own battery manufacturing facility, but also tapped into the rapidly growing market for the small batteries used in cameras, watches and calculators. Though the joint venture agreement was terminated in 1986, and the company name was changed to Sony Energytec, Inc., Sony was able to utilize the experience gained through the venture to develop the world's first lithium-ion rechargeable battery four years later.

In March 1968, Sony entered the music software business in Japan by establishing a joint venture with CBS, Inc. of the United States. The venture, later renamed "CBS/Sony Records," blossomed within ten years to become the number one record company in the world. The support provided by the CBS/Sony Group was critical to Sony's successful launch of the Compact Disc system.

In addition to the joint ventures, Sony also established a number of wholly-owned subsidiaries. In 1962, Sony established the chemical manufacturing and marketing subsidiary, Sony Chemicals Corporation, and, in 1969, Sony Magnescale, Inc., to manufacture the precision measuring instruments used in magnetic scales. Both of these companies are now listed in the Second Section of the Tokyo Stock Exchange.

Haier's diversification has taken several forms: joint ventures with both foreign and domestic companies, and mergers and acquisitions. Qingdao General Refrigerator Factory, Haier's predecessor, formed a joint venture with the German company, Liebherr, in 1984, to manufacture four-star refrigerators in China. In 1993, Haier signed a joint-venture contract with the Italian appliance maker, Merloni, to produce washing machines. Mitsubishi of Japan is among Haier's other joint-venture partners. In addition to absorbing advanced technologies from the venture partner, one of the big advantages of forming a joint venture with a foreign company on Chinese soil is the tax benefit. According to Chinese law, a joint venture does not have to pay taxes during the first two years, and pays only fifty percent taxes for the next three years.

Haier has also established a number of cooperative programs and partnerships with foreign companies to develop new products or new markets. One such program was with Philips, to develop Bluetooth technology for refrigerators. Another was with Toshiba, to develop commercial air conditioner products. Haier also had a program with Lucent Technologies, for its GSM technology.

Much in the style of Sony, Haier has diversified into fields that are outside its major fields of business. In 1994, Haier expanded into the bioengineering field by acquiring and forming two pharmaceutical companies—Qingdao Haier Pharmaceutical Company, Ltd. and Qingdao Haier Number Three Pharmaceutical Company—to develop and produce western and Chinese medicines.

This move raised some eyebrows among China's industry analysts, because of pharmaceutical industry's distance from Haier's major product categories and the losses that the companies had incurred in the first few years of operation. Since 1997, Qingdao Haier Number Three Pharmaceutical Company has gradually eased itself out of an all-time low situation, and sales have begun to increase by thirty percent each year.

In February 1999, Haier formed its International Travel Agency Ltd., hiring five hundred employees. The agency handles both industrial travel and business travel. In 2001, it catered to a total of over one million travelers.

In May 2000, Haier formed a joint venture with the Hong-Kong-based Fungchoi Printing Company to engage in China's 100 billion RMB per year printing business. The joint venture now prints posters, company catalogs and brochures, calendars, paper toys, periodicals and magazines, among other things.

Sony and Haier Branch into the Financial Services Field

In the late 1950s, on a visit to the United States to promote Sony's transistor radio, Morita was stunned by a towering white skyscraper soaring into the sky above Chicago. He was even more surprised to learn that it was one of the Prudential Insurance Company's office buildings. The fact that a life insurance company had such an enormous building and the association between financial institutions and skyscrapers stuck with Morita for a long time. At that moment, Morita's dream of a Sony financial company began to haunt him.

It took more than twenty years for Morita's dream to come true. In the spring of 1975, Donald S. McNaughton, CEO of the Prudential Company, who had met Morita long before, dropped by Sony to say hello. Prudential was one of the largest foreign stockholders in Sony, through its holdings of American Depositary Receipts. During their chat, Morita hinted that Sony would be very interested in starting a business operation with Prudential in Japan. No further discussion took place on the matter during their conversation, but when McNaughton left Morita's office, he asked one of the people escorting him to the car whether Morita was serious about a Sony-Prudential project. Morita immediately got back to McNaughton to reassure him that he was dead serious about his proposition.

Sony quickly set up a team to work on two fronts: to obtain permission from the Ministry of Finance (MOF) of Japan to set up a life insurance company, and to establish a management plan for an equally-owned joint venture between Sony and Prudential. While negotiations with Prudential did not present much problem, it took the MOF three long years to approve the establishment of an equally-owned joint venture between Sony and Prudential, and another two years before Sony Prudential Life Insurance Co., Ltd. was finally granted a business license in February 1981.

Sony Prudential Life Insurance was a big success, especially with its Life Planners. The company changed its name to "Sony-Pruco Life Insurance Co., Ltd." in September 1987, marking a turning-point in the company's management, with Sony taking up seventy percent of the stock and Prudential retaining the remaining thirty percent. In April 1991 Sony-Pruco celebrated its tenth anniversary, with a total insurance portfolio exceeding two trillion yen and total assets of more than 90 billion yen.

Also at that ceremony, the company's name was officially changed to Sony Life Insurance Co., Ltd. Two years later, in March 1993, Sony Life recorded its first non-consolidated fiscal year profit.

Haier is following a pattern similar to Sony's in getting into a life insurance partnership with an American company. Haier had been planning to diversify into the financial services sector for some time, since Zhang believed that would help generate more revenues for the company, in the long run.

Starting in August 2001, Haier began to invest heavily in this completely new field, mostly by buying shares in China's securities and banking companies. In early September of that year, Haier signed a Framework Agreement with the municipal government of Anshan, a city in northeastern Liaoning Province, to transfer its stocks in Anshan Trust Ltd., a publicly traded company whose net profit in 2000 had been 93 million RMB. Haier bought 200 million RMB worth of shares, which took up twenty percent of the total stock in the Trust.

Also in September, Haier bought heavily into the stocks of Qingdao Commercial Bank, making it the largest shareholder of the bank. In June 2001, the fast-growing Qingdao Commercial Bank which ranked sixth in the city of Qingdao with a profit of ten million RMB that year, announced its intention to increase its capitalization to 769 million RMB from 350 million RMB. Haier jumped at the opportunity, wishing to increase substantially its existing meager holding (0.65%) of the bank's stock.

The problem was that, according to Chinese commercial banking law, a single shareholder cannot hold more than ten percent of the stock in a commercial bank. What Haier did was to rally ten more companies that were affiliated with Haier to buy into the bank jointly. According to the Chinese *Finance and Economy* magazine, after the expansion, Haier and its affiliated companies held more than fifty percent of the bank's stock.

As a prelude to a more aggressive move in that direction, Haier formed the Qingdao Haier Insurance Company Ltd. on December 18, 2001, shortly after China's accession into the World Trade Organization. The registered capital for the company was six million RMB, with money coming from Haier Electric International Ltd., a subsidiary of the Haier Group, and ten other corporate or *legal person* shareholders. The company sells both industrial and personal insurance in the areas of automobile, enterprise property, employer liability, family property, construction, personal mortgage, and life insurance, among others.

On December 26, a week after the establishment of Qingdao Haier Insurance, and the day of Haier's seventeenth anniversary,

Haier announced that it would form a joint venture with New York Life Insurance Company to sell life insurance in China, pending approval by the China Insurance Regulatory Commission (CIRC). The joint-venture company, called Haier New York Life, was a fifty-fifty partnership between the Haier Investment & Development Company Ltd., under the Haier Group, and New York Life International, the overseas arm of New York Life Insurance Company, the largest mutual life insurance company in the United States. The new company had an initial capitalization of 200 million RMB ($24 million) and, in December 2002, started its initial operations in Shanghai, one of the four Chinese cities currently open for Sino-foreign life insurance companies.

Founded in 1845 and headquartered in New York City, New York Life Insurance Company is a Fortune 100 company, offering life insurance, annuities and long-term-care insurance. New York Life International's Asian operations include Hong Kong, Taiwan, India, Indonesia, the Philippines, South Korea and Thailand. In mainland China, the company has representative offices in Beijing, Shanghai, Guangzhou and Chengdu.

Gary Benanav, Chairman and CEO of New York Life International, considered the joint venture with Haier a major step in solidifying New York Life's presence as a global leader in life insurance. Over the years, New York Life had demonstrated its commitment to China, and Benanav looked forward to being a long-term partner with Haier.

It all started with a "matchmaker," someone doing business with Haier Hong Kong who happened to know one of the vice presidents of New York Life International (NYLI). According to Qiao Yide, NYLI's Shanghai representative, in a chat in August 2001, Haier showed strong interest in entering the financial service field, and wondered if NYLI would consider striking up a relationship with them.

Qiao was excited about Haier's interest. He obtained the contact number and called Cui Shaohua, head of Haier's capital management division in Qingdao. After a few telephone exchanges, they agreed to meet in Shanghai. In the months to follow, representatives from both companies met frequently to discuss the joint venture details.

In October, top New York Life corporate executives also flew to Qingdao to meet with Zhang and other Haier top executives.

Since this is a fifty-fifty joint venture, the contract terms specify that both parties have an equal number of directors sitting on the board. New York Life would nominate the first General Manager, to be confirmed by Haier. The negotiations basically went smoothly, although initially Haier had some concerns over the relatively long period of time required for the projected return on their investment.

NYLI went the extra mile to explain to Haier that, unlike the home-appliance industry, a new insurance company normally does not make a profit in the first six or seven years. But in the long run, it is a very profitable business once the customer base is established and clients are retained. Haier finally saw eye-to-eye with NYLI regarding profitability.

It had taken New York Life long years to return to the Chinese market after the Communists took over from the Chiang Kai-shek government in 1949. In 1994, NYLI set up its China office in Shanghai and, a year later, Qiao Yide was sent to the city to work on the company's China program. Other offices in Beijing, Guangzhou and Chengdu were soon set up. These offices had three missions: market research into China's insurance industry; networking with the Chinese government, regulatory agencies, peer insurance companies and media; and helping with the training of China's insurance professionals.

As with other foreign insurance companies trying to get into the Chinese market, New York Life faced two major challenges: the Chinese government's protectionism toward the industry and the scarcity of qualified professionals in the field. To boost the image of New York Life in China, the company had invested $180 million dollars over the previous several years in some not-so-profitable infrastructure projects, such as highway construction and sewage disposal programs. It had also donated 100,000 RMB to Fudan University in Shanghai, and Shanghai University of Finance, to set up scholarships to train insurance professionals.

After the American bombing of the Chinese embassy in Belgrade in May 1999, Sy Sternberg, Chairman, President and CEO of New York Life's corporate office, visited China. He came at a time when the relationship between China and the United States was at a very low point, to reassure the Chinese government that New York Life had been consistent in supporting China's economic growth, market openness and reform. During the U.S. congressional debate over China's Most Favored Nation status, Sy Sternberg testified in China's favor to the American lawmakers. In August 2001, Sternberg paid another visit to China, during which he met with the Chinese President Jiang Zemin. Before his visit, other New York Life top executives had met twice with the Chinese Premier Zhu Rongji.

All these paid off and, in December 2001, New York Life obtained permission from the China Insurance Regulatory Commission (CIRC) to move forward in establishing life insurance operations in China.

The choice of Haier as NYLI's joint venture partner was not a whim coming from some NYLI executive; rather, it matched the company's basic partnership criteria. NYLI was particularly impressed with Haier in that it shared NYLI's corporate concept, had deep pockets and an effective accounting system, and owned a nationwide customer base and service network.

NYLI had initially made a list of potential partners that included the top hundred Chinese companies. After using a process of elimination to exclude some obviously "impossible" companies such as tobacco companies and breweries, Haier remained on its short list. The reason that NYLI did not choose a Chinese insurance company as its joint venture partner was that NYLI had a precondition: if the joint venture proved to be successful, the original Chinese insurance company should cease to exist. This is an anticipatory measure to avoid future cutthroat competition between the joint venture and the original Chinese insurer.

This seems to be a view shared by other foreign insurance companies wishing to enter China. In 2000, the China Insurance Regulatory Commission approved the establishment of four Chinese insurance companies, with the intent that they would be "married" to foreign insurance companies as joint venture partners, but none of them had been chosen and all remained virgins waiting to get marriage licenses.

The marriage between Haier and NYLI looks like a good match. Both companies have promised that they will not form joint ventures with any other company in the life insurance field in China. A "marriage for life" seems to be in prospect.

At almost the same time as it started approaching NYLI for the joint venture project, Haier was holding talks with the Wuhan-based Changjiang Securities Company (CJSC) to buy into its stock. Like the Qingdao Commercial Bank, CJSC, a medium-sized securities company, was planning to increase its capital base from one billion RMB to two billion RMB. By the end of September 2001, the consensus was that Haier was going to be the primary shareholder in the newly organized securities company, holding fifteen percent of the company's stock.

To iron out the last rough edges of Haier's further expansion, CJSC held a shareholders' meeting in January 2002, to revise its charter to allow a single shareholder, in this case Haier, to own up to twenty percent of the stock in the company.

In March 2002, the Changjiang Securities Company, now with Haier as its largest shareholder, signed a Framework Agreement with the French-based BNP Paribas to establish the Sino-Foreign Joint Venture Securities Company. This partnership was the first of its kind after China's accession to the World Trade Organization. It became the second Sino-foreign joint venture investment bank, after the China International Capital Corporation (CICC). The joint venture company will provide its customers a wide range of financial services, including distribution, offering and underwriting of securities in the primary market, financial advisory, mergers and acquisitions and other financial services.

By any account, Haier's diversification into the financial services sector can be regarded as aggressive, maybe more aggressive than Sony's, in its initial stages. Given that a huge amount of investment money has been put into these ventures, Haier must be very serious about its moves. It is not clear, at this point, whether Haier is going to sit waiting for returns on its investment or, like GE, is going to fight an active battle in the ditches of finance, but Haier should expect to make a sizeable fortune from these highly protected businesses, whose profit margins could be astronomical.

6

The Haier Kaleidoscope:
People Behind a Brand Name

A Day with the Haier Employees: December 18, 2001, Qingdao

Ashining minivan picks us up at Number One Haier Road, where the Haier Group's headquarters is located. Today we will be shown one of the firm's largest and most modernized sectors—the Haier Air Conditioner Manufacturing Plant—on the east side of Jiaozhou Bay. The thirty-three-square-kilometer Qingdao High-Tech Industrial Park, which has proved very popular with investors, has housed quite a few world-famous brands. AT&T set up a joint venture there in 1993, and was followed by Coca-Cola, which has a thirty-million-dollar bottling plant in the Park. Other investors include Hewlett-Packard, Lucent Technologies and Fuso Chemical of Japan.

Haier's newest air conditioner, the MRV series, is also manufactured there. This new plant controls the firm's core business —residential and commercial air conditioners. In comparison with the same period in 2000, according to the company newspaper, *Haier News*, the number of exports has trebled. The plant is proud to be responsible for the advanced, state-of-the-art MRV series, which is hot in both Chinese and world markets.

Sitting in the van, we are waiting to move. We have noticed that we're not the only ones. Quite a few cars and minivans, parked under the swinging flags of several major countries with which Haier is currently doing business, are also waiting with their engines running. Two seconds ago, the minivan driver, Xiao Li, was paged. He is now talking rapidly over the company cell phone, with his back to us.

While we wait, we take another look at the unique, red-columned corporate building in front of us. We were told yesterday by a taxi driver, who happened to have been one of the many contracted suppliers for Haier for the past four years, that, from the sky, the square building with the glass dome resembles a turtle.

There is a turtle joke about Zhang Ruimin. Unlike some other corporate executives who take time off to play golf or go bowling, he almost never does any sports. Most of the time, he sits at his desk in his office, without moving an inch, for hours, like an old turtle keeping all to itself. But surprisingly, he has been in good shape despite his immobility. Once he joked about that, saying that his "life lies in inaction," as against the proverbial "life lies in action." Maybe he was referring to the ancient oriental culture in which a turtle is regarded as a symbol of longevity. In any case, the Haier building was built to last a thousand years.

We had spent the whole of the previous day inside the building, in various showrooms and conference rooms. Today, when we were inside again, we were told by Mr. Xie, of the Haier Enterprise Culture Center, that the twelve circular floors inside the square building provide thoughts of the flexibility required to deal with each and every specific issue. Together, the outward appearance and the inside design symbolize the Haier culture, which reflects the time-honored Chinese wisdom of "being tough and flexible at the same time."

"See the thirty-six dots of our company logo on top of the building? Those dots symbolize resourcefulness, as suggested in the famous thirty-six military strategies," Xie said in a spirited voice.

There is no doubt that Haier has imagination.

The driver's conversation with his boss, the company dispatcher, is now over. Joined by Liu Chunhua, our guide, whom we call Xiao Liu (meaning Little Liu), we hit the road.

As we drive along, we soon learn that Xiao Li, the driver, used to drive for cadres at the Red Star Electric Appliance Company, which was acquired by Haier in July of 1995. Asked about the merger (it has been said that the merger was a very painful experience for the Red Star employees), Li says that it didn't affect him at all.

"I'm a driver. What do I have to lose? Cadres everywhere need drivers." After a pause, he added, "Managers got hurt."

Red Star had over 3,000 employees, of whom over one hundred were middle-level managers. Quite a few were let go after the merger. Li says that he lost nothing but the pain of not being able to get paid on time.

"Now we get paid on time, base plus bonus."

"Bonus?" We are interested, thinking this must have something to do with Haier's market chain practice. This is the Haier way of assuming individual accountability. If a product doesn't sell in the market, or sells very poorly, everyone from design, manufacturing and sales is held responsible for it. And their pay is directly related to the product's market performance. We understand that the market chains practice works with people directly associated with products, but we are not sure how it applies to a company driver's bonus.

"Yes, bonus. It's calculated according to the miles we drive each day. The more miles we drive, the more pay we get."

We feel a bit guilty for having been late this morning, but it was not entirely our fault. The night before, Ms. Su, director of the Haier Enterprise Culture Center, had informed us that we would be picked up at nine-thirty a.m. from the Holiday Inn, a trendy hotel in the trendiest section of Qingdao, where we are staying. While we were having breakfast and comparing notes at nine o'clock in the hotel lobby lounge, Xiao Li arrived, half an hour ahead of time. In the end, he had to wait while we gulped down our *dim sums*. We cost him time when he could have been driving more miles and making a little more money. No wonder he got paged the moment we got out of our hotel. His boss must have thought he had already picked us up and dropped us off, and was ready for another trip to earn more bonus points.

"If you have a good relationship with your boss, you'll get more assignments and earn more miles, I'd assume?" Shawn wondered. China has always been famous for favors.

"Not in Haier. We have driving to do all day long."

"How so?"

"We calculate how much driving we have to do each day before we rent our cars." This time, Xiao Liu answers. Xiao Liu is the Director of the Enterprise Culture Department at Haier's Air Conditioner Division, and is our guide for today. He's been with the firm for a little over four years, one of the many college graduates who joined Haier in the summer of 1997.

"Rent?" We were again surprised.

"Yes. We used to own our cars, but not anymore. Renting is much cheaper. It's also maintenance-free. We are not in the car business, you see, and we don't want car maintenance. That's one of the features of Haier management: maintenance-free operation. You'll see what I mean when we get to our modern, completely automated warehouse. We keep goods flowing as fast as we keep cash flowing. Inventory eats profits. We don't want inventory."

As with every other driver in whose car we ride (a total of seven or eight), we ask Xiao Li how much he makes a month as a driver. We want to get a more complete picture of the pay schedule for this group of employees. Since wages are open secrets to everybody in the company and nobody really minds being asked about that, it is safe for us to ask without being embarrassing or embarrassed.

Xiao Li says that he makes an average of 2,000 *yuan* a month (the equivalent of $240), which is almost the same as what we have heard from all the other drivers we have asked. This is a little higher than they would earn if they worked for another company in the same city. We have previously asked the same question to Mr. Liu Wei of the Group's Overseas Development Division, who showed us around Haier headquarters the second day after our arrival in Qingdao. With a college degree and overseas working experiences, he makes about 10,000 *yuan* (the equivalent of $1,200) a month.

We later learned from Haier headquarters' Enterprise Culture Center, headed by Su Fangwen, that Haier has a very complicated pay system. There are altogether thirteen pay schedules in the company. Mid-level managers and up are salaried employees, while R&D personnel are paid according to the projects contracted or assigned to them. Lower-level managers receive wages based on their job positions and the level of technical ability required of them. Production workers are generally paid by the piece. All thirteen pay schedules are tied to the job performance of the employees or managers. While there is no ceiling to cap the pay, there is a floor, which is based on the minimum wage of the City of Qingdao, to safeguard the employees' standard of living.

We do not know exactly how much Zhang Ruimin is making as Chairman and CEO of the Haier Group. In August 2002, for the purpose of this book, we asked Su Fangwen about Zhang's current salary, and were informed by her office that Zhang's salary is now determined by a program set by the Qingdao municipal government, tailored specifically for top executives. According to our research, this program is called the "Entrepreneur Salary Program," initiated in 1998 by the Qingdao municipal government in order to reward more handsomely top executives in the city's large companies.

There are two parts to this salary program, the fixed part and the flexible part. The fixed part is the base annual salary, which has to do with the size of the company and the average salary of its employees. Chinese enterprise laws allow top managers in collectively-owned companies to receive up to three times the average wages of the company. The flexible, or risky part, as it is called, specifies that, after the company has achieved its projected goals and has made a profit, its top executives are entitled to take up to fifteen percent of the profit, after taxes and other necessary deductions. The program was first experimented with in 1998 at Haier and Hisense, another large company in Qingdao, and extended to ten more companies in 1999.

Contrary to a widespread belief that Zhang and other Haier executives do not own any company stocks, Zhang and other Haier executive have been in possession of some shares ever since the company went public in 1993. According to the annual reports of Qingdao Haier Co., Ltd., the publicly-owned subsidiary of the Haier Group, Zhang owned 4,800 shares of stock in 1993; 6,240 shares in 1994; 12,730 shares in 1996; and 25,814 shares in April 2001, when he yielded his position as the Chairman of Qingdao Haier Co., Ltd. at the end of the four-year term, while remaining Chairman and CEO of the Haier Group.

In 2001, Zhang received 73,101 *yuan* (the equivalent of $8,828) from Qingdao Haier Co., Ltd., while Yang Mianmian, the Haier Group President, received 70,931 *yuan* (the equivalent of $8,567) and held 37,173 shares of stock at the end of the year, up from 25,814 shares in April of that year.

Xiao Liu continues, saying that the firm has recently bought three Mercedes 500s, each costing 1.6 million RMB. One of them came to pick us up at the airport upon our arrival.

"Haier wants to give our guests the best treatment. A courtesy. Our CEO, Zhang, and President, Yang Mianmian, drive Mercedes 300s."

"We have costs, but we'd like to minimize cost. Haier is promoting zero inventory and zero distance from the customers. One way to do that is to use the customers' money to make the refrigerators. You see, our computer terminal is connected to all the satellite computers in all of our stores. When a purchase order is registered in a store, say an air conditioner, it goes directly to the headquarters' terminal. In seven days, the air conditioner is made and shipped to the store where the customer has made his purchase. Seven days are long enough to turn the money around—the customer has to pay the moment he makes the purchase," Xiao Liu says.

"That's an ideal situation for any manufacturer! But what if the customer doesn't want to wait?" Shawn asks.

"In our marketing department, we have two sales teams who are handling this issue, before sales and after sales. Our manufacturing department knows very well what kind of products the market is looking for, because they talk to the marketing department all the time. Today, we are not afraid of product shortages; we're afraid of oversupply. We don't want warehouses because we don't need warehouses. Every product is made with a customer waiting for it. You must have heard of our way of handling logistics. Water flows, cash flows, material things flow, too. To ensure this, we have a new company slogan that says 'Any product without an order is a wasted product.' You'll see for yourself when we arrive."

The minivan is on the newly built highway to Yellow Island, a newly developed High-tech Industrial Park, to which Haier's air conditioner manufacturing has recently moved. After an hour's drive and chat with Xiao Liu, we arrive at the Industrial Park.

Along Broadway stand three large, newly-finished, modernized, gray plant complexes, each a quarter of a mile long, belonging respectively to three competitors, Hisense, Aucma and Haier. They co-exist along Broadway, proud and bare. Construction workers, who must have been peasants on this tough land some five years ago, are building plants or are in uniform, guarding gates. They no longer depend on the mercy of Mother Nature to make a living. They must be grateful for the change.

We drive through a guarded gate and make our first stop at the manufacturing plant.

The young girl in charge of reception receives us with a nice smile. As she has done with many people before us, she leads the way among the various air conditioners in the showroom, wall-mounted, window-mounted, ceiling-mounted and central.

"These models," the young girl says, "can be picked up anywhere, from Haier's showrooms around the world. If they run out in our New York office, we'll ship it over. Domestically, we do free delivery and free installation." She sounds proud.

Haier is well known for free delivery and free repair, and has a very good reputation for service. Jeannie had personal experience of this in the summer of 2001. While she was in China, she bought a window-mounted unit for her great-uncle in Chengdu, Sichuan Province. A three-person team arrived at her uncle's home, punctually at three o'clock, the promised delivery time. The three young men in their early twenties had brought with them three things: a blanket to lay on the living room floor so as not to leave footprints on the carpet, some rags to wipe things clean after the installation was done, and a Haier service card that told her where to call if problems occurred. Sweaty and thirsty after working three hours drilling holes in windows in the afternoon sun, they declined the soda Jeannie brought for them, nor did they drink the tea her great-uncle made for them. They said they were not supposed to, according to Haier rules. After the job was finished, they showed Jeannie's seventy-seven-year-old great-uncle how to use the control panel, over and over again, till he was sure of its operation. Then the team leader took her great-uncle's telephone number, and told him that he'd personally call to make sure the air conditioner "works just fine."

Impressed with their excellent service, Jeannie subsequently bought five more Haier air conditioners, through the serviceperson, at a total cost of 14,800 RMB (3,000 RMB apiece, with 200 RMB total discount) for her mother-in-law, her two aunts and two cousins.

Her great-uncle kept saying, "China has changed. Competition has changed the young people. The young people have changed China."

Compared with Shawn's experience back in 1988, that was really a big change. Shawn was among the early-birds to be able to install a personal telephone in the city of Hangzhou, where he held a teaching position in the Department of Foreign Languages at Zhejiang University. He paid 300 RMB as the initial installation fee (a few months later the fee soared to over 2,000 RMB, as applications for installation increased considerably) and waited for three months before a team of installation workers from the municipal telecommunications department came to his apartment to lay the lines.

As was the general practice at the time, Shawn prepared ten packs of cigarettes (cigarettes being among the popular gift items in China, then) and presented them to the team of three the moment they arrived. During their work, Shawn and his wife served them drinks and *dim sums*, from time to time, which they took without any word of gratitude. After about two hours' work, both in and outside his apartment, the installers left a messy floor and word that the line would be connected within a week.

But after a week, nothing had happened. Shawn was anxious, and went to the local office of the municipal telecommunications department several times to push for connection. Two more weeks went by without any progress. Frustrated, Shawn picked up a pay phone and called the office of the municipal telecommunications department. It happened to be the service-day of the head of the department, and Shawn had the good luck to talk to the very person in charge. The head listened to Shawn's complaint, and promised that he would look into the matter as soon as possible. When he returned home, five minutes after the call, Shawn heard his phone ringing. It was a call from the local telecommunications office, informing him that the line had been connected, and was ready to use.

Shawn later learned, from someone working in the local telecommunications office, that everything had been done to his line the day of the installation, and all the local office needed to do was push a switch to get him hooked up. The reason they did not push the switch was that they had been waiting for Shawn to send them additional sweeteners, such as ten more packs of cigarettes, within a week of installation.

Shawn's problem was that he had not fully understood the meaning of the installers' words that "...the line [would] be connected within a week."

After the showroom, we move to the factory. It's very clean and roomy, completely different from the memories we have of factories in China. Young workers all wear gray uniforms, the color of the air conditioners they are making. (The driver wears a blue uniform while Xiao Liu wears a blue management uniform to separate him from the workers of this plant and this group. Obviously, the color of the uniform follows the system of individual accountability.) We watch in fascination while the frame of a wall unit is taken out of a cardboard box by one worker to be put over a compressor that is simultaneously taken out of another cardboard box by another worker standing opposite across a moving black belt. In a second, a fan and a few computer chips join the frame and the compressor. As the air conditioner-in-the-making moves down the belt, more parts are put on and screwed tight.

We move along with the black belt while the air conditioner takes shape. The Chinese manufacturing plant and the air conditioner are not props. Less than seven minutes later, the air conditioner is made, and, at its final stop, it is "dressed up" with the Haier logo—the Haier Brothers, a Chinese boy and a foreign boy joining hands—by two young men, one on each side of the moving belt.

They put on the last nine screws, and the air conditioner is ready to be packed and shipped to someone's living room.

"A product without an order is a wasted product," says the slogan on the wall over the moving assembly line. A digital clock tells the quota of the day: 800 units. By 10:45 a.m., the time we got there, 287 units were done.

On the opposite wall is the same couplet, illustrating the Haier spirit, which we have seen on the walls of Haier headquarters:

Haier Spirit: Serve the Country, Work Hard, Pursue Excellence;
Haier Style: Prompt Reaction, Act Immediately.

Next to the couplet is the much-quoted slogan that has made Haier products popular on the Chinese market: "Zero Defects."

"Do you have enough time to get the other 500 units done by the end of day?" Jeannie asks the last worker on the assembly line, a young man of about twenty.

"Yes." He looks toward the digital clock and the quota board. He then smiles shyly. "We only have to do 600 units per day. The other 200 are bonus."

We keep moving, and, following the products, come to the next building, connected to the assembly hall. This is the pride of Haier: the most advanced, completely automated warehouse, with a computer-control system for packing, moving, storing and loading products onto trucks. Since it was completed two years ago, it has been used by China as a model warehouse, and people from all over the country have come here to see it.

Once inside the guarded building (every single door and gate is guarded at Haier), we are greeted with six large TV screens on the wall of the Central Control Room. They monitor a warehouse that looks more like a huge basketball court. There are ten automatic carts shuttling back and forth, loading and unloading materials. Finished air conditioners from the assembly hall have already been packaged as they go through the underground tunnel that connects the two buildings. They are now moved automatically by the carts to the right storage spot, from which they'll soon be taken outside to the waiting trucks.

When he visited the Haier warehouse in August 2001, Milton Kotler, a U.S. marketing consultant and brother of the renowned Northwestern University marketing professor, Philip Kotler, was surprised to learn that there were only nine workers in the whole warehouse, doing the job that used to be done by forty people. Though Milton Kotler had some reservations about Haier's diversification strategy, he was very impressed by the efficiency of this modernistic warehouse.

Actually, Zhang Ruimin and other Haier executives hesitate to call this building a warehouse, for they believe that it is not a traditional warehouse per se. Rather, they prefer to call it a logistics or distribution center, because most parts or finished products do not stay long in the building, as would be the case in a traditional warehouse.

It's lunchtime. We ask to have lunch with the workers in their large dining room, for we miss that part of China—eating with friends—but Xiao Liu says that we are guests and should eat in the guests' dining room.

It's the same kind of fast food for all guests, foreign or domestic: a small plate of French fries, a small plate of salad, a small plate of pot stickers, a bowl of white rice, two pieces of sausage and two chicken wings or drumsticks, all on one platter. The only thing that changes daily is the meat part: chicken, fish, pork or beef. The Haier standard is the same.

"The only difference is that you can talk in the guest room. In the workers' dining room, forget about it," Xiao Liu told us.

The two of us, and Xiao Liu and the driver Xiao Li who dine with us, have the same kind of food on a nice platter. Zhang Ruimin doesn't like preferential treatment in any area, especially in the kitchen. Once, on a Chinese TV program, he made a special point of it: cadres and workers must be treated equally, and the ladle must be the same size, as at McDonald's.

Xiao Liu tells us that the workers have the same kind of portion for their lunch. He is sipping a can of Coca-Cola. "The food is sold for four *yuan* (equivalent to fifty cents) a plate, but the workers only pay two *yuan*. The other two *yuan* are paid by the factory as a food subsidy. All the young workers on the assembly line you saw earlier eat breakfast, lunch and dinner in the factory dining room. Their food cost is subsidized by fifty percent. Four people share a dorm room, free of rent. They also have medical coverage and a social security fund."

"Most of them are rather young. Some of them should be in college," Jeannie sighs.

"If they can afford it. They have to pass the entrance exam and they have to be able to afford the tuition before they can have a college degree, like me. I think America is the same, isn't it?" Xiao Liu remarks. "I want to go to America, one day, to study management."

We learn that Xiao Liu graduated from the Light Industry Institute of Shandong Province, with a major in mechanical engineering. After coming to Haier, he chose to work in the Information and Cultural Department for his internship. He distinguished himself during his internship and, after a short period, was hired by the Enterprise Culture Department of the air conditioner division as an Assistant Director, and later promoted to the directorship.

After lunch, we are going back to the headquarters. As we pass the gate, the Haier company logo on a cargo truck suddenly catches our eye: the red square and the surrounding blue dots. Suddenly, that logo seems to be everywhere—on the building, on the cars, on the trucks and on workers' uniforms. We turn to Xiao Liu and see the same logo on his blue working uniform, one on the arm, another on his chest.

"What's the relationship between the red square and the blue dots?" Shawn asks, expecting to hear a different answer.

"Simple: we act alone, yet we also act together. The red square is our headquarters, and the blue dots are the many Haiers around the world."

"How many blue dots are there?"

"Thirty-five, and there is one red square. That makes a total of thirty-six, symbolizing the thirty-six military strategies in ancient China, which means to be resourceful. You see..."

"Among the thirty-six strategies, 'Keep running' is the top strategy," Jeannie bursts out. Immediately, she corrects herself: "Not 'Keep running,' 'Keep moving forward.'"

That is true. Keeping moving has been the Haier way of growing, from a company on the verge of bankruptcy to a national and international brand that has not only dominated China's domestic home-appliance market, but also captured sizable market shares in the United States, Europe, Southeast Asia, and the Middle East.

Shawn tries to be philosophical. "The proof of the growing is in its moving."

Manager Stories

At Haier, "80/20" means that twenty percent of the leaders are responsible for eighty percent of the job. By extension, if there is any production error caused by an employee, the management should bear eighty percent of the responsibility. This is a rather heavy burden on the Haier managers, and it is like the Sword of Damocles, which can fall at any time, hanging over the managers. Many, from workshop supervisors to division general managers, have been exposed and criticized in the company newspaper, *Haier News*, run by the company's Enterprise Culture Center.

Haier is known to be very tough on its middle-level managers. There is a rule at Haier that, if a manager receives three written criticisms (two oral criticisms count as one written) within a year, that manager has thirty days to make improvements. If no improvement is made within that period, the manager should be demoted or released from his managerial position. After a manager has received two written criticisms or the corresponding oral ones, the *Haier News* will carry an article in the form of a warning on behalf of the Group President to that manager, whose name is released. That usually implies that there is only one more chance for the manager to fix the problems or correct the mistakes.

Li Kaifeng, Director of the Electrothermal Department

On April 29, 2000, the Microwave-oven Factory under the Electrothermal Department was moved to the Development Zone Industrial Park. By May 11, it had not resumed normal operations, which caused the *Haier News* to run an article comparing the move with that of the washing machine factory, in 1997, under the directorship of Chai Yongsen, now Executive Vice President of the Haier Group.

The article pointed out that the washing machine factory move was a more strenuous situation—a bigger factory size, and fewer resources—but it did not affect the factory's productivity. When asked why the microwave-oven factory move had slowed down production, Li Kaifeng commented that it had taken some time for them to become adjusted to the new environment. The article concluded that, because Li thought it normal to have some adjustment period, it was nothing out of the ordinary that production should slow down a bit. The article ended by criticizing Li for not being able to keep in line with the top management's thinking, and urging him to think seriously about Zhang Ruimin's remark: "If others can do it, you should be able to do it, too. Otherwise, you must leave the competition."

Yu Zida, General Manager, Haier Group's Electronics Division
Yu was the man sent by headquarters to handle the Haier Hefei strike case in June 1998. He exhibited leadership in handling the crisis, and was later promoted to head the Group's Electronics Division. But that position did not make him immune to criticism by the newspaper. Early in 2000, after a number of corporate-wide management overhauls, referred to as "integration and business process reengineering," the division had lost some market share for their TV sets.

Yu's performance was apparently disapproved of by Zhang Ruimin and Yang Mianmian, who had inspected the division and talked to Yu several times. In May 2000, a department head from some other division within the Group purchased a thirty-four-inch TV from Yu's division, and was informed that the TV would come in on Saturday. But on Saturday, that department was further notified that the TV would not come in until the following Monday. Then, on Monday, the department was told that there would be no delivery because the Electronics Division's service people were taking a training course, and they should come to pick up the TV themselves.

The May 31 issue of the *Haier News* carried an article on the story, demanding to know if Yu, as the head of that division, had been aware of the problem. If not, the newspaper challenged, Yu might have missed some other problems in his division. The article ended by urging Yu to pay more attention to criticisms from within the company. Otherwise, people would seek compensation from him, according to the company's market chain practice.

Initially very upset by the criticism, especially by the suggestion of seeking compensation from him, Yu wrote a letter to the newspaper at the end of June, admitting that he had not previously quite understood the significance of the overhauls, and had been a bit resistant to change, which accounted for a number of problems the division had experienced. After the newspaper warning, he had used some new approaches to promoting their products, including big-van tour promotions in the countryside and aggressive promotions in big cities. Toward the end of June, the division's color TV sales had increased by thirty-seven percent. Yu attributed the improvement to an open mind that was receptive to change.

Yu was promoted to Haier Group Vice President in 2002.

Zhang Liquan, Deputy General Manager, Haier-Merloni Washing Machine Division

After serving as Deputy General Manager of Haier-Merloni Washing Machine Division for ten months, Zhang was dismissed from his position by Haier top management for a number of reasons. The main reason cited for his discharge by top management and admitted by Zhang himself in a working summary report was that he had ceased to be creative and innovative in his thinking, which had caused stagnation and dwindling market share for their products. He was specifically criticized for not having a sharp mind for the market. Among other things, he had turned down an order for 10,000 washing machines.

Lin Xitang, Director of Customer Service at the Washing Machine Division

Before being transferred to his new position, Lin had been working in another division for quite some time without impressing the top management with a satisfactory job performance. The top management wanted to give him another chance to distinguish himself in a new environment. Shortly after the transfer, he was sent to solve a service problem. The top management was upset when they learned that he had spent three days out of the city without meeting the customer even once.

It was about two o'clock in the afternoon when he returned to Qingdao. Instead of reporting to work, he went straight home. During the next ten days, similar things happened twice more. In the January 12, 2000 issue of the *Haier News*, there was an article on Lin's unsatisfying performance which triggered a series of discussions. Lin subsequently made a self-criticism, but it was regarded by some as not "deep" or sincere enough. He was soon removed from his position.

These stories show that life for Haier managers is not as easy and enjoyable as it is elsewhere. If they want to keep their positions and pay, the managers must first of all stay in line with the thinking of the top management, especially that of Zhang, who takes every opportunity to preach the importance of being creative and innovative in one's thinking. Zhang has made "being creative" the cornerstone of the Haier enterprise culture. A pattern can be found in the above stories about Haier managers in hot water: if they want to get out of it, they must first of all identify their problems with the "root cause," which almost invariably is their failure to keep in line with the thinking of the top management. Before any business or management action is taken to fix the problem, self-criticism is required of these managers to acknowledge their distance from that cornerstone principle and to express their willingness to catch up.

The stories also demonstrate that any Haier manager who is not head over heels in love with Zhang's thinking risks being marginalized or relegated. It takes a strong mind and body to keep afloat among the Haier managers.

Women at Haier

According to ancient Chinese philosophers, everything in the universe is made from *yin* and *yang*, elements that depend upon each other. There can be no light without darkness, and no life without death. *Yang* will be settled by *yin*, and *yin* will grow by *yang*. *Yin* and *yang* integrate and move together. The ancient Chinese also believed in the harmonious union of *yin* (female energy) and *yang* (male energy), to form an ever-changing combination. Just as day gives way to night, something hot can grow cold....

In the Haier Group, if Zhang and other male employees stand for the *yang* element, Yang Mianmian and other female employees symbolize the *yin* element. One man and one woman, that was how a world was originally created. And so is a company.

More than once, we have been told that, although her name suggests "soft as cotton," Yang rules with an iron fist. Actually, she is a bundle of energy barely contained in her dark blue business suit. In action on factory floors or at negotiating tables, she is always energetic, passionate and outspoken. In addition to being the President, she also wears the hats of Vice Chairman of the Board of Directors, and Deputy Party Secretary of the Haier Group. In any sense, she is the very right hand of Zhang and commands an unequivocal second position in the Haier hierarchy.

When it comes to dealing with middle-level managers, there seems to be a tacit agreement between Zhang and Yang in that Zhang plays softball while Yang plays hardball, much like the traditional Peking opera in which the one wearing the mask of the hero coaxes (*chang hong lian*) and the one wearing the mask of the villain coerces (*chang bai lian*).

There is a story about Yang in the *Haier News* that shows how she "rules with an iron fist."

February 16, 2000 began another exciting day at Haier, for its top management gathered in a conference room of the Haier Building where a "horse race" had just started.

"Horse race" is a term used at Haier to refer to applying for posted positions through open competition, rather than being handpicked by someone higher up. Under this practice, every employee has an equal opportunity to get into a horse race to distinguish him- or herself.

In this particular "horse race," three candidates from three different divisions were competing for the position of Head of the Refrigeration Division. They were Mr. Liu Xiangyang from the Refrigerator Division, Mr. Ma Jian from the Freezer Division, and Mr. Wang Chunming from the Supermarket Division. They had delivered their campaign speeches and gone through on-the-spot question-and-answer sessions, which they had all handled with confidence and ease. It was almost noon, and the panel of judges was hard-pressed to make their choice, since all three candidates seemed bright, in one way or another, and one of them must be voted on.

Just at that moment, a female voice, firm and loud, broke in.

"In my opinion, none of the three candidates was qualified for the position!" All eyes shot to the speaker. It was Yang Mianmian, then Executive President of the Haier Group.

All of a sudden, everybody was holding his or her breath, and dead quiet covered every inch of the conference room.

Yang continued her comments.

"None of you three is competing for the position with a broad vision of the development of the Refrigeration Division over the long run. In your campaign speeches, I did not see any detailed research you have done regarding the past of the Refrigeration Division, so as to picture its future, which means you do not regard the Group's long-term development as your own responsibility. How can we bestow such an important position on those who lack a sense of responsibility for the Division's future?"

Yang's words, like drops of water thrown into a pot of boiling oil, immediately evoked a heated discussion among the panel members.

Some argued, "Since we must choose one of the three, what's the point of being too hard on the candidates?"

Others said, "The position of Head of the Refrigeration Division is very important, and we should not make do with just anybody."

As a result, nobody won the competition, because none of the candidates was regarded as fully qualified for the position.

"Rather go without than have someone shoddy," Yang explained after the meeting.

Based on Yang's suggestion, the Haier Group decided to keep the position open for six months before starting a new "horse race."

To ordinary Haier employees, Yang is their respected President, and the pride of the Haier women. *Contemporary Managers*, a Chinese business magazine, ranked her among the top ten Chinese women managers of 2001. In September 2002, Yang was selected as one of the top ten Chinese businesswomen at a national conference jointly sponsored by the China Social and Economic Research Center and *Chinese Women* magazine. She is one of the three women executives who are on both lists.

Zhang Ruimin once praised Yang highly: "President Yang possesses all of the three characteristics which the ancient Chinese considered a human being should possess: the aspiration to do something (to make Haier a global brand name); the knowledge to do something (to have a clear mind and make realistic analyses of problems or possess problem-solving power); and the ability to do something persistently (not only to do a good job at one particular time, but to keep doing a good job for many years to come)."

An Guizhen is another high-ranking woman in the Haier Group. Energetic and full of innovative ideas, An started from the bottom and worked herself all the way up to Deputy Chief Accountant and Deputy Director of the Capital Promotion Division. In 1999, when Haier began its business process reengineering, it was An who put forward the suggestion of moving the finance departments from each individual division to the Haier Group's direct control, so that they could exercise more effective supervision. An's suggestion was accepted, and she was put in charge of this reform. But that was just the beginning of An's initiatives. During the financial reengineering period, she suggested using a capital flow process, that is, setting up a market chain system of "SS" (*suochou*/*suopei*, meaning reward and compensation) to cover all the financial departments in the company.

Due to this financial reform, Haier's capital turnover sped up by 28%, and its working efficiency doubled in 2000, despite a shortage of finance staffers.

An also engineered the Haier system for cash transactions, which has not only solved the lingering problem of accounts receivable, but also helped Haier reach zero accounts receivable and zero bad debt.

Su Fangwen, Director of the Haier Group's Enterprise Culture Center, is concurrently the chief of the Party Propaganda Department of the Group. She reports directly to Zhang Ruimin and Yang Mianmian and enjoys their trust and support. A journalist before joining the Haier Group in 1988, Su never dreamed that her knowledge and expertise would flower at Haier.

During its early stages of development, Haier had recognized the importance of establishing its enterprise culture and educating its new employees in the basic values of that culture. After joining the staff of the Haier Enterprise Culture Center, an organization aimed at implanting Haier's culture in every employee's mind and building up a rainbow between management and employees, Su made it a rule that she would give an introductory speech each time new employees came in. She would introduce the Haier culture to the newcomers, so as to help them understand the company's goals before they were put into working positions. She started the weekly Haier newspaper, *Haier News*, which provides the soil to nurse the enterprise culture. Many daily managerial issues are brought up for heated discussion in the newspaper. Proper behavioral standards are reinforced; poor performance is exposed; and, in many cases, employees' voices are heard.

Su and the newspaper have played so important a role in the company that Zhang once praised Su as "the one who inserts the company's philosophy, as well as its values, into people's minds."

In today's still-male-dominated business world, women at Haier have been doing as excellent a job as their male counterparts. Women occupy twenty percent of the managerial positions at Haier. Women employees at Haier, just like their male counterparts, work hard to realize their career dreams, for Haier has provided them with a stage leading to success.

There are numerous small innovations at Haier named after the women employees who invented them, such as "Aiying's Three-step Working Procedures" in refrigerator leak-hunting, "the Xiaoling Wrench" and "the Yunyan Mirror," etc.

In mid-April of 2001, Haier sent a delegation to Pakistan to attend the opening ceremony of the Haier Industrial Park there. What was special about the delegation, in the eyes of the locals, was that one third of its members were women, and the keynote speaker—Yang Mianmian, President of the Haier Group—was also a woman!

Employees and Their Families
Some say that the Haier culture is a family culture, caring for one another, with genuine feelings flowing from one heart to another.

This statement is not far-fetched. In the Confucian system, an official leader is like a father to his subjects/workers, and is expected to take care of food, clothing, habitation and everything else. In Zhang's Haier, the corporation has dating services to help the young people find perfect matches. They also help host wedding ceremonies and provide loans so the newlyweds can purchase apartments—Haier owns many apartment buildings in Qingdao.

Not only does Zhang have to take care of his employees, he has to take care of the employees' families, parents (benefits), spouses (finding jobs) and children (funding school projects). In return, all that Haier asks from its employee is what has been expressed in the mission statement: give 110% of you and your time.

As we go over the hundreds of stories, photos and writings about Haier employees which we gathered during our China trip, we are struck by the many similarities between Zhang and his employees. They mirror each other in words and actions, and link with one another through genuine sentiments and emotions. The following are four articles written by Haier employees and their family members. They are on different topics, but in the same voice: the simple, unpretentious, crystal-clear Haier voice. Their actions, no matter how trivial, bring new meaning to the most commonplace things and open a window into the minds and hearts of ordinary Chinese workers.

I'm a Little Fish in the Sea

The early winter sunshine shone through the window and glided over Mr. Hou's face. If I had not noticed his swollen lower jaw, I would never have guessed that he had been the victim of a terrible car accident a month ago, or that, at that time, he felt totally finished...

In fact, I was in a state of unconsciousness until I was sent to the hospital by passersby. Everything was blank, and stood still, at that moment. Faintly, I heard somebody whispering into my ear, "Please hang on, Hou Junhua! Please hang on..." Siren, ambulance, and then I was wheeled quickly through the long corridors of the hospital. And after that, all sounds died away...

In the hospital ward, the aroma of the tea floated in the winter sunshine. Time was trickling by, in the silence. After being silent, myself, for a while, I could see that Hou Junhua was on the verge of tears.

Death was standing so close to me, grinning hideously. If it had not been for the whisper that kept on calling me earnestly, I would have kept on sleeping and never come to consciousness.

Later, I was told by my family that it only took about eighteen minutes after I was sent to the hospital before Mr. Lian Tieqian, head of our division, and Mr. Wang Ling, director of the department, rushed to the hospital to see me. They helped with my registration and pushed my gurney to the emergency room. They kept on calling me during the time I was in a coma, in the hope of passing the message to me: I would come to life. On the day of the accident, they spent the whole night in the hospital, and did not go home until I was in a stable condition. Under the persistent persuasion of my family, they reluctantly dragged their exhausted bodies away. Their uniforms were stained with blood, here and there, like red silk cotton flowers blooming under the sun...

During my stay in the hospital, the Union arranged for delivery of my meals every day. After the operation, my colleagues even cooked nutritious soups for me, daily, which was admired a lot by my ward mates, who all thought that I was so lucky to have so many brothers at home!

Also, during the period of my recovery, the Union brought me many books to kill the time with. I remembered coming across a novel by the Japanese novelist Haruki Murakami, who wrote the bestseller *Norwegian Wood*. There is a sentence in the novel which always lingers in my mind. "The fish said, 'I cannot see your tears because I'm in the water.' The water said, 'But I can feel your tears because you are in my heart.'" This reminds me of Haier. After going through ordeals and upheavals in life, I suddenly realize that I, myself, am the little fish in the Sea of Haier.

—Xiao Jia, Electric Department

Because You Are with Me

It's been ten years since I started working at Haier. Having witnessed the path Haier has traveled, I always feel proud of the company's accomplishments. As a Party member in charge of the Development Zone projects, I always have confidence in overcoming whatever difficulties I encounter. From work, I get a sense of fulfillment.

For the past six months, I have not spent a single Sunday at home, leaving all the family chores to my wife. She didn't understand and complained, "What the hell are you doing all this for?" I told her that I was doing something pioneering, and there were sacrifices I must make.

One Saturday afternoon, I received a phone call from my wife when I was in the middle of negotiating with some Japanese businessmen. I was told that my son was running a high fever, and he had had a seizure. I told her not to worry too much, and said I would go to the hospital when the negotiations were over. My wife got very angry at me, saying, "You care for nothing but your work." Then she hung up the phone in a rage.

When I got to the hospital, it was half past seven in the evening, and our son, Shuaishuai, had fallen asleep. My wife was watching him quietly in the hospital bed. I saw my wife's bloodshot eyes, and felt a pang in my heart. I told her that I had asked for a leave of absence and that I would stay with our son that night so she could go home to take a nap.

The next day, I had to return to the company, because the refrigerator factory was moving its equipment. I promised my wife I would come back to the hospital that evening, but I did not. Since we were allowed only a short period of time for moving, we had to work at night in order not to slow down production. For two consecutive nights, no one from our team returned home to sleep. When I hurried to the hospital the third day, my son had almost recovered. When he saw me, my son put his hands around my neck, crying, "Daddy, Daddy, please don't leave me." My eyes were wet and for the first time, I strongly felt that my son was in desperate need of paternal love, of which I had given him too little. I stretched out my arms to embrace him, but the moment I touched him, I passed out and fell on the floor. That frightened my wife. When she learned from the driver that I had been without sleep for three days and nights, she threw herself into my arms and burst out crying. She said that she now understood me. That night, the eyes of the three of us were all red.

On my son's birthday, I did not have time to go home. I bought a toy car and asked someone to give it to him as a present. That day, my wife called and said in a choked voice that she and our son were expecting me to do a better job, which might be the best gift I gave them.

In the new millennium, there are still too many things to be done and the same busy story will continue. But it is comforting to think that, because my wife and son are with me, days won't be as long and difficult as before.

—Zhang Liping, Technology Equipment Department

Proud of My Daughter Working at Haier!

When we are getting old, we always love to have our kids running around by our knees, to enjoy the happy family life together. Counting the days on the calendar on the wall, I knew my daughter wouldn't come to see me for another two weeks. My daughter works in the wine-cellar section at Haier, and in her heart, there is only Haier. "Ma, the wine cellar is in big demand. Market is very important!" Yes, the market is important; Ma is not.

Friday night, my daughter called. "Ma, you always complain about my working too long and too hard at Haier. Tomorrow, our unit is having a family trip, to tour the Haier Industrial Park. After the tour, you'll have a better understanding of me and my work, I'm sure." I put down the phone, wondering whether Haier is truly so amazing.

The next day, the moment I got out of the Haier shuttle bus that had brought us to the Park, I was impressed right away by the magnificent Haier Building in the traditional Chinese style of red and gray. The big Culture Square, the pagoda and gazebo, the windmill, the gurgling stream and the fleet of boats—they looked as if they were pictures within a picture. The uniformed Haier employees walking by us looked serious and hurried, as if they had so much energy that they had to spend it on their jobs, which gave them the sense of pride. In such an environment, how can any employee not try her very best? I was truly proud of my daughter who can work in such an excellent company!

In the showroom, I listened to the tour guide introducing their amazing products, from refrigerators to wine cellars to computers, TV sets and cell phones. It was my first time hearing about the futuristic network household appliances of so many kinds and models. Many had been shipped and sold overseas! The trip was truly an eye-opening experience!

Upon returning home, I told my neighbors about what I had seen at Haier. They said, in admiration, "Look, how proud you are to have a daughter working for Haier!"

Being the mother of a Haier employee, I may have to do more house chores for my kids and help them with raising their children. But I'm pleased to be able to do those things for an employee of such an excellent company!

Daughter, Mom will help you and be your strong support. Your excellent performance at work will be the best reward for your mom!

—Wang Zhengpei, a retired teacher, mother of Shen Ruihong, Wine Cellar Division

Girl and Café

My girlfriend is a Haier employee, or a "Haier person," who is used to reading late into the night while drinking coffee to stay awake. To tell the truth, I don't particularly like her to be a "night cat," nor do I drink coffee, the "imported Chinese herb medicine" of bitter taste.

Other couples date under the moonlight or listen to the tides coming in from the sea, but we swim in an ocean of books to "improve our knowledge." She comforts me by saying, "As long as I'm with the one I love, I don't mind where I'm doing the dating. Haier is growing so fast that I must learn to keep pace. Otherwise, Haier will dump me one day and you'll dump me afterward."

The good thing is that, like other girls of her age, she enjoys shopping. But she doesn't go to the cosmetics counter, or the fashion area. Instead, she goes to the household appliances section to "observe the customers' faces." Why?

"True, Haier products sell very well, but we need always to see what customers are looking at—places they'd like to see improvement. Their reaction to our product is extremely important."

Like her girl friends working at Haier, she'd take out some tissue to wipe off the dust from the Haier products on display, if she sees any. Why?

"I don't want to see any dust on our product."

Nothing but amazement. Suddenly, I understand that life is like drinking a cup of coffee. Sweet or bitter depends on the person who drinks it. Haier guys think it is sweet and so does my girlfriend.

—Quanwei, boyfriend of Qiqi at Technology Division

These stories have forged a sturdy chain, to link Haier not only to Haier employees, but also to their families, with each individual functioning as a different link, according to their positions in the unbroken chain, because each one is someone to the others. Some of the things that have happened to Haier employees and their families will be difficult for people in the West to imagine, and more difficult to emulate. Chinese culture emphasizes the harmony of the family and the collective good of the community and the country, as compared to Western culture which stresses individualism and personal freedom. In Chinese culture, standing in the center of a family or a community is not a single person, but persons in a relationship that combines them all.

Without the other, without oneself. In this relationship of complementarity, if the central virtue is benevolence, the golden mean is the principle or standard of achieving balance or central harmony through proper action. This is a simple and powerful social syntax that extends into not only each family, but also the corporation. It influences how business is managed and done. Just as with the oxygen in the air, a Chinese person cannot stand alone without the support of others, or a relationship. (In ancient Chinese culture, cruel and unusual punishment always took the form of exiling a man from his family and friends, so he would suffer alone on the wild frontier.)

After all, all Chinese are related to one another in a very complex way of being one (self) and two (the other) at the same time. Benevolence, love, charity, filial piety and friendship exist not in oneself, but in the other, when the other is affected accordingly. In this sense, relationship is vital in the Chinese culture.

Relationship or "*guanxi*" provides stability and balance. Simple and naïve, the above stories of families illustrate team spirit in its simplest way, and any average Haier employee can identify with them. Like a signifier, the story's social meaning is readily conveyed to a community that has a standard code of behavior deeply rooted in its cultural makeup and in the mentality of the people.

Admittedly, things like what has occurred at Haier are not happening everywhere in China today, when too many people are looking at the material side of things. There must be something special or magnetic about Haier that has attracted people to its banner and held them together. People at Haier attribute that to the Haier enterprise culture.

President Yang Mianmian once proudly proclaimed that excellent leaders build excellent people, and excellent people produce excellent products. Yang's words have been quoted by Haier employees around the world, in Haier industrial parks and plants. The power of the role model is infinite. As Confucius says, "He who exercises government by means of his virtue may be compared to the north polar star, which keeps its place and all the stars turn towards it."

Immersed in such a culture, one could hardly imagine behaving otherwise.

7

Market Chains and BPR:
A Haier Revolution

(BPR: Business Process Reengineering)

Market Chains

According to Zhang Ruimin, Haier has experienced three stages of growth: brand name building, diversification, and globalization. While the first phase focuses on the quality of products and the second one on market penetration, the third phase concentrates on the company's overseas expansion. It is during the third phase that Zhang developed his market chain approach, an accountability system which links every employee to the market performance of a product.

This system examines how internal services, such as designing, manufacturing and marketing, are related to a product's final market performance (cost, profit and other issues) and how they are the responsibility of each employee.

At first glance, we would assume that Zhang's idea is to tie every employee's salary to the performance of a product on the market. For example, after a product designer working in a Haier refrigerator lab has designed a refrigerator, the fate of the refrigerator on the market will directly affect or even decide the income of the designer. Haier Air Conditioner Development Division chief Wang Zhentai says that a designer has no monthly salary. How much the designer gets as his monthly pay depends on the sales of the products developed by the designer. There is also a certain formula to calculate the actual pay.

Take, for example, a project that costs the firm 100,000 RMB to develop. When the project is done, and the first 50,000 units have been sold, the payout to the designer would be 30,000 RMB. After mass production begins, if sales hit 50,000 units a year, the breakeven point has been achieved. On the basis of increments of 30,000 RMB, when sales hit 100,000 units, the designer will be paid 60,000 RMB. If the breakeven point is not achieved, the pay to the designer will be reduced according to the formula. If sales were 20,000 units short of breakeven, the income would only be 10,000 RMB, with the designer incurring a debt of 40,000 RMB to the company. Therefore the designer has to speed up developing other products to make up for the debt.

So, at the end of the day, product sales push the designer into the market as well, because his income is decided by the market. He cannot just sit in the office, drawing according to his imagination. Every single product design has to go to the market to be tested before it can be produced.

After the product gets onto the market, when there is a problem, the designer must react immediately to solve it. Otherwise, his or her pay will be greatly affected. Furthermore, someone downstream, be it a manufacturer, a marketing specialist, a shipper or a salesperson, will ask for compensation from the designer.

This method has worked well in Wang's department. Most products they have designed have become market successes. According to Wang, many designers who have worked under him are making big profits and enjoying their jobs immensely.

There are also people who are living with a huge debt on their backs. When the debt reaches a certain level, they have to leave the firm.

It is easy to understand the first part of the market chain theory—an employee's income is tied to the market performance of his or her product. But such an understanding is only half the story. In fact, the market chain approach has a theoretical foundation that is reminiscent of quality-improvement expert Philip Crosby's idea of serving your customers *internally*—your customer is the next downstream user in the product value chain. It can also be regarded as a derivative of Michael Porter's value chain theory.

In April 2001, at the Wharton School of the University of Pennsylvania, Zhang was asked about the difference between his market chains and Porter's value chain. In Zhang's opinion, Porter's

In 1984, Qingdao General Refrigerator Factory, predecessor of the Haier Group, had a deficit of 1.47 million RMB. Machines were old and factory window frames were taken down by workers to make fire for heating. *Courtesy Haier Group*

In 1985, 76 refrigerators made by the factory were found defective. Director Zhang Ruimin ordered the workers responsible for the defects to smash the refrigerators with a sledgehammer. *Courtesy Haier Group*

The Haier Group Headquarters building in Qingdao. There is a red column at each corner of the building. *Courtesy Haier Group*

Haier University, located in the Haier Industrial Park in Qingdao, is primarily a training center for Haier managers. *Courtesy Haier Group*

CEO Zhang (right) gave out distribution awards to overseas managers. *Courtesy Haier Group*

CEO Zhang (left) awarded training certificate to a Haier America employee, 2001. *Courtesy Haier Group*

CEO Zhang with Prof. Lynn Sharp Paine at Harvard Business School. March 1998. *Courtesy Haier Group.*

CEO Zhang (far left) speaking at the International Institute for Management Development at Lausanne, Switzerland. October 2000. *Courtesy Haier Group.*

Haier's fully-automated logistic center in the Haier High-Tech Industrial Park in Yellow Island, a Qingdao suburb. There are nine people operating in the center. *Courtesy Haier Group*

Assembly-line workers at the Haier Air Conditioner Manufacturing Plant in Qingdao. December 2001. *Photo Taken by Shawn Ye*

The founding of Haier America Trading in New York, 1999. Left to right: Diao Yunfeng, Haier Group Overseas Division; Zhou Yunjie and Chai Yongsen, Group VPs; Yang Mianmian, Group President; Jack Dushey, Haier America board director; Zhang Ruimin, Group CEO; Michael Jemal, Haier America President; Shariff Kan, Haier America VP; David Dushey, a guest. *Courtesy Haier Group*

Haier America exhibiting at the International Consumer Electronics Show (CES) in Las Vegas. January, 2002. *Photo Taken by Shawn Ye*

The Haier Building at 1356 Broadway, New York. *Courtesy Haier America*

Main Hall of the Haier Building in New York. *Courtesy Haier America*

Grand opening of the Haier Building in New York. March 4, 2002. Left to right: Michael Jemal, Haier America President; Zhang Ruimin, Haier Group CEO; Zhang Hongxi, Chinese Consul General to New York, Frans Jamry, President of Haier Europe. *Courtesy Haier America*

CEO Zhang (second left) chatting with his Qingdao colleagues at the grand opening of the Haier Building in New York. *Photo Taken by Shawn Ye*

Haier manufacturing facilities in Camden, South Carolina. *Courtesy Haier Group*

Inside the Camden facilities. *Courtesy Haier America*

Left to right: Michael Jemal, Haier America President; Zhang Ruimin, Haier Group CEO; Frans Jamry, President of Haier Europe. *Courtesy Haier America*

Authors with the Haier executives. Left to right: Yang Mianmian, Haier Group President; Jeannie Yi; Zhang Ruimin, Haier Group Chairman and CEO; Shawn Ye. Haier Headquarters Conference Room, Qingdao, China. December 20, 2001. *Courtesy Haier Group*

value chain emphasizes the long-term profit of the company, while the market chain stresses the maximum satisfaction of the customer. Zhang maintained that, in the Internet age, the value chain theory has become inadequate. Because there are many other companies trying to enter the chain to erode your values, one company alone can no longer handle all the links in the chain. All one company can do is take good care of the most important link in the chain—the market.

In 2000, Professor William A. Fischer of the International Institute for Management Development (IMD) in Lausanne, Switzerland, wrote a case study titled "Building Market Chains at Haier" to introduce the concept and practice.

Located on the shores of one of Switzerland's most beautiful lakes, and about forty minutes by road or rail from Geneva, IMD is one of the world's leading business schools, with over fifty years' experience in developing the leadership capabilities of international business executives at every stage of their careers. Professor Fischer's principal teaching and research interests involve the management of technology, including the management of the creative processes within R&D, the creation and coordination of a presence in international technology and technology transfer. He was a development engineer in the American steel industry, and served as an officer in the United States Army Corps of Engineers.

For more than fifteen years, he worked with the World Health Organization on strengthening research and development institutes in developing countries in Asia, Africa, the Middle East and Latin America. During 1998 and 1999, Professor Fischer was executive president and dean of the leading business school in China—China Europe International Business School (CEIBS) in Shanghai, a joint venture supported by the European Union. Between 1976 and 1996, he was on the faculty of the Kenan-Flagler Business School at the University of North Carolina at Chapel Hill, where he was the Dalton L. McMichael Sr. Professor of Business Administration. In 1980, Fischer participated in a joint U.S. government-Chinese government venture in Dalian, a seaport city in northeastern Liaoning Province, which provided managerial training to senior level Chinese officials.

Since that time, he has remained consistently involved in the Chinese reform experience, including consulting for a variety of multinational corporations, government agencies (both U.S. and Chinese) and international aid agencies. He has visited China professionally yearly since 1980, and has written extensively on Chinese economic reforms.

We are reproducing below the second half of Professor Fischer's case study "Building Market Chains at Haier," with permission from IMD. The whole case study is attached at the end of the book as Appendix F.

(Excerpt begins)

In late 1998 Haier began to experiment with a market chain strategy to reinforce the market focus that Mr. Zhang Ruimin often spoke of. The market chain had been inspired by Michael Porter's value chain, but was, in fact, quite different in both philosophy and in objectives. According to Mr. Zhang Ruimin:

> The concept of value chain developed by Porter emphasizes marginal income and aims to realize profit maximization, while we regard maximum customer satisfaction as our goal. We take customers as being most important, so in our market chain everybody is a market, and everybody has a market. This way, inside-employees can begin to feel market pressures even though they are inside the organization: Everybody faces the market, and everybody supplies their best procedures!

The essence of the market chain was that every unit, every operation and everyone was linked directly to a customer, and every unit/ operation/body was also someone else's customer. In this way, everybody in the enterprise, no matter how deep inside the firm, felt market pressure directly. As an example, the environmental testing laboratory was depicted as having the design department as a customer. Design expected that the laboratory would provide timely service, meet time deadlines, and show integrity in the testing it performed and the data it produced. Production, in turn, was seen as being a customer of design, depending on design for manufacturable products. In another example, Mr. Wang Yangmin, director of manpower resource development for the Haier Group, was portrayed as having the job of "finding ideas and solutions to settle productivity problems of the factories. In this way, the factories are his customers." He was also the customer of top management to the extent that they needed to develop group-wide policies pertaining to manpower development. Madame Shi Chunjie, information center director within the Haier Group's plan and development center, was described as heading-up a group that had formerly been directors of the whole group (planning and development had effectively played that role in the centrally planned economy which had preceded the reforms), but that now had to sell its planning services to others within Haier, who then become its customers.

The management of facilities in Haier was also described in market chain terms: The integrated technical facilities department set the standard charges for equipment management, which was responsible mainly for reducing downtime according to customers, i.e., product divisions. It integrated the equipment management in the group and provided the third party's integrated services of purchasing, maintenance and preparation of spare parts. After negotiations between the technical facilities department and product divisions, the standard charges were written in a contract. The technical facilities department was thus the supplier to the product divisions, providing equipment management with its equipment managers as executors, while the product divisions were the users of equipment and the market of the technical facilities department.

Haier University, which was scheduled to open in December 1999 for the internal training of Haier's staff and management team, was described as both a customer and a supplier for the production functions. The University was expected to respond as a supplier to two major customers—the production functions and senior management—in creating educational offerings that met their needs, and would be, in turn, a customer of the production functions to the extent that the production functions wanted it to add new capabilities to their existing portfolios.

One of the appeals of market chains to Chinese managers, according to Mr. Zhang Ruimin, was that "the traditional Chinese approach to being a manager is different from that of the West. In China, people would rather be a big manager in a small company, than a small manager in a big company." In other words, "Better be the head of a dog than the tail of a lion....Chinese managers want to do everything with their own ideas." Mr. Zhang Ruimin believed that market chains made it possible for Haier employees to approach being big managers in a small company, even though they were in the very middle of a 20,000 employee organization. In a sense, everybody was the senior manager of his or her own target market. Or, generally speaking, "Everyone is a boss!"

Market chains were also useful in overcoming the dysfunctional nature of hierarchy and relationships based on mutual obligations (*guanxi*), which have historically characterized Chinese organizations, and which, in the words of Mr. Zhang Ruimin, were "usually speed-absorbers":

> Since we are not an SOE, relationships are not so important to us. Also, we say that 'Haier is a race-track,' and we want everyone to race to see if they have the ability to rise to the top. Everyone shows their ability through competition. We continuously redesign our group structures to make our firm more market-oriented.

SST: Claim Compensation, Claim Payment, Stop!

Aside from the idea of using the chain metaphor to reinforce the requirement for everybody at Haier to be customer-focused, the market chain concept also had a second major element to make it work effectively, and which was referred to as SST. The acronym SST was derived from the sounds of three Chinese words that defined how the market chain should work:

· *S (Suo Chou): Claim for compensation*
If you can do your job well, you should claim compensation from the employees after you (your customers downstream in the market chain);

- *S (Suo Pei): Claim for payment*
  If you cannot do a good job, the employees after you (your customers downstream in the market chain) should claim payment from you;

- *T (Tiao Zha):*
  If there is neither a claim for compensation nor a claim for payment, [computer] systems will take it as of no record. This is the so-called Stop!, which means that the immediate downstream process cannot go on. In case of Stop!, the responsible party should pay the claims.

An example of how SST worked could be seen in the relationship between Haier University and a production function. If the production function asked for a certain training course to be designed for its people, and the University delivered a high-quality program, it could expect to be paid for this service, at the negotiated rate, even if the production function chose not to do the program but still used some of the ideas anyway. If the University failed, it should not expect to be paid, and the customer might even claim some compensation for being unsatisfied. The final decision as to whether or not to pay, however, was up to the customer—and the customer is always right! As a service provider, Haier University's words, in this instance, don't count; only the customer's do. This leads one manager to observe that "within Haier, we treat service as a product."

The need for Stop! originated from the recognition that Haier Group had been growing at 80% per year, but that the quality of its human capital had not been increasing that fast. So, it needed some sort of standard to monitor the first two Ss in SST. Thus, the rationale behind the T was: "If you don't meet the standard: Stop! This standard was set-up by the customers, and if the customers believed that the product or service was not meeting the standard, they could stop the process."

To some extent, the origins of some of the SST philosophy might be traceable to the so-called Fan Ping incident of July 12, 1995, following Haier's acquisition of Qingdao Red Star Electrical

Appliance Factory. At that time, the factory had already changed its name to the Haier Washing Machine Co., Ltd. The quality control inspector, Fan Ping, was fined 50 *yuan* for a failing in her job. Her case showed that loopholes existed in management. Thus, managers from the Haier Group held that it was not only Fan Ping but also her supervisor who should carry the responsibility. This judgment aroused an enthusiastic discussion in the Haier Journal because none of the bosses had ever been fined for problems in quality control before. In the end, the person in charge at the higher level fined himself 300 *yuan* after handing over a written self-criticism.

At the beginning of the launch of SST, there was considerable resistance to it because of issues of *face* and *guanxi*. These have gradually been overcome, however. According to one manager:

> We overcame face and *guanxi* resistance because now we have to claim compensation for performance. In the past we were all good friends, and we didn't want to claim compensation from a friend, so we always tolerated mediocre performance. Now, however, if my product does not satisfy my customers, they will claim compensation from me; so I am forced to ensure that my suppliers do a good job. In other words, the market chain idea is working because of 'popularization through necessity.'

Issues of Implementation

One manager at Haier observed that:

> The traditional Chinese mentality is not to be innovative. We are content with maintaining the status quo, and we would prefer to stay on a team and never move—to have something stable. In the beginning, people were concerned about *face* and *guanxi* but, step-by-step, they realized that they are all in the chain, so relations became harmonious.

This same manager believes that a year into the experiment,

> The benefits include the pushing of everyone into the marketplace, so that they have to think about the needs of their customers, and they are forced to be innovative. The system

also encourages leadership, because if you are in more chains, you can claim more compensation, so leadership leads to larger salaries.

How to allocate overhead, always a sticky issue in such pricing schemes, was determined by negotiations between suppliers and customers. The negotiations were based on the previous year's status quo, i.e., "the bottom line." As for each project, less input for more output was encouraged. Returning to the equipment management example:

A contract established by the technical facilities department and product divisions clearly specified that for product divisions, 1 minute above the defined downtime limit agreed by the two parties, should result in a penalty of 1 *yuan*, while 1 minute saved can be rewarded with 1 *yuan*. It also defined service projects that, if completed by product divisions, would result in the technical facilities department paying them. After the service contract had been established, the technical facilities department changed its original concept and approaches to equipment management, and dis-aggregated the objectives required by product divisions, (i.e., markets) down to every equipment manager, maintenance worker and piece of equipment, as well as to every month, every day and every moment. It tied each person's performance to his or her wages so as to ensure clear objectives and responsibilities. Every month, the technical facilities department charged product divisions according to the total downtime, while equipment managers and maintenance workers got compensated according to the downtime and services within their functional areas. Likewise, if the technical facilities department was not doing a good job, product divisions could claim compensation and also source outside equipment management service. As a result, the technical facilities department had to provide superior services and a satisfactory price. In this way, what we've done is to take a seemingly isolated transaction, deep inside the organization, and make it into a big chain connected to the market place.

Next Steps

The next steps in Haier's market chains concept was to expand the dimensions that were covered. A senior manager put it this way:

> We'd like to establish a multidimensional matrix structure to create flows: material flows, cash flows, overseas flows and knowledge flows—all of which would be market chains. This is administratively very complicated, and we are presently thinking about how to do it.

(Excerpt Ends)

There are some interesting stories at Haier about claims for compensation between co-workers, as well as between workers and managers.

In the beginning, workers were not very comfortable seeking compensation from their colleagues. Zheng Wen, a worker from the air conditioner division, felt very upset when he was handed a ten-*yuan* claim form by Liu, a downstream co-worker and his roommate in the company-provided dormitory, because he had delayed the production process a bit. Liu was not at ease either, having held onto the compensation coupon for a long time before handing it over. For several days after compensation, Liu avoided Zheng, because he had a guilty conscience.

In mid January 2000, Lou, a direct sales representative stationed at Shanghai No. One Department Store, placed orders for some air conditioners with Ren, the manager of the supply center. According to Haier rules, Ren had to reply to the order request within two hours and supply the ordered products within thirty-six hours. Something happened on the Ren side which caused a twelve-hour delay in delivery.

Lou immediately issued a compensation form to Ren for the loss that he had incurred. That was a big story among Haier managers and employees, for it was the first case in which a manager was fined by his subordinate.

But the practice soon grew common, and no one now feels uncomfortable about it. The practice has even reached the employees' families. Li Wei, a fifth-grader and daughter of Wei Xijun at the Freezer Division, wrote to the company newspaper to tell her story of "SST" at work in her family. She said her mother had brought Haier's "SST" into the family to cover a variety of matters, including eating, studying and sleeping habits. If she did not make her bed, did not wash her socks or did not go to bed as scheduled, she would be "S"ed by her mother in the form of a monetary fine, which might cost her a month's savings, or in the form of physical punishment, such as mopping floors for a week or being prevented from watching TV for three days.

The good part of her story is that it was a two-way street, and she also had the right to "S" her mother, sometimes. When, one day, her mother did not go running with her in the morning as they had agreed, she claimed compensation by "ordering" her mother to buy three books for her.

The direct result of the market chain practice at Haier is two-fold. On the one hand, it has ensured Haier products' marketability—every single product is designed with its market in mind—and, on the other hand, it has guaranteed its advantageous position in market competition. For instance, during the summers of 1998 and 1999, oversupply of electric and electronic products on the Chinese market impacted many powerful companies, mostly Haier's competitors. Even Changhong, China's largest TV manufacturer, had to cut its prices by thirty-five percent to make sales in the saturated Chinese market.

But Haier maintained its prices, and overall revenue in 1999 increased to 26.86 billion RMB, from 16.8 billion in 1998.

Business Process Reengineering (BPR): A Haier Revolution

The concept of Business Process Reengineering (BPR) was first advanced by Michael Hammer and James Champy in their 1993 international bestseller, *Reengineering the Corporation: A Manifesto for Business Revolution*, which has since become a management classic for mid-sized and large corporations. In the book, Hammer and Champy impart the basic management principles of process redesign. They call on business leaders to examine their core processes, such as order fulfillment, and encourage them to redesign those processes to their maximum efficiency.

When he was visiting a car assembly line in Germany, Zhang Ruimin was amazed by the individualized cars the company had produced—the first car was black, the second white, and the third blue. The equipment loaded was also different: one with a Sony stereo, another with a GE one.

He was told that these cars were being custom-made for people who had already paid for them. Zhang believed that that was the real "new economy," the buzzword that was on everybody's lips in China at the time.

Ever since then, Zhang has been an enthusiastic advocate of making individualized products for customers. He incorporated the notion of satisfying individual customer needs into his market chain concept.

Zhang realized that, in order to be successful with his market chain goal, he must absorb and consolidate different management methods and styles. According to him, China missed the first and second management revolutions, represented by Taylor's scientific management in the late nineteenth century, when China was fighting against invading world powers, and Total Quality Management, practiced by Japanese companies in the 1960s, when China was fighting an internal war—the Cultural Revolution.

Now Haier is making up for the two missed lessons by adopting OEC management and catching up with the third wave of the management revolution, which highlights product individuality, by applying Zhang's market chain theory.

While OEC management primarily aims at solving problems from within the company, the market chain method looks to link the inside of the company with the outside market's need and demand. Zhang regards implementing OEC management as "doing things right," and the market chain as "doing the right thing."

Zhang maintains that there is a big difference between "doing things right" and "doing the right thing." He gives an example: if an assembly line worker does everything according to specifications and requirements, and produces quality product off the production line, he is "doing things right." But since his products do not have a buyer, he is not "doing the right thing." One must be "doing the right thing" before he can be "doing things right."

By 1998, after a number of mergers and acquisitions during the previous seven years, Haier had grown much larger, and was moving toward its third phase of development—globalization. Zhang realized that, to compete at the international level, Haier must be more efficient in meeting customer needs and augmenting production speed. But the company was facing a grim situation in the wake of its aggressive expansion. There were too many self-sustaining walls between and among the divisions and departments within the Group, which made efficiency at the Group level a thing of extreme difficulty. Zhang thought that something radical must be done to the corporate structure before he could strengthen the company's competitiveness and further his market chain practices. His decision was to adopt Hammer's concept of "Business Process Reengineering."

Zhang orchestrated the Haier Business Process Reengineering in two phases, the first focusing on organization restructuring and resources integration and the second on making everyone in the company a strategic business unit (SBU).

BPR Phase One (September 1998 to December 2000)

In a May 2001 interview with the Chinese magazine *IT Management World*, Zhou Yunjie, Haier Group Vice President, said that, since September 1998, Haier had been in continuous reform in technology, organization and business processes. Comparing these reforms to reengineering a fast, heavy truck while it raced down the highway, Zhou conceded that he was just like a mechanic on the truck with a wrench in his hand; it was Zhang, Haier's top man, who would give instructions on how to constantly rebuild, fix or add weight to the truck without reducing its high speed.

It all began in September 1998, when Zhang put forward his ideas of the market chain and Business Process Reengineering (BPR) at a management meeting. In order to achieve the goal of the market chain, which is to link every employee's work with the market, Zhang wanted to give the whole company structure a root canal. At the heart of Zhang's BPR was a corporate structural overhaul, which would change the traditional pyramidal structure into a flat, web-like one, through which the divisions and departments within the group could interact with each other without having to go through their functional bosses.

In the traditional pyramid system, each division had been a profit center with its own R&D, procurement, production and sales departments. Each of these departments had been responsible to its immediate boss. All they needed to do was what they were told to do. No borders were to be crossed or trodden upon by other departments within the division, still less across divisions.

For a long time, this system had worked very well for a collective enterprise like Haier, which required uniformity and conformity both politically and administratively. Under that system, the Haier Group headquarters had been the planning center; the divisions had been the management decision-making centers; the departments had been profit centers; the factories had been cost centers; and the work teams had been the quality centers. None of them except the sales department had needed to face the market directly.

But when the company had grown bigger, especially when it was facing pressure from increasing competition by foreign multinationals, the system had become inadequate and unfit. Because everybody was responsible only to his or her immediate boss, it had become impossible for the whole company to respond quickly to the market.

For the first six months after the meeting, Zhang focused on educating managers and workers on the need for change, emphasizing taking down walls between departments and divisions and being prepared for structural change. In March 1999, Zhang started his first organizational change—to transform the company's pyramid structure into a matrix structure focused on project operations.

If we look at the matrix structure as a coordinate system, the horizontal axis is where the functional departments sit, such as planning, procurement, accounting and sales, while the vertical axis is where the projects are positioned. As far as the functional departments at Haier were concerned, the joins were what they needed to work on. The new structure maintained all the divisions and their R&D, procurement and sales departments, but the divisions were no longer self-contained entities. Rather, they should interact with other divisions on certain projects.

The advantage of this system was that it enabled the divisions to pull resources from different departments within the division to form project teams, so that they could turn out new projects more quickly. These project teams were given the power to deal with the whole business process, from project design to marketing and sales. The major drawback was that members within project teams were still mostly responsible to their own bosses from their respective departments. If a department head was not interested in certain projects requiring interaction, those projects would be delayed or otherwise affected. On the other hand, the project teams had too much power in their own business dealings and less coordination among the divisions, even among departments within the divisions. Aside from that, the corporation had little control over these project teams, because orders were no longer to come straight down from the top.

For Zhang, the matrix system was still a far cry from the market chain in his engineering plan.

After practicing the matrix system for a few months, Haier decided to put a stop to it. But Zhang had learned a very important lesson from the practice: it should not have been the division that tried to complete the whole business process; it should have been the job of the corporation to reengineer bigger business entities that could coordinate similar business processes in all divisions. These business entities should be independent in running their own businesses.

Zhang figured that the matrix practice was one step closer to his market chain idea, but had not arrived at its heart, because everyone had not been in contact with the market. He decided to implement a more radical business process reengineering (BPR).

He knew that, for a company of Haier's size, BPR could not go very fast, or it would be like removing the chassis of a fast-moving truck while it was driving down the highway. But it should not go too slowly, either, for that would hamper his agenda.

In mid-August 1999, Haier top management started to take the procurement, sales, accounting and export departments from each of the divisions to form four bigger, independent divisions, which came to be called the Commerce Flow (Sales) Development Division, the Material Flow (Logistics) Development Division, the

Capital Flow (Finance) Development Division, and the Overseas Development Division. Together, these four divisions were called the Development Divisions.

The new divisions were under the Group control, and their heads reported directly to the Group President. Their responsibilities within the Group were to coordinate similar business processes in the whole Group and, as profit centers, they were to deal with the market directly and independently. These constituted the Group's core business processes.

The next step was to establish sub-business-processes or sub-divisions within each of the core processes. For example, under the Material Flow Development Division, there were three sub-divisions: Procurement, Allocation and Warehousing. Under the Commerce Flow Development Division, there were more than ten sub-divisions, such as the East China Division, the North China Division, the Northeast China Division, the Northwest China Division, etc.

Similar operations were performed on supporting departments. Relevant departments from each division were reshuffled to form corporate-wide R&D, Human Resources, and Customer Relations Divisions (referred to at Haier as the 3Rs) and Total Planning Management, Total Quality Management, and Total Equipment Management centers (referred to as the 3Ts). The 3Rs are development-supporting processes, while the 3Ts are basic supporting processes. They were independently run business centers that not only provided services to the Group's core business processes on a fee basis, but also offered services to the outside market as business entities.

The factories or plants were rearranged to form seven product divisions: Refrigeration, Air Conditioner, Washing Machine, IT Products, Kitchen, Bath and Electric, Technology Equipment, and Direct Affiliates such as Communications, Housing and Biological Engineering. They were the Group's manufacturing facilities in the industrial parks across the country. The division heads also reported directly to the corporate President.

Under each division, there were several sub-divisions. For example, Refrigeration had such sub-divisions as Refrigerator, Freezer and Supermarket Equipment.

After considerable reengineering, Haier's original pyramid and matrix structures had become a flat, web-like structure with three major interactive processes: the Development, or core, process, which was made up of the four development divisions; the Functional, or supporting, process, which was composed of the 3Rs and the 3Ts; and the Product process, which was composed of the seven manufacturing facilities. The new structure moved the company a further step closer to Zhang's market chain concept, according to which everyone at Haier should be in contact with the market directly.

Post BPR, the Commerce Flow Division and Overseas Development Division are responsible for setting up Haier's global sales and marketing networks and soliciting orders from their customer base worldwide. Supported by the 3Rs, the various product divisions manufacture products according to orders that flow in through the Commerce Flow Division. Relying on the group's global supply resources, the Material Flow Division sets up its purchasing and shipping systems using the JIT (just-in-time) approach. The Capital Flow Division takes care of the whole Group's overall budget and accounting matters.

The following example shows how the new system works since BPR:

After some market research, a staff member in the Market Resources Department at the Commerce Flow (Logistics) Division finds that a shopping center has a growing demand for domestic mobile phones. He submits his analysis to the Sales Department of his Division. The Sales Department sends out a representative to that shopping center to pitch their products. He subsequently gets an order for three hundred Haier mobile phones. He forwards the order to the Planning Department, which confirms the order on its computer system. The Commerce Flow Division then places an order with the factory under the IT Product Division for the phones to be manufactured.

The factory makes its production and purchase plans, and places an order with the Material Flow Division, which makes purchases from its suppliers. The purchased materials arrive at the factory at the designated times, and the factory finishes the production according to the schedule.

Once the three hundred mobile phones are made, the factory commissions the Warehousing Department of the Material Flow (Logistics) Division to handle their storage. The Commerce Flow Division soon picks up the goods from the warehouse, and ships them to the shopping center. Cash is paid on delivery to the shopping center. After confirming that the payment has been made, the Material Flow Division pays the suppliers.

In March 2000, Haier formed its e-commerce company, serving both business (B2B) and individual (B2C) customers. The goal of the company was to satisfy the individual needs of customers at the fastest possible speed. Zhang's goal was to form a dynamic system that centered around orders and drove the material and capital flows.

On the manufacturing side, Haier deployed a number of programs, such as Material Resources Planning (MRP), Manufacturing Resources Planning (MRP II), Enterprise Resources Planning (ERP), Computer Integrated Manufacturing System (CIMS) and Concurrent Engineering and Agile Manufacturing. With such systems, Haier could maximize the coordination of manufacturing among its production facilities, while retaining flexibility of product variety for the best customer satisfaction.

For example, on March 24, 2000, the Hualian Company in Hebei Province placed an order through Haier's website for five commercial air conditioners. The order was received by the Purchasing Department of the Material Flow Division and the Commercial Air Conditioner Factory of the Product Division. Haier's computer system immediately showed the factory's material shortage status. No meetings were necessary, because each department knew what it was going to do. The Purchasing Department immediately bid for compressor prices on the web, and the Material Allocation Department delivered all the required material to the factory within four hours. By the end of March 31, the five air conditioners were made and ready to be shipped from the warehouse.

The Heart of the Matter: Logistics
To Zhang Ruimin, the most remarkable achievement of phase one of BPR is its logistics or material flow reform. On March 31, 2001,

Haier held a symposium on Haier's experiment in order-oriented logistics, at which Zhang elaborated on the path Haier had traveled.

Why order-oriented logistics or material flow? Zhang maintains that, in the Internet era, if a company does not implement an order-oriented logistics method, that means it does not have any material to flow. The driving force of a company is orders, without which it ceases to operate. If there are no orders, there is no material flow. A company must do everything around orders—purchasing for orders, manufacturing for orders and marketing for orders. The most important step toward achieving that is to invigorate the material flow or logistics.

Under traditional management, factories made their purchasing decisions according to plans. Because there were no orders, the purchases were merely for inventory purposes. Zhang compared individual warehouses to individual reservoirs that did not interact with one another. Zhang wanted to lift the sluice-gates of the reservoirs and make them flow like a river. His magic touch was the JIT (just-in-time) method. JIT purchase is buying material or supplies according to need. JIT delivery involves the carefully scheduled release of material or parts, and JIT allocation means temporarily storing parts or raw materials in the warehouse, and sorting or grouping them before delivering them to the production site.

Zhang considered inventory not only as taking up a sizeable amount of capital, but also as causing a lot of bad debt. For electronic products, it was especially so. Since technologies change very quickly, when new products are made, the prices for older products and the raw materials for making older products will drop considerably. The only way out for excess inventory is to sell it at reduced prices. No matter what a company may say in their promotion, the pressure to sell at reduced prices comes from too much inventory.

Zhang blamed disorderly competition and price wars in Chinese consumer markets on lack of material flow, because many companies did not manufacture for orders but for inventory. For many companies, price wars led to losses, which, in turn, led to production stoppage or bankruptcy. Zhang's conclusion was that, if a company does not employ an order-oriented logistics method, its production will eventually come to a halt.

What does logistics mean for Haier? Zhang contends that it means two things for him: a management revolution and speed.

Order-oriented logistics required business process reengineering, which further required Haier to change its traditional pyramidal management structure. That was a difficult revolution, one that Haier went through with great pain and many twinges. With the backup of the new management structure, Haier was able to implement its order-oriented logistics experiment.

Zhang regards speed as Haier's competitive advantage, especially in its worldwide competition with multinationals. While it takes multinationals a month to turn out a new product, it takes Haier only a week to do so.

What Has Haier Achieved from Order-oriented Logistics?

For Zhang, the Haier logistics reform is like a revolution under his control. It has helped sharpen the company's core competitive edge. By the end of 2001, Haier had basically arrived at its goal of achieving the three zeros: zero inventory, zero distance from customers and zero operational capital.

Zero Inventory: by using JIT purchasing, JIT delivery and JIT allocation methods, Haier minimized its inventory and made its warehouses places for temporary storage and transfer. Previously, Haier had used over 2,000 suppliers, both at home and abroad, for its 15 billion RMB parts and raw materials purchases. After the logistics reform, the number was reduced to less than 900.

But this was a painful process, given that Haier had to cut ties with over 1,000 noncompetitive suppliers, most of them domestic companies that had profited from the business relationship with Haier over the past years. When they learned that Haier was going to dump quite a lot of suppliers, many were fearful of losing a steady source of income, and did everything they could to remain on Haier's supplier list. Some went so far as to call Haier managers and staff members who had the power to decide who was going to leave, threatening to harm them.

According to Zhou Minjie, then Deputy General Manager in charge of supplier regrouping within the Material Flow (Logistics) Development Division, almost everyone in his office had received calls threatening to injure their legs or fingers, but they did not budge.

Zhou said that what made him feel good was that he did not have to face pressure from the corporate top executives as to who should not be dropped, because no Haier top executives were personally involved with the suppliers to be dumped. Therefore they did not have to fear repercussions, as was the case with some other companies facing similar situations.

Before the new logistics method, the average storage time for Haier products was thirty days (the Chinese national average is still about fifty days), before being shipped out to customers. After the logistics reform, the average turnaround time was reduced by sixty percent, and Haier's warehousing space has also been drastically reduced, from over 200,000 square meters to just 26,000 square meters. In addition, the use of ERP software effectively shortened the company's response time to orders, increasing Haier's ability to process its orders by over fifty percent for the first five months of 2001.

Zero Distance from Customers: Haier has set up fifty-two product-transfer centers across the country, which can deliver its goods into the hands of its customers at the highest speed possible. Within six to eight hours, Haier can ship out its products to its center-city customers, within twenty-four hours to regional customers and within four days to major distribution-chain areas.

Zero Operational Capital: Following Dell Computer's model, Haier required customers to prepay for their customized orders before it paid its suppliers. For Zhang, cash flow is more important than profit, for, without cash flow support, a company can go bankrupt, even if its sales are strong. That has accounted for the bankruptcy-in-the-black of many companies. That is also the reason that the Chinese securities regulatory agency has ruled that public companies in China must provide a cash-flow statement, in addition to an income statement and balance sheet. Haier's Internet payment-rate is eighty percent and its timely payment-rate is one hundred percent. The Internet payment system has saved Haier suppliers about ten million RMB a year.

BPR Phase Two (January 2001 Onward)

Starting in 2001, Haier began the second phase of its Business Process Reengineering, this time focusing on making everyone in the company a strategic business unit (SBU). The term "SBU" is normally applied to a department or division within a corporation which is a profit center, but Haier top management goes one step further, aiming to make every employee in the company an independent profit center. The rationale behind this is that, under the market chain, since everybody—not just a department or division—faces the market directly, it makes sense that everybody can work as a strategic business unit. The purpose of doing this is to maximize the production efficiency of each employee in the company.

Employees are required to fill out an SBU OEC Form (see Chapter 3) with an emphasis on profit-and-loss analysis. The form has sections of projected monthly and daily income in a given year for a particular employee, and the actual daily income based on a variety of parameters such as sales, expenses, gross profit, percentage of the profit, etc. From the form, an employee knows how much he or she will make on a particular working day.

The form is computerized as a Microsoft Excel file, with embedded formulas that are capable of daily updating.

We have obtained such a form from Haier headquarters for Zhang Yongzhao, the purchasing manager of steel plates at the Material Flow Development Division. The information and data last entered on the form were for June 28, 2002. Zhang Yongzhao has a projected annual salary of 57,253 RMB. Depending on how much he purchases and how well he controls the expenses allowed him, he can make more or less than the projected amount. On June 28, 2002, his projected income was 186 RMB, but he did not purchase as much as planned that day, which resulted in his making just 157 RMB.

Because the all-SBU program leans strongly on the quantitative measurement of job performance, everything is calculated and put under scrutiny. This is a more sophisticated way than the OEC model of linking one's job performance with one's economic output, and many people, especially some managers, feel very uncomfortable with it. They believe they have lost some control over their subordinates, because employees are more concerned about the market side of their jobs than about taking orders from their administrative bosses. As a result, the implementation of the program has been slow, and there has been some reluctance, or even resistance, on the part of both managers and ordinary employees.

According to a July 23, 2002 report in the *Economic Daily*, a leading Chinese business newspaper, one lower-ranking Haier manager openly defied the program by lashing out, in an inflammatory way, against SBU. He was a section head in a functional department who had been able to lord it over his staff, but with the introduction of SBU, his words seemed to carry less weight with his subordinates, and he felt less powerful and more frustrated.

Zhang Ruimin, the CEO, had anticipated difficulties in implementing the program, and set out to educate the employees, especially the managers, about the necessity of adapting to change.

A number of activities show that Haier has been moving in earnest toward that goal.

On May 6 and 7, 2001, Haier had a two-day management conference on BPR, to push the all-SBU program. Zhang made a speech at the close of the meeting to address the issue. He called on the managers to take a more active part in the program, saying, "The essence of management lies not so much in knowing as in doing. Managers must first of all put their words into action. In addition, it is not enough to make just yourself an SBU; you must make every employee under you an SBU, too."

In January 2002, when celebrating Haier's record-breaking worldwide sales of 60.2 billion RMB, Zhang reiterated the company's tasks for 2002—speed, creativity and SBU. Once again, Zhang stressed that, if everyone becomes an SBU, customer loyalty will be enhanced.

At the end of June 2002, Haier held a meeting to celebrate the eighty-first birthday of the Communist Party of China. As Party Secretary of the Haier Group, Zhang awarded prizes to some of the outstanding Party members who had distinguished themselves in implementing the all-SBU program. Among them were Liu Xiangyang and Wang Li, two division general managers whom Zhang praised for quickly switching roles in Business Process Reengineering and having kept pace with the process.

When asked by Wharton's Professor Marshall Meyer, in April 2001, about the ultimate goal of the market chain, Zhang replied, "I think the goal is to make everyone at Haier an SBU. That way, an employee is no longer a liability or debt to the company, but capital. When each of our 30,000-plus employees becomes a strategic business unit, a practice no other company has ever implemented, Haier will have achieved something remarkable."

That "remarkable" thing is what Zhang calls the Haier Revolution, which is still going on.

8

Zhang Ruimin:
The CEO Who Leads

Zhang Ruimin, son of an ordinary Chinese textile worker, was born in Laizhou, Shandong Province on January 5, 1949, the same year the People's Republic of China was founded. It didn't take long for Zhang's generation to discover that China was standing hungry on an international stage that had no place for it.

Like everyone in his generation, Zhang went through rigorous years of elementary school education under the cult of Mao. Middle school and high school included Communist refinements geared toward "three big things": joining the "Red-Scarf Team," a Chinese version of boy and girl scouts, joining the Youth League and joining the Communist Party.

In his youth, Zhang went through the Great Famine (1960 to 1963), and fully understood the meaning of the word "starvation." When the Cultural Revolution began in 1966, Zhang joined the Red Guards and, like all other Chinese youths of the time, traveled to Mao's birthplace, Shaoshanchong in Hunan Province, to pay homage. Later, he went to Beijing, capital of China, where Mao served as Chairman of the Communist Party.

Between 1966 and 1969, the Cultural Revolution took center stage in Chinese life, and the schools were closed down completely. Although Zhang was in senior high school in 1968, he lost the chance to go to college. Being the only child in the family, he didn't have to go to the countryside to be "reeducated" by peasants, as millions of Chinese youths did at the time. Instead, he got a job in a metal-processing factory in Qingdao, as an apprentice, a position that was the envy of the day.

In the factory, Zhang worked hard, and was made a model worker, a model Communist Party member, a team leader, a workshop supervisor, and Deputy Director of the factory. He was later promoted to Deputy Manager of the Household Appliance Division of the Qingdao municipal government, a position he held until December 1984, when he was appointed Director of the Qingdao General Refrigerator Factory, the predecessor of Haier.

There are quite a few stories about Zhang during his pioneering years in the Qingdao General Refrigerator Factory. Many people remember him as the one who really took the interests of the employees to heart. The most popular story was about Zhang going to borrow money from the peasants for the sake of his employees.

"In a few weeks, it would be Chinese New Year. Zhang tried very hard, and got five kilograms of fish for each employee for the New Year. But he also wanted to give each of them a little cash bonus," recalled Han Shufa, the factory driver. Several times, in 1985, he had driven factory leaders to nearby villages to borrow money, so workers could have salaries.

"Where could we go to borrow money in those days? Banks wouldn't lend a penny to us because we were a collective enterprise and we had no connections anywhere. The factory was losing more than 1.47 million, and could go bankrupt anytime. Zhang had no choice but to go to the nearby Big Mountain village one more time. The factory had only two old East Wind three-wheelers and a broken truck. I drove a factory deputy director three times to the commune, and kowtowed three times.

"Three days before the Chinese New Year, the money was approved. Zhang notified the accounting department and got into a three-wheeler without a top. He had to go to the commune savings bank, twenty miles away, to get the money. It was biting cold, and the wind slashed our faces and hands."

Mr. Wang Donggui, the village Party Secretary who had agreed to lend the money to Zhang, recalled an interesting anecdote.

"Zhang had just taken over the refrigerator factory. The factory was doing very poorly, and the employees all wanted to go to Red Star. It was the Spring Festival, and there was no money to be given to the employees, not even two *yuan*, for a bonus. Zhang was very anxious, and came to me saying he must get some money for his workers to celebrate the Chinese New Year with. I told him okay. I asked him to stay and get warm first. I knew he never drank, but I told him he must drink. Otherwise, I wouldn't lend him the money.

"He got drunk that day. He was willing to get drunk in order to borrow the money, so that his workers could have something for the New Year. No wonder, in a few months, Zhang got the factory going, and soon he returned me the money. Zhang Ruimin has vision, credit and class!"

Two days before the New Year, the money was in the employees' hands. They were overwhelmed with joy and gratitude.

Zhang is a disciplined man, and is always hard on himself. In early 1985, the German company, Liebherr, agreed to set up a joint venture with Qingdao General Refrigerator Factory, and their technology was to be shipped to Qingdao.

Yu Limin, now working in the President's Office, was an ordinary employee at the time, handling everyday business and running errands. He recalls: "It is by far the hardest thing to get all the necessary approval stamps from Beijing for such a joint venture program. The Germans were convinced we could make it, but in Beijing, we didn't have connections, and they didn't believe us. Once, when we were in Beijing, trying to get a stamp on a purchasing document to allow us to buy the German technology, people inside the office told us to wait outside. We knew they didn't want to take care of us. Nevertheless, we went out and waited in the snow for two hours before someone looked out the window and saw us covered in snow.

"They were moved, and stamped the purchasing document. During those early days, we tried harder to save money for the factory than we tried to save money for our own families. People saw us rush to Beijing and Guangzhou and in and out of the gates of the State Economic Planning Commission, thinking we were the lucky ones, to travel a lot. But they didn't know that at night, behind the closed hotel doors, we were eating leftover noodles."

Another employee, Mr. Zhao Guobin, who now works at the Air Conditioner Factory, was then working with Zhang on a daily basis, and was very impressed by his frugality. In August 1985, he and Zhang went to the Shandong Provincial Foreign Currency Division in Jinan, capital of the province, to apply for foreign currency exchange. (Foreign currency was, and still is, controlled by the government. The only circulating currency in China has been the Chinese *renminbi* or RMB.) In order to do business with foreigners, Chinese companies had to get approval for foreign currency exchange.

"In order to save travel costs, Zhang suggested that we stay in a cheap hotel. So we checked into the Jinan Military Hostel, for four *yuan* a night—five times cheaper than the regular hotel. The temperature in Jinan was about 100°F that day. Inside the tiny room with no fans, it was even hotter. The two of us could not sleep, so we took turns spraying cold water onto the cement floor to get cool.

"About two in the morning, I was too tired to continue, so Zhang took over. At six in the morning, we got up and borrowed two bikes to ride to the provincial office in order to save some bus fare. Seeing us sweating all over when we got there, people in the office were very sympathetic, and one of them sighed, 'There are still people who care about doing business. Foreign currency documentation should be approved for them.'

"After we had received the approval documentation, we jumped onto the overnight train back to Qingdao. Because it was a travel season, we couldn't get a seat, and had to stand overnight in the join between two cars."

Even fourteen years later, when Haier had become a giant and Zhang had been granted a Presidential reception in Manila, capital of the Philippines, where Haier built its first overseas Haier factory, he was still a frugal traveler. He never flew first class if he was traveling alone, and he would content himself with a bowl of noodles at the airport, like any other traveler. Business has changed, but Zhang remains the same—a hard working employee.

Because of the Cultural Revolution, Zhang missed the chance to go to college, but in the 1980s, he enrolled in an on-the-job, distance-learning MBA program offered to corporate managers by China Science and Technology University. He got his MBA when he finished the program in 1988.

Zhang has been the head of the company since 1984, though its name has changed many times and it has grown from 800 employees to over 30,000. At the time of this writing, he is Chairman, CEO and Communist Party Secretary of the Haier Group, the paramount leader of the company in every sense of the word.

An Interview with Zhang Ruimin and Yang Mianmian

On December 20, 2001, we interviewed Zhang Ruimin in his headquarters conference room in Qingdao.

Zhang sat opposite us across a large conference table. He is unusually tall for a Chinese—over six feet. He looked tired, though he was dressed in a suit and tie, and his hair was neatly combed back. He had just returned from a trip to Hong Kong. The previous day, before he got a moment for himself and his staff, he had had to entertain guests from Canon, and then he was off again for a provincial meeting with higher-level Party leaders.

On the afternoon of the interview, he was scheduled to fly to Jinan, capital of Shandong Province, for a business meeting. His blue chopper, Haier One, was waiting for him in the meadow behind the Haier corporate building.

On his right sat Yang Mianmian, the President. Next to Yang was Ms. Su Fangwen, the company's Enterprise Culture Center chief. At the far end of the large room were rows of comfortable, wine-colored sofas, arranged conference-room style under a large Chinese painting of pine trees.

Before interviewing him, we had walked the four main roads in front of the corporate building, which he had named after the four big seas and rivers of China—the Yellow River, the Yangtze River, the Yellow Sea and the Bohai Sea. We also found that the central road directly leading from the gate to the building was symbolically named "Pacific Avenue." Haier was moving out by way of China's waterways and across the Pacific Ocean to America and other parts of the world.

We had also ridden company shuttles that took employees and visitors to their different destinations around the Haier Industrial Park. In front of the Haier Central Research Institute, we made a stop to take a picture of the billboard at the bus stop. "Is the moon in the West fuller than that in China?" the billboard asked.

Unquestionably, Zhang felt great pressure to catch up with the West. He also had great conviction and strong motivation. In front of Haier University, we had pondered long and hard over the school's guiding principle: "Be realistic, be pioneering, and be realistic."

There are various sculptures around the Park, including the famous five-dragon clock given to Haier at the 1996 Olympic Games and a group of mama, papa and baby elephants that symbolize prosperity and happiness in the Chinese tradition. The sculptures and the square, gray-and-red headquarters building, supported by four solid columns symbolizing the four legs of Haier business—manufacturing, trading, financial industry, and high-tech—all spoke of Zhang's ambition.

We started by asking him about his 1984 appointment to head the nearly broke company.

"My official boss told me to take over the Qingdao General Refrigerator Factory. I was the fourth person they had asked to go there in a year. The factory had been losing money, and was on the verge of closing down..." He must have told this story a thousand times. He looked exhausted.

"So your boss in the municipal bureau had asked both you and Yang Mianmian to..."

"No, they asked me, and I chose Yang Mianmian to come along with me."

"Why?"

"I chose her because she was the best. She was an excellent engineer, and she was very passionate about her job. Also, Mianmian is from the south. You know people from the south traditionally have more business sense than people from other parts. And she was married to a Shandongese. She combines in herself the shrewdness of a business woman from the south and the down-to-earth working attitude of a Shandongese in the north."

The Shandongese have been known for straightforwardness and hard work. This fine characteristic of the Shandong people has been built into the Chinese consciousness through popular cross-talks by and about Shandong. The men from Shandong were strong, and considered the best husband material.

"In Yang Mianmian, all of these fine qualities were wonderfully combined. She has made great contributions to this firm."

Yang Mianmian nodded her head and smiled broadly. She was proud, and with good reason. She complements Zhang very well. If

Yang is the *yin* element, Zhang is the *yang*. At each turning point in Haier's brief history of eighteen years, Yang Mianmian was there. At sixty-one, Yang Mianmian still maintains the same posture of abundant energy and confidence.

"As a team, Chairman Zhang and I have gone through many things together. He strategizes; I implement. And we did it." Yang Mianmian's eyes were shining when she turned to her boss.

"But you took the job because you also saw some opportunity, and that has made all the difference." We showed him a photo we had taken two days before at the Haier Museum of Science and Technology. It was the photo of the sledgehammer which had been used to smash the seventy-six defective refrigerators. "This hammer has not only produced quality products but has opened up a Haier Road in America! The Chinese have been seeking jobs in America for over a century, and now you give *them* jobs!"

His eyes suddenly brightened, and we saw a CEO in action, a charismatic man, not a tired man trying to get another necessary chore over with, or meeting the press or writers who want to make their names by writing his stories.

The interview was moving to Haier's management, and those people who want to learn from it.

Su Fangwen answered for Zhang. "Many visitors have come for our management secrets, but none has really learned them. That is because we have good employees and visionary leaders. Besides, our enterprise culture cannot be duplicated simply." She had mentioned this point to us during the past three lunches in the guest dining room.

There, we had run into reporters, corporate leaders and professionals from academic circles, from both China and overseas. Among them was a Chinese-Japanese scholar studying the Haier management style for his post-doctoral thesis.

"We have good employees because we have good leaders. If you want the train to run fast, the engine has to be good." Yang Mianmian smiled.

"We summarize as we go along," Yang Mianmian continued. "Haier has developed so fast and has grown so big that we have to deal with new issues all the time as they surface. A leader must be a role model. Excellent leaders build excellent people. Excellent people produce excellent products."

This last sentence from Yang Mianmian had become the Haier motto, and was present in almost all the Haier plants across the world.

"The essential point is having good software—that is, good-quality people must exist before good machinery and other hardware, to ensure the success of a business."

Zhang agreed. "It's good to work hard, but no one should get burned out. A leader must be able to inspire and care for the people working under him, and to make the able and the less able serve each other like a family. It is upon that foundation that a good society and a good business can be built. This idea is not mine; it is borrowed from Confucius and Mencius. You must have strict discipline, but you must also rule with your heart."

Zhang continued: "In the early stages of our development, we merged with and acquired eighteen money-losing factories. Those enterprises needed capital injections, but good software was far more important than capital injection at the very beginning. So we sent our people over with the Haier culture."

Our question moved to globalization.

"As Haier moves onto the international platform and becomes global, how do you control your business? How do you take care of issues such as loyalty?" we asked.

"As for business, we have a sophisticated system that does global settlements, just as investment banks do. As for people, we hire the same type of people, people who are trustworthy and passionate and know and love what they do."

"For example?"

"Michael Jemal, president of Haier America. He used to be our distributor. He knows what he's doing, and is proud of working for Haier. He is a member of the Haier family in America. Our effort is to try combining his goal with the company goal, and provide him with the right platform to succeed. In turn, he hires the same type of people and makes them successful with the same principle.

"To manage people overseas, you cannot go to extremes," Zhang continued. "For instance, we have a worker in our South Carolina facility who liked to listen to rap music while working. While he worked, he danced and moved his body to the rhythm. We had never run into a thing like that in China.

"At Haier headquarters, the first thing all new employees have to learn is how to walk—walk in a straight line. We believe in strong discipline. That's why the new employees have to go through one month of military training. If you lower your standard of employee requirements, your quality will suffer, then your product will suffer and, eventually, your customer will suffer. Without customers, we have no business. So what we did was promote and praise another worker, who worked alongside this employee, for his proper attire and proper manner at work. After a while, the employee who liked to listen to the music and dance while working no longer brought his stereo to work. It took patience. But, as Confucius says, deal with problems in the mean."

He went on to explain.

"We have vigorous training for new employees. But again, you must have balance, too." Zhang was more excited. "This is where we find our Chinese culture more efficient, such as the teaching of the Mean. The Mean is our standard. We can use standards derived from what Confucius calls *zhong*, the mean, to guide us on our path. The mean is the center, the balance point. If you demand too much and make people feel pushed all the time, you eventually push them out. Treat people like family members, and with a longer view.

"Let me give you another example. We had a new employee in our South Carolina plant. She got sick after only a few days on the job, and was hospitalized. Our local office sent flowers to her. The employee broke into tears. True, companies don't like to see employees get sick. It means a loss of work and money. To run a successful business, one cannot be too short-sighted. You have to create a family environment through genuine care and consideration, a sense of belonging, like a home. Bottom line, you spend more time at the workplace than at home." Zhang's tone was gentle, but his words were powerful, and carried heart-felt sincerity.

"History gets written while it develops and moves ahead," Zhang said in a conclusive tone. "At the very beginning, we only wanted not to starve—to eat to our hearts' content. Then the business got bigger and bigger. The pressure was also getting bigger and bigger.

In the past, I only needed to take care of about 800 workers. Now I have to think about more than 30,000 employees. This is a very big pressure which leaves me little time for my family." He looked a bit weary when he finished his last sentence.

We had heard a story about Zhang's family life. When Zhang invited his wife of over twenty years for a walk on a May Day holiday, his wife, who had been accustomed to being left alone on holidays, was so taken aback by the invitation that she didn't at first realize what he was saying. Then she broke into tears. In the ten years since Zhang had taken the job at Qingdao General Refrigerator Factory, this was the first time he and his wife had taken a walk together.

Zhang was the only son in his family. His mother, like many Chinese women of her generation, didn't know how to read or write, but she knew every single heartbeat of her son. "When I hear Ruimin's footsteps on the stairs, I know everything is fine with him. Then I can go to sleep."

"What did you do when you saw your wife shedding tears? Did you dry them for her?" Jeannie asked Zhang.

Everyone in the conference room seemed to be sweetly surprised by this very feminine question.

Zhang was silent. There was genuine sorrow in his eyes—he always looked a bit sorrowful.

"*Wo...mei fazi*—I...have no other way." He grew silent again.

We had previously heard from Mr. Xie, of the Enterprise Culture Center, that Zhang's wife was a Party secretary in a textile factory in Qingdao, and a very low-profile person. For a long time, their son's teachers had had no idea who his father was, because his mother had always instructed him to fill in the school registration or record forms with her name as parent, omitting his father's. "I wonder whether the school thought the boy came from a single-parent family," Xie joked.

His son is now a student at the Wharton School of the University of Pennsylvania.

When Zhang Ruimin took over the Qingdao General Refrigerator Factory in December 1984, he set the date of December 26 as the birthday of the factory. Haier now regards 1984 as the official year of Haier's establishment, and all Haier documents began with that year.

We brought up a question regarding this date in our interview.

"Why did you choose December 26th? That's Mao Zedong's birthday. Are you implying..."

Having grown up in China, we have always been sensitive to Mao's birthday. Like all the Chinese of our and Zhang's generation, we had celebrated Mao's birthday every year until his death in 1976. By naming the same date as the birthday of his factory and his rule, was Zhang continuing Mao's tradition, or was this Zhang's denunciation, a breakaway?

"There's no special meaning," Zhang answered simply. "The day I reported to the factory was December 22. A few days later, it would be Mao's birthday. I talked with Yang Mianmian and a couple of other managers and we decided on the date of December 26 as the factory's birthday. It's only a matter of convenience; there is no political implication."

"But you respected Mao. For instance, you copied the 'school principle' in Mao style on the central wall of the Haier University. You constantly emphasize the importance of being practical and realistic, which are frequently quoted Mao doctrines. Also, you traveled all the way to the hometown of Jiao Yulu, who was a role-model Mao had set up for the whole nation to learn from. And, like Mao, you want to do something big..."

Zhang was silent, and looked at us as if he were a bit intrigued. We could not tell for sure if he took secret pleasure in the implication, but we had little doubt that he was an admirer of Mao and a practitioner of many of Mao's teachings.

Zhang's Strategies for Haier after the WTO

Zhang considers China's entry into the World Trade Organization (WTO) more a challenge than an opportunity for Haier. Domestically, Haier will face tougher challenges from foreign conglomerates in China's appliance market, such as Whirlpool and Electrolux. Almost all multinationals will eventually enter this huge, unconquered market. With strong capital backing, their strategy is "winner take all," leaving nothing for the unfit in the competition.

Kodak has set up numerous processing centers across China, with the intention of taking the whole film market in China. Coca-Cola has set up many production facilities in major Chinese cities. If the two of them put in one or two billion U.S. dollars as additional investment money, they can easily take a much larger chunk, if not all, of China's film and soft drink markets.

Internationally, Chinese companies will face anti-dumping regulations and non-trade-tariff barriers from many countries. The European Union has imposed a 21% anti-dumping tax on all Chinese microwave ovens. To buffer the tax, Haier opened an assembly factory in Italy, which reduced the tax to 9%. Now Haier is producing microwave ovens in Italy to avoid the anti-dumping tax.

Under U.S. law, Haier's exported refrigerators must meet the country's ever-higher energy-consumption standards, which adds extra costs to satisfy those benchmarks. With its refrigerators designed in the U.S. and some of them even produced in South Carolina, Haier is in a much better position to deal with such issues.

Zhang concluded that, in order to meet the challenge of the multinationals, Haier must become a multinational itself. If you are going to "dance with the wolves," you must become a wolf yourself. Otherwise, you cannot escape the fate of being eaten by the wolves. It worries Zhang that many Chinese companies are still playing the part of lambs, which, in Zhang's opinion, will put them in a very dangerous position.

The first strategy Zhang adopted to make Haier a strong multinational was to build up localized structures, both at home and abroad. Haier now has ten industrial parks around the world, which can be divided into three groups. The group in the greater Qingdao area serves as the company's export base, taking advantage of China's lower labor and material costs to make products primarily for export purposes. The second group, centered around the Hefei Industrial Park, makes products for the domestic market. The third group comprises all the industrial parks and manufacturing facilities overseas, including those in the United States, Europe, the Middle East and Southeast Asia. Zhang viewed these facilities as bases from which to build the Haier brand name in localized environments.

Zhang emphasizes that Haier should first of all strengthen its domestic competitiveness by taking full advantage of its strong sales and service networks. He contends that now, at least, foreign multinationals cannot compete with Haier in these two areas. He also sees the very great importance of localization of design, manufacture and sales in foreign lands, citing as an example the ability to bid for government purchases in the United States.

Zhang's next step is to build a global center that can pull together all the resources around the globe to coordinate its design, manufacturing and sales activities. He is very impressed by General Motors' around-the-clock design, which takes the advantage of time zones in different locations around the world. He is very much attracted by the GM model, and will do everything in his power to catch up.

Zhang's Strategies for Haier to Win in Domestic Competition

For more than eighteen years, Zhang has been successful in trying to dodge price wars in China's appliance market. He wants to fight and win value wars, not price wars. Zhang admits that it is understandable that sometimes price wars are unavoidable, especially for a country like China that is going through the transition from a planned economy to a market economy. Normally, companies that have lost price wars should exit the market, so that a new market order can be established as a result. It perplexes Zhang that a lot of state-owned companies can still exist, even though they have lost a great deal in price wars. After a period of adjustment, these companies can launch another round of price wars, which drags other companies into a new vicious circle of cutthroat competition.

For Zhang, the best way is to stay out of these lose-lose price wars by sticking to set prices as much as possible. He feels confident that his customers value Haier products because of their high quality and excellent service. His solution to growth is to raise the rate of capital return by increasing marginal profits and speeding up capital turnover.

Zhang's ideal business model is Dell—taking money from customers before shipping customized products to them. With a more liquid cash flow, he can run his business without much burden. He considers a high capital-return rate to be of vital importance to Haier—its employees and its shareholders—without which Haier would not be in a competitive position to win market share and retain employees.

He wants to do more about capital and brand management in the future. Using Haier's good reputation, he hopes to raise more capital, which will, in turn, help Haier make more and better products. As for brand, Zhang's goal is to make Haier a truly global brand, like GE, Sony and Nike.

He has a lot of admiration for Nike. With only about 1,000 employees and no manufacturing facilities, the company has customers all over the world, selling sneakers made by OEMs in quantity every day. Zhang believes that is the true power of a global brand.

"Capital is the boat, and the brand is the mast." Zhang believes that the relationship between capital and brand is the same as that between a boat and its mast. Capital is used to make boats of all sizes and shapes.

"If I have a lot of capital, I can make a lot of boats—small boats, big boats, fast boats, and ocean-going boats. But if the mast is not made right, either not big enough or the wrong size, how can the boat go far? If the mast—the brand name—is big and strong, it can take the boat really fast and far, and then we can make a bigger boat."

Manage with Traditional Chinese Values

In an interview with *Forbes* magazine, Zhang says that his management theories are largely influenced by ancient Chinese philosophy. He especially emphasizes the three principles of Confucian doctrine. The first is to observe the three cardinal guides (ruler guides subject, father guides son, and husband guides wife) and five constant virtues (benevolence, righteousness, propriety, wisdom and fidelity). The second is to emphasize the importance of education and self-cultivation for the betterment of the society. The third principle is that no official title should pass from father to son, to ensure equal opportunity for everyone to compete and excel.

When asked again by China Central TV reporters, Zhang stressed the Confucian concept of family in a web of relationships, helping one another evolve. For Confucius, there is no place for individualism or "self" in such human relationships. At the heart of everyone's roles and relationships is a unified entity—the family and the complexity of relationships that constitutes it. The goal of living, then, is to achieve harmony and enjoyment for oneself and others through acting appropriately in prescribed and predetermined roles in such relationships.

Zhang maintains that, since we all live within the web of family relationships, it is entirely natural that we should project this concept onto a business community such as the Haier Group. Etymologically, the Chinese character "business" reveals the importance of a person or persons. Remove the symbol for "person," and "business" is "nonexistence."

Similarly, the core of Confucian teaching is the concept of *ren*, or benevolence. In the Confucian community, be it a family or an organization, benevolence is made up of relationships between persons higher up and persons lower in position. Therefore, the ruler is father to his people, the son of Heaven who is a faceless amalgam of ancestors, containing all the virtues combined. Accordingly, the teacher is a "father figure," which accounts for the Chinese saying "A teacher for a day, a father for life."

An interesting example of this can be found in Jiang Zemin, the Chinese President, who paid a special visit to Professor Yu H. Ku during his United States trip in October 1997. According to Jiang, Ku had taught him calculus at Shanghai Jiaotong University some fifty years before, though Dr. Ku could only remotely remember the relationship. A Ph.D. in mechanical engineering from MIT in the 1920s, Ku had served as president and dean at several universities in China in the 1930s and 1940s. He had also held high-ranking government offices (Chief of the Department of Education of Shanghai and Deputy Minister of Education under the Chiang Kai-shek government) before emigrating to the United States in 1950. At the time of Jiang's visit, Ku, at ninety-five, was a retired professor from the University of Pennsylvania, living in the Philadelphia area.

"Treat your family members properly—this is the root of becoming a person," taught Confucius in *Analects*. One of the most important concepts of Confucianism is "propriety" (*li*)—a code of formal behavior for stabilizing and disciplining our ever-changing circumstances. "Propriety" covers everything from table manners to the three years of mourning after the loss of a parent, from the institution of parenthood to the appropriate posture for expressing commiseration. It is this social syntax that brings the particular members of the community into meaningful relationships, while proper conduct locates them appropriately, one with the other.

Throughout the classic Confucian writings—*The Analects, The Great Learning* and *The Doctrine of the Mean*—both Confucius and Mencius believed that human nature was intrinsically good, though human conduct could be negative. *Ren*, or benevolence, is the ultimate fountainhead from which all virtues flow: wisdom, love, compassion and equality. *Ren* refers to humankind, human nature itself, and always includes others. The ideogram for *ren* includes the ideogram for "two," implying that dialogue and communication are part of *ren*. To be is to be in a relationship.

Zhang has been following such Confucian guidance in managing his company. He has incorporated some of the Confucian philosophies such as the concepts of benevolence or *ren,* propriety or *li*, integrity and duty, into the Haier enterprise culture. Under him, Haier has become a home or family where proper behavior rules.

The actions of Zhang and his Haier have brought Confucian virtues together by living them. In being benevolent, honorable and sincere, they have found themselves naturally doing the right thing and being courageous enough to act upon their convictions with integrity, no matter how simple and naïve they may sometimes appear.

The fruits of such management are apparent in Zhang's company. Sports activities, family days, employee-appreciation days and regular family tours conducted by the company for Haier employees' family members, as well as the stories and cartoons in the *Haier News*, all illustrate such efforts. Zhang and his team have created an atmosphere in which employees feel encouraged and appreciated.

Having been a worker himself for twelve years, Zhang is keenly aware of the importance of appreciation by one's boss. He shows appreciation to his employees for the smallest achievement, whether in product design, manufacturing, marketing, business management, operations or accounting. The employees at Haier act upon the strong motivation that comes from their CEO, who encourages everyone to be creative or innovative.

"Everyone should be encouraged to innovate, and those who contribute more to the product should benefit more." Still, he wants to acknowledge all employees, especially workers on the factory floor, when they do something out of the ordinary. Consequently, Haier names products, parts or even manufacturing practices after the employees who are responsible for their innovation. That way, Zhang says, all the employees know they have a chance to become special in the organization.

Zhang compares the force of creativity in each individual with the fountainhead or origin of a river. Many "origins" form a flowing river, and flowing rivers with a common goal gush into an open sea. Zhang regards Haier as the sea, and has written a memorable company mission statement combining one's job and one's duty to one's company (small home) and one's country (big home) through an analogy of the sea.

In the mission statement, Zhang tries to convey the sense of obligation an individual must have toward his two homes—company and country. He also strives to instill a sense of history in the consciousness of Haier employees by bringing past and future together.

The following is the last section of his statement "Haier Is the Sea," which we saw written on the wall of the central hall in the Haier Museum of Science and Technology. Zhang's calligraphy makes each word jump out of the wall, a splash of ocean blue, punctuated with Zhang's vision, ambition, and determination.

> Like the sea, we should make contributions to society and mankind. As long as our love of society and mankind is "sincere and forever," Haier will last forever, the way the sea does. Every member living within its boundless limits will be rewarded handsomely for his or her effort to maximize the company's well-being while contributing to society. Haier and society will become one and the same.

People, especially reporters, are often curious to know what has propelled Zhang to shoulder the huge burden of his country and his company. Zhang's answer has been consistent: the ancient Chinese teachings.

"There are three books I often read, and I draw strength and inspiration from them. They are Confucius' *Analects*, Lao Tzu's *Tao-De Ching* and Sun Tzu's *The Art of War*." Zhang believes that one of the underpinnings of Confucianism is the state/ruler providing for the family/subject and the family/subject supporting and obeying the state/ruler. In the line of Confucian thought, an official (a company head) is head of the household (company) who provides for the children (employees). In return, the father figure wants his children to obey the rules he has set, and do everything they can to maintain the unity of the household.

On several occasions, Zhang said that he has drawn inspiration in running his company from the following Taoist teachings:

All things of the world originate from visible beings,
And all visible beings originate from invisible beings (Tao).
(Lao Tzu, *Tao-De Ching*, Chapter 40)

To put it another way, this somewhat esoteric doctrine means that there must be something abstract (invisible beings) preceding something concrete (visible beings). Zhang has been very unhappy about situations in which he believes that people pay too much attention to the visible and too little attention to the invisible. For instance, every time officials from higher up inspect a company, all they want to know about is the visible—the number of production units, the revenues and profits, etc. Rarely does anyone pay attention to the invisible, that is, the company's culture.

To Zhang, a company without a culture is like a person without a soul. The soul he finds for Haier is the "invisible" in Lao Tzu's *Tao*, or "the Way."

Tao gives birth to the One (unified thing),
The One splits itself into Two opposites (*yin* and *yang*),
The Two gives birth to another (Three),
And the newborn Third produces a myriad things.
(Lao Tzu, *Tao-De Ching,* Chapter 42)

To apply the Tao to human activities, such as running a business the size of Haier, Zhang finds in the doctrine some unutterable prophesy that explains the necessity and importance of establishing an enterprise culture that governs the thinking and behavior of all people in the company.

Zhang has applied many of the military strategies expounded in *The Art of War* by Sun Tzu, to his business practices, either in strategic business planning or market tactics. Zhang acknowledges that "Sun Tzu has helped me formulate management styles and business competition strategies."

When he was planning for his three phases of business development strategies, Zhang followed Sun Tzu's teaching, "Know your enemy and know yourself, and you can fight a hundred battles without peril. If you are ignorant of the enemy and know only yourself, you will have equal chances of winning and losing. If you know neither the enemy nor yourself, you are bound to be defeated in every battle." ("Attacking by Stratagem" in *The Art of War* by Sun Tzu)

In the first phase of brand name building, Zhang knew that the market needed quality products, and Haier, though capable of making them for the market, must expend tremendous effort to meet challenging product requirements. Guided by that wisdom, Haier spent seven years working on just one product—the refrigerator—and established an excellent reputation for a strong brand name.

When it comes to specific business tactics, Zhang is a firm believer in Sun Tzu's weaknesses-and-strengths scenarios.

"The law governing military operations is like that governing the flow of water, which always evades high points and chooses lower courses. To operate an army successfully, we must avoid the enemy's strong points and attack his weak points." ("Weaknesses and Strengths" in *The Art of War* by Sun Tzu)

An example can be found in Haier's assault on the U.S. market with compact refrigerators, a product area where most major U.S. appliance makers were relatively weak, because they did not care too much about this not-so-profitable category. Had Haier tried to enter the U.S. market with large-size refrigerators to compete head on with GE and Whirlpool, Zhang would have met his Waterloo with the first engagement.

A Fighter Prepared to Be a Martyr

In a speech Zhang made on April 18, 1997, to graduate students at Tsinghua University in Beijing, regarded as China's MIT, he expressed his ambition to uplift China's image in the world.

"Mr. Sun Yatsen once said, 'We should aspire to big things, not big positions.' For me, the big thing to do is to make Haier a first-rate company in the world, to make it the backbone of Chinese enterprises. Maybe I will not see that happen, but I am sure that, someday, Chinese enterprises will certainly be among the world's strongest players."

Reiterating that high aspiration, Zhang spoke from his heart in the following interview with the Chinese media, which we have excerpted from a Chinese publication:

> During my primary schooling, I learned that, from the Opium War in 1840 until the Westernization Movement, a movement to introduce Western techniques initiated by *comprador* bureaucrats in the late nineteenth century, China had always hoped to make herself more prosperous and economically stronger. Now that we have the opportunity to reform and open our doors to the world, we should seize the chance to build up a real Chinese brand name in the world. In my opinion, to live is to do something for the country. Only when our country is stronger will it be able to secure its international status in the world. Since I am in no position to decide big issues, what I can do is start with some down-to-earth work.
>
> Without the support of such belief, I am afraid I would have given up my effort a long time ago. Because when you look around and think a bit, you will feel sad or even distressed. By saying that, I do not mean to lecture you on general principles or impress you with high-sounding words. The truth of the matter is that I do live by such beliefs. Otherwise how can you justify yourself, while many people around you gain a lot more by doing less or nothing? Some people even act in defiance of the law but still live comfortably.
>
> A state-run enterprise, even if it loses money, is always excused for various reasons. Our case is the contrary; no matter how hard we have worked, we will be faulted, here and there.
>
> It is not that Haier has done something extraordinary, but that China has produced nothing we could boast to the world about since the Opium War. *Nothing!*

Take Japan as an example. In wartime, she launched the Meiji Restoration, aimed at making Japan rich and building up its military might. Now that we are in a time of peace, the economy should lead the way.

Think of this: China was no good in terms of military strength during the Opium War. And if China is still no good in terms of the economy, and cannot catch up with the developed countries during peacetime, what else can China do?

When you are in Germany, the German people show their pride in themselves by saying that the German nation is a great nation; when you are in Japan, the Japanese people talk about how proud they are of their country; when you are in Korea, the Korean people, too, boast about the nation that created their economic miracles.

When it comes to China, what should we Chinese be proud of? When I was at Harvard, delivering a lecture, the Chinese students there told me that, while they could make a lot of money abroad, they were unable to name a single brand name China had produced which could represent the national economic strength.

Other international students at Harvard can boast, "We are German and we have got such brand names as Benz," or, "We are Japanese and we have got Toyota and Sony." But what kind of brand name do the Chinese have?

The Chinese economist Wu Jinglian once told me that China is a country without corporate cultures. And I think this is sadly true. Now we are under a market economy, which results in intense competition, but the country still remains in a state of disunity. During wartime, disunity might cause the whole country to be trampled upon. Under a market economy, disunity will not give a country the competitive edge.

In the final analysis, when we talk about a brand name, we are talking about the outward appearance that characterizes a nation.

[*Zhang was asked about how he thinks of the reform of state-run enterprises.*]

To tell the truth, I have no idea what the people at state-run enterprises are really thinking of. But one thing is clear: in the current situation, we have done our best as an enterprise in China; at least, I feel so. Certainly, there are people who are very smart and very bright. To these people, it is another story.

As for me, there is not a minute that goes by when I do not think of the company. But even so, things are very, very difficult for me. A lot of business executives have all kinds of excuses. For instance, some say they need to have some hobbies. Since the foreign businessmen all play golf, they should play golf too.

I am not saying that they cannot play golf, but I think it is absolutely impossible to build up excellent businesses in China without the sacrifice of one generation of Chinese entrepreneurs. Looking around at the businesses in the world, you will note that a whole generation was sacrificed in the United States, in Japan and even in Korea. The generation who built up the business all made personal sacrifices.

When I was in Japan, the Japanese said, "We had been fighting for a five-day work-system for so many years. We worked extremely hard before we were granted the five-day working system. But you Chinese are really unbelievable, for your working efficiency is still very low, yet you observe the five-day system anyway. How will you be able to compete with others in the future?"

One Japanese entrepreneur said to me, "Do you know how I did my work at that time? Every morning, after I got up, I tied a towel around my head and started working on modeling. I kept on working till my wife brought me some food. After taking some food, I immediately resumed work. We never had a schedule indicating the time for going to bed. If we were too sleepy to go on, we would doze for a while, and then, back to work. There was no fixed schedule for breaks during the daytime. We just kept on working like robots."

I do not mean everyone should do the same, but we started at such a low level and our foundation was so shaky...

[*"How many hours do you work per day?" asked the reporter.*]

For me, I always work at least twelve hours a day. That does not mean that I do not want people to enjoy life, by no means at all.

The enterprises in Guangdong Province were pioneers in reforming and opening doors to the outside world, and they built up the businesses themselves. But, while commenting on these enterprises, the deputy editor-in-chief of *Southern Weekend* newspaper once said that now many enterprises in Guangdong seemed to have lost their direction. Now that they have made a lot of money, what else are you busy for?

He asked me if I could go there to give some talks. I asked him what topic I should talk about. He said that the southern entreprencurs no longer found any fun in running their businesses. To them, working had become a kind of burden and suffering. So it's better to play around and enjoy.

Such an attitude really sounds disturbing. The state-run enterprises do not want to work because they do not make a lot of money, but these entrepreneurs do not want to work because they have *made* a lot of money.

I told the editor-in-chief, "Let me put it this way: A Zen story tells that, thirty years ago, an old monk saw a mountain as a mountain, and a river as a river. After he had encountered Zen, when he saw a mountain, the mountain did not look like a mountain; when he saw a river, the river no longer looked likc a river, either. However, after thirty years, when he became a Zen Master, he saw, again, a mountain as a mountain and a river as a river.

So what are you going to do with it? Just hang on there until you have reached such a state of revelation. Then you will attain enlightenment. Otherwise, you will not see the light. There is nothing in the world that is not painful. Having delicacies of all kinds every day is also a pain. (Yan and Hu 2001, 491-93)

In *The Competitive Advantage of Nations*, Michael E. Porter, one of the two Western business theorists Zhang admires most, the other being Peter Drucker, points out that good corporate leaders believe in change. "They harness and even create external pressures to motivate change... As a result, leaders are often seen as statesman, though few would describe their own actions that way." (Porter 1990, 615)

Without question, Zhang Ruimin falls within, if not exceeds, Porter's definition of a good corporate leader.

9

Going Global:
Asia, The Middle East and Europe

Haier's ultimate goal has been to go global and become a multinational like GE, Matsushita (Panasonic) and Sony. Zhang's strategy for reaching that goal is what he calls the "three one-thirds," which means that, out of all Haier products, one-third is made and sold domestically, another one-third is made domestically but sold overseas, and the third one-third is both made and sold overseas.

There are three phases of Haier's globalization tactics. Phase one: focus on the social awareness of the Haier brand name. Phase two: localize design, production and sales. Phase three: pull in local resources of capital and human talent.

Most companies adopt a step by step, or "first the easy, then the hard" approach when they enter the global market. Companies generally choose to enter those markets that are familiar to them or geographically or culturally close to them, before getting into unfamiliar and geographically or culturally remote areas.

Many Chinese companies start their overseas operations in Hong Kong, for that reason. In the late 1970s, some Chinese companies set up businesses in Nepal and Tanzania, because China had provided economic and technical assistance to these countries since the early 1970s, and they were familiar with the social and economic conditions in those regions.

In operations, Chinese companies normally begin with trading before setting up overseas sales outlets or investment offices. The advantages of such an approach are lower capital outlay and limited risk, but these operations are usually of small scale, with inadequate manpower and scant chance for growth.

There is also the dilemma that many of the managers and sales representatives who are sent from China leave the offices after they have familiarized themselves with the market in the overseas countries. They either go to work for larger companies or simply set up their own companies, invariably taking with them all the customers they have worked with.

Experiences have shown that an overseas company operated that way is almost a guaranteed money loser. Running overseas companies in that fashion is a constant pain for the parent company in China.

After an initial period of trial-and-error that was not much different from the experience of other Chinese companies, Haier adjusted its basic strategy in entering the global market to "first the hard, then the easy," which means getting into the markets with tougher entry requirements first, and then entering the markets with lower entry requirements. The hard markets are basically those of developed countries, while the easy ones are those of developing countries.

The rationale behind Zhang's adoption of this strategy was that, if Haier had already built its brand name in the developed markets, such as the United States and Europe, it would be a lot easier to sweep the easier markets. Zhang once commented, "If we can effectively compete in the mature markets with such brand names as GE, Matsushita and Philips, we can surely take the markets in the developing countries without much effort. It is just like what we did with the domestic market. After Haier refrigerators had taken Beijing and Shanghai, we met no difficulties getting into medium and small cities."

Haier's "first the hard, then the easy" strategy in getting into international markets reverses conventional thinking. Conventional wisdom says that it is relatively easy to export to third-world countries, but the influence of a company's brand name is limited. Prior to Haier, the Western countries had, by and large, ignored Chinese brand names. That actually gave Haier a chance to crack the hard nut with almost no competition from within China.

Tactically, Haier got into the hard market by launching one product at a time, rather than a number of products at the same time. The entry cost for adopting this approach is lower. In the European market, especially in France and Italy, Haier first promoted its air conditioners. Because the air conditioner market there was relatively new, it did not make a lot of difference if they were made in Japan, Korea or China. After it had established its brand awareness in those markets, Haier edged in with refrigerators and washing machines.

Among the developed countries, Germany has the toughest entry requirements. If Haier met German requirements, it could meet requirements in other counties without much difficulty. Haier spent a year and half experimenting with German benchmarks.

One of the tests was resistance to electrical short-circuits due to leaking. A refrigerator was hung in the middle of a room, with water coming from all sides. It was a very tough test, but Haier's refrigerator passed it. What was hurtful to Haier was that, even though the benchmark had been passed, the Germans still refused to accept Haier refrigerators, arguing that, since Japanese refrigerators had not been accepted into the German market, how could it be possible that a Chinese company had made it?

Haier requested a blind test of its refrigerators along with other major brands in the German market. All trademarks were stripped off the machines for the test, and the Haier refrigerators came out with the most pluses, even more than those made by Liebherr—Haier's German teacher. Some German importers were so impressed that they placed an order for 20,000 Haier refrigerators on the spot.

It took Haier seven years, from 1991 to 1998, to become a globalized company, during which time it exported its products widely to all major parts of the world. But that was not Zhang's ultimate goal. What he had in mind was the globalization of Haier, with Haier ending up as a multinational, fully localized in the global markets.

"Globalization equals localization" is what Zhang has often been quoted as saying, which is his version of the so-called "global localization." In the face of the World Trade Organization (WTO) and the world of the Internet and e-commerce, for any multi-billion dollar corporation to survive, globalization is a must.

For many years, Haier had been an "original equipment manufacturer" (OEM) in the United States and European markets, with only a small portion of its broad product assortment represented. Haier recognized that, in order to expand its global reach and strengthen the Haier brand name, a strong commitment to the international market was a necessity. To be successful, they needed a better, broader understanding of the global market.

According to Zhang, the most important aspect of Haier's globalization is to localize its business operations in a foreign country by hiring local people, building factories in the local area and promoting the products in local markets. Since local people know their market, their people and their psychology, they can handle promotion and services better than people sent from the source country. Local people can also deal more effectively with local issues and problems, such as laws, taxes and resistance to foreign brands.

This chapter will offer a brief overview of the path Haier has traversed in its pursuit of globalization.

Haier Asia and Haier Middle East

Haier first tried its hand at the international market back in 1992, when its products entered the Indonesian market under an "original equipment manufacturer" (OEM) arrangement. Sapporo, an Indonesian company attracted by the quality and style of the Haier refrigerators, decided to undertake a joint venture with Haier. This was Haier's first manufacturing facility overseas and, by agreement, Haier held the majority of stock in the joint venture. In August 1996, the joint venture, Haier Sapporo Indonesia, started to make refrigerators for the local market. The facility was not big, but a huge Haier billboard on the highway attracted a lot of attention.

Cities in Indonesia often had power-shortage problems, and the voltage was not very stable. The spending power of middle and lower wage earners was limited. Taking these considerations into account, the Haier joint venture made energy-saving, flexible-voltage refrigerators, washing machines, air conditioners, microwave ovens and hot-bathing equipment. The products are sold in over three hundred shopping centers, and an average of 100,000 units of the combined products are sold every year.

According to the Indonesia Statistics Association, by the end of 2000, Haier freezers had taken 28% of the Indonesian market, while its ice-cream freezers had taken 50%, thanks to their stylish design and practicality.

In June 1997, Haier went into a joint venture with the LKG Electric Company in the Philippines to manufacture refrigerators, freezers, air conditioners and washing machines. The products bore the Haier brand, and were also sold to some neighboring areas.

Two months later, a Malaysian company approached Haier, suggesting a joint venture to produce washing machines and other appliances.

According to Zhang, this practice overseas had given Haier experiences that became useful in its later expansion into other, more distant areas. The Philippines experience was especially valuable in that the country's omnipresent American influence taught Haier a lot of things that could be used later in the United States.

In the 1960s and 1970s, American products dominated the Middle Eastern appliance markets. In the 1980s, the Japanese began to enter those markets, and took a large share from American companies. The Koreans made their way into the markets in the 1990s. Though Korea was a latecomer, their products quickly grew to take a majority of the markets in the Middle East.

Now it was China's turn. In February 1999, Haier Middle East was formed in Dubai, the United Arab Emirates.

In August 2001, Haier introduced its new color TVs at an exhibition in Saudi Arabia. The products at the show included seven series, with twenty-one models of color TVs especially designed for consumers in the Middle East. Seventy-five of Haier's dealers in Saudi Arabia attended a separate meeting held by Haier, and some of them received awards from the Haier Group for aggressively promoting the Haier products.

According to Al-Jazirah, one of the three largest media in Saudi Arabia, Haier's success lies in its quality high-tech products and attractive designs, which have posed a challenge to the existing dominance in the market by other foreign brands.

By the end of 2001, Haier had had joint ventures with companies in Iran and Algeria to make washing machines, refrigerators and air conditioners. Haier has established an efficient network of after-sale services in the Middle East. In Saudi Arabia, its services even extend to very remote villages in the desert. Haier has launched rather aggressive promotions in the Middle East to increase its strong presence, by attending trade shows (for example, at the SIMA in

Syria), and advertising on buildings and billboards (in such Saudi Arabian cities as Riyadh, Jeddah and Dammam). In Damascus alone, Haier ran advertising in four major streets.

According to a Haier company document, by 2001, Haier's washing machine market share in Iran was twenty percent, and its air conditioner market share in Turkey was also twenty percent.

On the last day of 2001, the Jordan Haier Middle East Trading Co., Ltd. (JHMET) was officially established. The company would develop business in some Middle Eastern countries including Jordan, Lebanon, Syria, Palestine, Iraq, Egypt and Kuwait. The joint venture had its first shareholders and board of directors meetings in Amman, capital of Jordan, on that day. At the meetings, they proclaimed that the purpose of the company was to expand the Haier market share and raise the brand's reputability in these countries. Haier also invested in Jordan to build manufacturing facilities which would make household appliances. By arrangement, eighty percent of them are to be exported to Jordan's neighbors.

On June 26, 2002, Zhang Ruimin had a five-minute telecom-satellite conversation with the Jordanian King, Abdullah II, which was televised publicly in Jordan. The King had just attended a ribbon-cutting ceremony for the new office building of the Jordanian Ministry of Investment in Amman. Obviously impressed by Haier's products and their investment in Jordan, the King wanted to have a talk with the head of Haier. The King told Zhang that Haier enjoyed a good reputation in Jordan, and that he and the Jordanian government would make efforts to create a healthy environment for Haier's development in Jordan. The conversation was, of course, all diplomacy and custom, but the mere fact that the King had called spoke volumes about his appreciation and support of Haier operations in his country.

On April 10, 2001, Zhang and his delegation arrived at Lahore, in Pangop Province in Pakistan, to attend the cornerstone-laying ceremony for the Haier (Pakistan) Industrial Park. Haier was said to be the first foreign household appliance producer who had ever invested in Pakistan. But the Haier (Pakistan) Industrial Park was the Haier Group's second overseas industrial park, after the Haier (U.S.) Industrial Park in Camden, South Carolina.

The Pakistani government was very pleased with the investment. One day after the ceremony, President Talare met with Haier CEO Zhang Ruimin and his delegation at the Presidential Palace.

Haier (Pakistan) Industrial Park covers 150,000 square meters. It is a joint venture between the Haier Group and the Pakistani R Group, the largest dealer in household electrical appliances in Pakistan, with the largest marketing and sales networks in the country. The first construction phase of Haier (Pakistan) Industrial Park was designed to produce one million units of refrigerators, washing machines and air conditioners. Once fully completed, the Industrial Park would become the biggest, most diversified and most technologically advanced household appliance production base in Pakistan. The main construction project was completed in September of 2001.

In May 2002, the facility rolled out its first products.

Pakistan has a population of 170 million. The demand for household appliances had been high, but the market had relied primarily on imports. Prior to the establishment of the Haier (Pakistan) Industrial Park, Haier products had been selling well as imports in the Pakistani market, and had become popular with local customers because of their reliable quality and special design. Haier's sales volumes in Pakistan had been growing at the rate of eighty percent a year.

On April 12, 2001, shortly after the Pakistan trip, Zhang and his colleagues attended the opening ceremony for Haier Bangladesh, a joint venture with Hayes (Bangladesh) Ltd. (HBL). Located in Dhaka, HBL has a forty-one year history, with assets of over $50 million and 1,500 employees. The company has been active in the fields of telecommunications services, home appliances and office automation.

Back in July 2000, the Haier Group formed a joint venture with HBL, called "Hayes-Haier Appliances Company Ltd." The joint venture is currently assembling Haier air conditioners, washing machines, refrigerators and freezers for the Bangladeshi market. Some of its products are exported to countries such as India and Nepal. The product range will be expanded to TV, audio-video products and small appliances.

Like Pakistan, Bangladesh is a developing country with a large demand for household appliances. Zhang and his team were quite surprised by the disparities they saw in both countries. Mules were walking beside Mercedes-Benzes, and rickshaws were still the main means of transportation for many people. Not only were the buses full of passengers, but their racks were full of people, as well.

Despite all this, what met their eyes as they drove through city streets was the advertising of such familiar names as Sony, Toshiba, Siemens, Philips and, of course, Coca-Cola. The market was unmistakably there, and their competitors were by no means less developed in the less developed countries.

Japan has long been considered the last and most difficult Asian market for foreign companies to invade, especially for non-OEM Chinese brands. But the long-standing wall broke down on January 8, 2002, when the Haier Group and Japan's Sanyo Electric Co. announced that they had agreed to form a broad business alliance to gain a stronger foothold in each other's market for electrical appliance products. Zhang Ruimin, CEO of Haier, and Satosh Iue, President of Sanyo Electric Co., attended a press conference during which they made the announcement jointly.

Under the terms of agreement, cooperation between the two companies covers four aspects: the sale of Sanyo products under the "Sanyo" and "Haier" brand names in China through Haier's networks; the establishment of a joint venture for sales of Haier products in Japan; the promotion of cooperation at points of production; and the supply of Haier with key Sanyo devices and technological collaboration.

Sanyo's purpose in making this move was to increase the company's competitiveness in China by using Haier's extensive sales-and-service network. Haier's was to enter the Japanese market by using Sanyo's distribution and service outlets. Specifically, Sanyo hoped to boost its annual production in China by around 100 billion Japanese yen over three years, from the current 165 billion yen.

Sanyo and Haier also set up a joint venture to promote Haier's home appliances in the Japanese market. That was an unprecedented move, because no other major Japanese electronics company had ever established a company in Japan that specialized in promoting

Chinese products. According to the joint venture agreement, Sanyo Electric holds a sixty-percent stake in the new company, called "Sanyo-Haier Corporation," to be capitalized at 500 million Japanese yen (U.S. $4.2 million), while Haier controls the remaining forty percent. With headquarters in Moriguchi City, Osaka, and Toshiaki Iue as its first president (Iue had previously been Executive Managing Director at Sanyo Sales & Marketing Co., Ltd.), the joint venture started operations on April 1, 2002, with a staff of seventy-six, to be increased to one hundred fifty over a three-year period.

Beginning in mid-May, the joint venture started selling eight types of Haier small and mid-sized appliances, including three models of refrigerator and two models of fully-automatic washing machines, at large-scale appliance stores across Japan. The company's sales target was ten billion Japanese yen (U.S. $85 million) for 2002, to be increased to thirty billion yen in 2004 (U.S. $250 million). Sanyo Electric will offer such services as customer support.

On May 20, Zhang Ruimin flew to Japan to attend the Future of Asia Forum, which coincided with the Sanyo-Haier initial sales launch of Haier products.

After the forum, Zhang paid a visit to Japan Bridge Commercial Street in Osaka, where Haier products were sold along with Japanese and Korean commodities. He made a modest comment on Haier's entry into the Japanese market.

"Japan is the last competitive market for Haier products. Japan is known as the kingdom of household appliances. It will take a long time for local consumers to accept Haier products. We hope to hear customer's opinions directly from the shops. This will be helpful for our future production."

The Japanese response to the Haier products was generally positive. The Haier brands, as well as other Asian brands, such as LGE and Daewoo from Korea, are being accepted by Japanese users because of their lower prices and unique designs. According to the Jasco Rifu Store in Miyagi Prefecture, Haier's refrigerators enjoyed 3,000 units of monthly sales in February and March of 2002. In its May 25, 2002 issue, *The Daily Yomiuri*, one of the largest English-language newspapers in Japan, quoted the manager of one of the local electrical chain stores where Haier products were being sold as saying, "From seeing the Haier appliances, we know they have a thorough knowledge of the Japanese market."

The next steps in Sanyo-Haier cooperation will involve the launch of a Sanyo wholly-owned subsidiary in Qingdao, China, to manufacture and sell small reciprocating compressors for refrigerators. The newly launched company, called "Qingdao Sanyo Electric Co.," is scheduled to start production in December 2002. It will provide compressors to the Haier Group and other Chinese domestic refrigerator makers. The company also plans to export compressors. With a staff of four hundred, the company plans to turn out one million compressors in the first year, hoping to increase the number to two million units in the near future.

As a spin-off of the joint venture project, Sanyo has agreed to supply key devices and technologies to the technology-savvy Haier, with which it hopes to augment the company's competitiveness in future products.

The Haier-Sanyo alliance was a smart strategy that enabled both parties to take advantage of each other's marketing resources. It helped Haier break down entry barriers and build its brand name awareness in Japan, and increase Sanyo's existing market share in China.

Shortly after Haier's announcement of its cooperation with Sanyo, this win-win model was repeated in Taiwan. In February 2002, Haier formed a strategic alliance with Sampo Corp., one of the largest appliance makers in Taiwan, to sell each other's products using the distribution channels each owns in its own market.

For political reasons, Taiwan had long prohibited manufactured imports from China, but the simultaneous entry of Taiwan and mainland China into the World Trade Organization, at the end of 2001, forced the island to open some of its markets to mainland companies. Since then, Taipei has passed laws allowing Chinese companies to invest in 58 of Taiwan's 108 business sectors, including real estate, hotels, restaurants and accounting. It also allowed imports of some 2,000 products, such as PCs, fax machines and bicycles— products made by Taiwanese factories in China.

Taiwanese companies began to invest on the mainland in 1992, and have so far set up about 40,000 factories and businesses there.

But, unlike the mainland which welcomes and encourages Taiwanese investors, Chinese companies were not allowed into Taiwan.

To circumvent the barrier, Haier, which had always longed to have a foothold in Taiwan in its overseas expansion, jumped at the strategic alliance opportunity when approached by Sampo.

According to the partnership agreement, Haier would distribute Sampo appliances in China, where the Taiwanese company has four plants which had been manufacturing mostly for export. Sampo had been trying to sell in China, but distribution had been difficult for them. Now sales in China will be made a lot easier by using Haier's distribution channels.

Ho Heng-chung, Sampo's CEO, revealed that the agreement called for the two companies to cooperate in order to create up to $300 million in sales over the next three years. With about eighty percent of Sampo's sales currently coming from the domestic Taiwan market, the alliance partnership will help Sampo get more direct access to the overseas market. Taiwan's appliance market is very limited, and Sampo, like many other Taiwanese companies, faces pressure to open new markets in order to survive. Under this agreement, Sampo will also be able to sell, among other things, DVD products and flat-panel monitors to China and other overseas markets through Haier outlets. In return, Haier products are to be put onto the store shelves of Sampo, which owns nine hundred outlets across the island.

The first shipment of Haier products marketed in Taiwan was 50,000 TV sets. Other Haier products Sampo carries include refrigerators, air conditioners and washing machines.

Haier Europe

Haier products were first exported to Europe in the early 1990s, first to the UK and Germany, then to France and Italy. After several years of export experience, Haier decided to launch its own brand name in Europe.

February 18, 1997 was a big day for Haier. For the first time, the Chinese delegation, of which Haier was a part, had its own exhibition stands at the Cologne Appliance Exhibition, which is held every other year in the beautiful German city on the Rhine. Half of the Chinese display items came from Haier. In addition to taking orders from merchants all over the world for its refrigerators, washing machines and air conditioners, what made Zhang Ruimin, then Group President, and Yang Mianmian, then Vice President, most excited was the ceremony to award the Haier Product Exclusive Distribution Certificate to twelve agents and sales representatives from such European countries as Germany, Holland and Italy.

It was the first time in the history of the Chinese home appliance industry that a Chinese company had awarded certificates to foreigners for distributing their products overseas.

The ceremony took place in a five-star hotel in the city, with twenty German middle-school students at the entrance, welcoming the guests with Haier flags. More than two hundred guests showed up, among whom were the Chinese Ambassador to Germany and other high-ranking Chinese officials. The news conference was simultaneously translated into four languages: German, English, Dutch and Chinese. Media from German and Dutch television stations and newspapers were invited. Almost all of them were curious about Haier, since it was from a developing country entering the market in developed Europe.

"In Europe, Chinese products have been known as low-price and low-quality items. Can Haier turn that image around?" asked a reporter from the Dutch NOVA Television.

"It is exactly for that purpose—to change the negative image of 'Made-in-China' products—that we have chosen to enter the international market with our own brand. Actually, we passed the ISO 9001 benchmark earlier than some of the European brand name companies, and our products have been selling in the European market for five years. Consumers in Europe have had some new experience with these products of ours by using them," Zhang replied, matter-of-factly.

"What are Haier's criteria for choosing agents and distributors?"

"Our goal is to build a global brand name. Any distributor who shares our goal and promotes our brand name products along that line is eligible. We are not just exporting our products for foreign currency; we are building our brand and providing the best quality products to European customers."

The highlight of the conference was the certificate-awarding ceremony. A photograph shows a group of Chinese sitting in the front row, with Chinese flags on the table in front of them, and a group of European agents and distributors standing in the back row, holding Haier certificates in their hands.

Mr. Lu Qiutian, the Chinese Ambassador to Germany who attended the ceremony from start to finish, commented, not without emotion: "As Ambassador to Holland, Romania and Germany, I have worked overseas for more than twenty years. I have attended many ceremonies, but this was the first time that I have ever witnessed us Chinese awarding distribution certificates to foreigners. I cannot say how proud I felt. No other Chinese company could cause such a sensation at an international exposition." He then pointed to the photograph. "In the photo, the Chinese are sitting, but what that truly means is that we have stood up in the international market."

In November 1997, Haier formed a joint venture with a Yugoslavian company in Belgrade to produce multitasking air conditioners with the Haier brand. That was Haier's first European manufacturing project.

The year 2000 saw the founding of Haier Europe by Frans Jamry in Italy, with headquarters in Varese, a northwest-Italian city close to Milan. Haier Europe coordinates the sales and marketing efforts of Haier products across thirteen European countries. In addition to the headquarters, Haier Europe has eight offices that deal with businesses by the country or countries—Italy and Switzerland, the UK and Ireland, France, Germany and the Benelux countries, Spain and Portugal, Greece, Poland and Scandinavia. The major product categories include refrigerators, freezers, washing machines, dishwashers, microwave ovens and small appliances designed to satisfy the needs of the European market.

Frans Jamry was a former senior sales executive at the Italy-based Merloni Elettrodomestici, the third largest appliance maker in Europe. After he left Merloni, he set up his own trading company, selling GE, Whirlpool and Siemens products. In April 1998, he noticed Haier products in the European market, and was impressed with their design and quality. Through an introduction by a friend in Hong Kong, he paid a visit to Haier headquarters in Qingdao, where he saw the manufacturing facilities and talked to Haier executives. He was so impressed with Haier management and product lines that he immediately decided to carry Haier products.

What made Jamry, a forty-year veteran in the appliance industry, really excited about Haier was an occurrence that took place in the autumn of 1998. In August, he submitted to Haier a design plan for a series of home appliances tailored to the European market. When he arrived at Haier a month later, all the designs had been made into sample products, awaiting his approval in the showroom.

It might have taken a European manufacturer two years to develop such a series of products, but, at Haier, it was just one month. Jamry said that, in Haier, he could see the Philips of twenty years before.

Haier Europe developed an impressive corporate-image campaign across Europe to create strong brand awareness. This was combined with a clear policy of presenting high-quality products and high specifications, as well as visual and functional designs that would appeal to European consumers. Steady progress took a great leap forward with the introduction, in 2000, of Haier products designed exclusively for the European market.

Haier Europe planned the local development of new products for the European markets, so that the taste and style of the European consumer were reflected even more effectively. Along with trade marketing campaigns in key countries, Haier Europe launched a higher level of consumer advertising and promotion.

At the Cologne Appliance Exhibition in March 2001, Haier put up advertisements side by side with the well-known European brand "Miele" at the entrance of the exhibition hall. In Paris, Haier neon advertising can be seen competing with that of Toshiba on the top of a building. Sales promotion and advertising were strengthened in 2002, with the distribution of eye-catching pink-cube displays for retail outlets throughout Europe. Consumer advertising, which started in the UK in 2001, have been extended to other European countries, with a doubled budget for advertising and promotion.

In June 2001, Haier spent eight million U.S. dollars to purchase an Italian refrigerator plant belonging to Meneghetti Equipment in the northeastern city of Padova. The first European acquisition by Haier, this purchase was an important step in Haier's localization strategy in developed countries, following the opening of its South Carolina refrigerator facility in 1999.

The new company would concentrate on built-in refrigerators and freezers. With a production capacity of 250,000 units per year and one hundred employees, Haier hoped to expand its product range and production capacity. Haier also planned to purchase Meneghetti-produced built-in ovens and hobs and market them in China under the Haier brand name.

Frans Jamry was excited about the purchase, believing that the acquisition would allow Haier to enter the rapidly expanding built-in sector in Europe and provide the opportunity to develop new products from a European manufacturing base.

On February 27, 2002, the HomeTech exhibition was held in Berlin. Over seven hundred appliance makers and dealers from thirty-nine countries competed against one another in cutting-edge technology, style and comfort. The exhibition became a display-window for Haier's strong presence in the European domestic appliance industry, with its family series and Bluetooth Internet-enabled series.

Bluetooth technology, which uses low-power radio waves to eliminate the wires and cables used for product connectivity, was developed by Ericsson, the Swedish technology group, in 1994. Haier formed a strategic alliance with Ericsson in 2001 to accelerate the application of this technology.

Haier showcased over fifty styles of refrigerators at the exhibition. The Dutch-style Haier refrigerator caught the eye of many show attendees. Unlike the traditional design that has the freezer on top and the fridge below, the Haier refrigerator was just the reverse— with fridge on top and freezer on the bottom. The new cubic wind-curtain technology is capable of reducing temperature fluctuation and increasing the degree of food freshness. On the outside, a height-adjustable handle was the hit of the day.

Haier chose Milan's ExpoComfort Fair to set its foot on the threshold of the Italian air conditioner market. During the exhibition, which took place in March 2002, Haier presented a new company, Haier A/C Trading, which has offices in Rendine Lago, near Treviso, Italy. The new company now distributes Haier air conditioning products in the Italian market.

Haier's stand at ExpoComfort showed the company's most important ranges, among them the MRV and the Internet-ready range. MRV is Haier's air conditioning range based on inverter technology, which enables it to modulate compressor power-consumption. The MRV range is also capable of improving performance with great energy conservation and temperature stability.

To comply with Europe's high standards of environmental protection, all Haier A/C products include the new refrigerant, HFC-407c, a very volatile gas that does not damage the ozone layer of the atmosphere. Haier A/C Trading was awarded ISO 14001, the international system for environmental protection and CFC-technology-free certification.

On March 7, 2002, a bigger Haier project, the Haier Train, began its tour around France. Organized by Haier France in collaboration with the Chinese embassy and the Chinese Tourist Agency, the train was a traveling exhibition of Haier products, followed by a section dedicated to introducing Chinese culture. The train was regarded as a miniature of China, in which visitors could discover the nature, the arts and the technological evolution of China. In each city, visitors to the train participated in games to win big prizes, such as a tour to China or a Haier appliance.

The Train was the first full-swing advertising activity organized by the Haier Europe operation in France. Composed of seven cars and each furnished as an exhibition hall, the Haier Train left Paris in the evening of March 7, heading for eleven large and medium-sized cities, such as Lille, Strasbourg, Lyon and Marseilles. It stopped for one to three days in each city before arriving at its final stop in the western city of Rennes. The trip lasted over twenty days and covered more than 2,500 miles. During the trip, people got to know Haier's products as well as China's history, culture and tourist attractions.

Haier Europe plans to introduce more new products to the EU market, such as the extreme range, the new range of built-in models and Haier brown goods and mobile phones. Specialty and niche products will include coolers, a chest freezer with a drawer, stainless models and frost-free and American style refrigeration.

The company's promotional programs include displaying a wide range of Internet-enabled products using Bluetooth technology in showrooms, at leading stores and trade shows Europe-wide, including the Electrical Retailing Show at the UK's National

Exhibition Center and the MOW Fair for built-in appliances in Germany.

In 2001, the Haier Group reported a worldwide consolidated sales revenue of $7.3 billion U.S. dollars (7.5 billion Euro), having sold three million refrigerators, two million washing machines, one million TVs and two-and-a-half million air conditioners.

According to statistics provided by the Zhongyikang Economic Consultation Co. Ltd. under China's State Statistics Bureau, Haier's domestic market shares in 2001 were as follows: refrigerator, 31.2%; air conditioner, 25.5%; washing machine, 30.5%; and freezer, 41.8%.

The figures for Haier Europe were quite modest for 2001—one hundred million Euro, with 1.2 million items sold (40% refrigerators/ freezers and small appliances, the rest being washing machines, dish washers and microwave ovens, all imported from China). In Italy, the company sold 50,000 units of appliances. The goal for 2002 was between 100,000 and 150,000 units. In Europe, the target for 2002 was 1.5 million units. Since the European market is still sluggish, an increase of 20% is a considerable challenge.

Haier Europe will continue using traditional channels for market penetration. The company's strategy is to bet everything on the brand rather than on the price. Price reduction will be the last thing they will consider doing.

Right now, Haier products are not sold through larger-scale distribution outlets, but through independent specialist retailers. This was a carefully deliberated choice. According to Raffaele Casilli, who formerly worked for Philips and is now managing director of Haier Italy, "In big stores we would simply be one of the many products available, whereas in smaller outlets, the specialist staff are able to underline our unique characteristics."

This approach has been strongly encouraged by the higher profit margins conceded to dealers as an incentive to sell the Haier brands.

In the space of ten years, from 1992 to 2002, Haier's globalization effort has paid off with considerable success. By August 2002, in ten economic centers around the world, Haier had eight design centers outside China, two overseas industrial parks, and thirteen overseas factories. As of August 2002, according to data we have obtained from Haier headquarters, the Haier Group had a worldwide workforce of 31,281, of whom 20,651 were located in the greater Qingdao area, 9,975 in other Haier facilities in China, and 655 were employed by overseas Haier companies. The company also claimed to have 58,800 sales agents and 11,976 after-sales services in 160 countries and regions.

With products in 86 categories and 13,000 models, consumers throughout the world now enjoy a variety of Haier household appliances such as refrigerators, freezers, air conditioners, washers and dryers, wine cellars, air purifiers, microwave ovens, electric irons, TVs, DVD players, computers and mobile phones, among others.

10

Haier America:
What the World Comes Home To

Prior to 1994, as with other overseas markets, Haier's home appliances were sold in the U.S. market under "original equipment manufacturing" (OEM) arrangements. Sales volumes were low, and product categories were few.

In 1994, things began to change. After visiting more than fifteen major appliance factories in five different countries in search of a quality supplier of major appliances, Michael Jemal, then a partner in an import company called Welbilt Appliances, based in Great Neck, New York, was impressed with the Haier Group. Jemal believed that Haier's capabilities—the manufacturing process, quality control and finished products—were equal or even superior to any other facility he had observed. The things that finally attracted Jemal to the Haier Group were its management and its desire to become a global company.

In life, there are no coincidences. The story of how Jemal found Haier is amazing, if not fated. As he was winding down his twenty-one-day trek to search out new suppliers, on his way home, as fate would have it, he noticed a large billboard in a major Chinese airport. Asking a local Chinese what company it was for, he noticed the proud expression on the person's face when he stated that Haier was the most respected company in its field.

Jemal immediately decided to visit Haier headquarters in Qingdao. The visit to Haier took place at the time when Haier was selling its products to American import companies that were only interested in getting the lowest prices. None of them was willing even to think of allowing the Haier brand on the products. None of them except Michael Jemal.

During his initial meeting with then Vice President Wu Kesong, Jemal was challenged to buy 150,000 compact refrigerators from Haier, with the understanding that, if he were successful, he would be granted exclusivity and the promise of a long-term relationship. The total market for that type of appliance in America was less than 1,500,000 units, which meant that Haier was ambitious enough to think it could achieve a ten-percent market share. With no brand awareness and just three models that could meet U.S. energy and safety standards, this was a serious challenge.

Jemal jumped at the opportunity anyway, thinking that 150,000 was just the tip of the iceberg. By year's end, the sales tally exceeded 165,000 units, a market share of over ten percent.

Born and raised in New York, Michael Jemal is a third-generation Syrian-American. His grandparents lived in a town called Aleppo in Syria. They left the country before 1920, because of persecution of the Jews. His parents were born in the United States, and have never been to Syria. Neither has Michael Jemal.

His father was in charge of a store in New York, and his mother raised the four children. Michael has two brothers older than he, and one younger sister.

Jemal went to private elementary and high schools, where he took great interest in learning Hebrew and Spanish. Today, he works at learning Chinese. After graduating high school, he went to Baruch Business School in New York. While attending college, Jemal was eager to get first-hand business experience, so he went to work at a cousin's import-export company called "Global Imports" in New York City, which specialized in battery sales.

His first duty was to keep track of stock levels. He worked there for a little over one year, spending his time talking to customers and learning how to merchandise and market the product line. One of the greatest lessons he learned from that business was to recognize the contribution that employees make. To his surprise, at the end of six weeks of work, his immediate boss awarded him a holiday bonus of $75 for the special attention he had given to the aging of the inventory.

He didn't think what he had done was so special. Apparently, one day, as he was looking over the stock, he discovered some inventory that had been hidden away unsold for over three years.

Nobody had paid any attention to it. When he brought this to the attention of his manager, the manager told Jemal to mark the inventory down to fifty percent of the original cost.

Not believing his ears, Jemal asked if the product was still good. The answer was yes, but the company had changed its packaging, because none of the existing customers would want the old packaging anymore. What Jemal did was simple: he called a list of accounts who, for one reason or another, were no longer buying from Global, and who, therefore, didn't know about the change in packaging. The result was that the inventory was sold in just two weeks, yielding a profit of thirty percent and a total value of over $50,000.

This was a very gratifying experience for Jemal, who still enjoys the realization he derived from the incident that it is important to spend time with employees, and to show appreciation for their efforts.

After one year, Jemal decided it was time to start his own business. At the age of nineteen, he opened his first retail store, selling electronic products and appliances. This, Jemal says, was an invaluable experience. Although he regrets not finishing college, and hopes to return someday to get a degree, he feels that what he has learned in business retail is something only experience can teach. It is to this that he owes his success and his knowledge of manufacturing, import and distribution.

Spending time on the sales floor trying to understand a customer's preference is something Jemal believes severely lacking in the appliance industry, and in most distribution businesses in general. After ten years in the retail business, Jemal was successfully operating thirteen stores.

Then he stumbled onto the business opportunity that would take him into his new career. In 1994, as a customer of a company called "Welbilt Appliances," Jemal learned that some of his purchase orders would not be filled. He inquired further, and found out that Welbilt was in the process of closing down.

Welbilt Appliances was a distributor of appliances such as refrigerators and microwave ovens, and small kitchen appliances such as bread makers. It had sales of over $100 million per year, but was losing over seven million. After making the right contacts, Jemal was able to assemble a team to purchase Welbilt after about ninety days of due diligence. He sold his own stores, and became Executive

Vice President of Welbilt Appliances. He tapped some industry professionals with the right experience to run Welbilt. Since this was a business that was hemorrhaging money, the management team had to work fast to make the right business decisions to turn Welbilt around.

To some extent, from an operating standpoint, they were successful in bringing the business to breakeven, but sales had suffered, and the challenge now was to develop new areas of growth for Welbilt. After a series of small acquisitions of companies and distribution agreements, Jemal met up with the Haier Group.

In March 2002, in an interview with Shawn at the newly opened Haier America building at 1356 Broadway, Jemal recounted his earlier work experience, and how he met Haier.

"In 1994, we started an association with Haier as a distributor. There are certain benefits to distributor-manufacturer relationships. But because Haier is so special and has the great ability to grow, and the brand is a global brand, I believed that the company should be more than a distributor. It should be a joint venture, with plans to become a major force in the United States. So we began developing new products and new markets. Our relationship then became a much closer one. In Qingdao, you see how big Haier is now, but in 1994, it was not as big. Yet we saw the future. We realized what the future could bring, because Haier was moving very fast and has an excellent reputation. So I spoke with Mr. Zhang Ruimin, and mentioned that Haier should have its brand in the United States. I said that Haier could be very strong."

Jemal said that Haier top management was very receptive to his suggestion of a joint venture, because they had already had an excellent relationship since 1994. "The idea was natural, because we always believed that this was the right thing to do." He added: "People sometimes ask me if we have problems with communication because of the language barrier. I can honestly say that, even though I do not speak Chinese, there is no such language barrier. We both speak the same language, we both want the same for one another, and that is to make the Haier company and the Haier brand grow."

While agreeing to form a partnership was easy, it took time to work out details, such as the location of the company and the number of employees to be hired.

"As for location, we chose New York. The reason we picked New York was that I believed that the main business should be in New York. A lot of companies have very beautiful offices, but are surrounded by golf courses or very quiet environments. What I wanted was to have an office and a showroom in a very busy district, where consumers could come in and take a look at the products and, at the same time, be surrounded by other businesses, and not by trees and golf courses.

"My enjoyment is really to be close to stores. Any employee can walk into a store to see what's selling, what's not selling, what's in customers' bags and what they are buying or not buying. We can also be close to other businesses and learn from other businesses."

In March 1999, Jemal formed a joint venture with the Haier Group called Haier America. They moved into 45 West 36th Street at Seventh Avenue in Manhattan, renting the entire fourth floor in the no-frills building, half for offices and half for a showroom. They hired seventeen people to start with, a number Jemal later thought a bit conservative for such an operation.

Compared with the situation Sony had faced when it started its American operation in 1960 (Sony Corporation of America, a wholly-owned subsidiary, with a team of thirteen people, including its soon-to-be legendary president Akio Morita), in a rat-infested office-warehouse at 514 Broadway, Haier America's initiation seemed to be blessed. Unlike Sony America's almost-all-Japanese workforce, Haier America's was an almost-all-American team, with only the accountant being sent from China.

Jemal set the sales goal for the first year at fifty million dollars. He remembered with some amusement that, when he discussed this sales projection with Haier, "Some people in Haier management said that this was a very big number, and sounded too big, and maybe impossible. But in reality, in the first year, we made $50 million in sales."

The challenge for Jemal was to get his products into as many stores as possible, and expand distribution channels, especially in the chains, where sales were considered significant. It was of primary

importance to have well-designed, quality products, but that was
not enough. In a market dominated by big brand names, such as
GE, Whirlpool, Maytag, and Frigidaire, why should customers buy
a brand that they had never heard of? Haier's competitiveness had
to lie in product differentiation and, to some extent, price.

"The most important thing is to have the products customers
need. We worked hard to make quality products, and the designs
and features they want. We developed many new categories of
products. One example is the wine cellar. When we came out with
the wine cellar, a lot of customers already had suppliers of compact
refrigerators, but did not have a wine cellar. Our cosmetics and design
were new and innovative, something we developed. After six months
of engineering and design, not only did we have new customers and
new products, but we created a new category. Because of the good
experiences our customers have with the newly designed wine
cellars, more were willing to try other new offerings of ours, such
as freezers and room air conditioners. Future growth, however, will
be in the core appliance categories, such as larger-sized refrigerators
like those we build in the U.S., laundry equipment and dishwashers.
So our strategy was really to design the product they need first, and
at the same time develop products that help build our image."

When Haier first developed the wine cellar, nobody believed
that it would sell. At one trade show, Jemal showed a picture of the
wine cellar to a store manager. He took the picture and laughingly
told Jemal that nobody was going to buy this, because it had to be
built into a cabinet.

Jemal asked him why, and the answer was, "All the other
manufacturers' units work that way."

Jemal said, "Okay, I understand your point, but I disagree. You
try it and you'll see. You are my customer. Tell me, would I ever
offer you products that you would have a problem selling?"

The approach worked well for Jemal. This same customer now
buys about five hundred units every month from Haier America. In
the end, this buyer also bought a Haier wine cellar for his own house.

Now Haier has a full line of wine cellars in both built-in and
free-standing models, with bottle capacities ranging from twenty to
one hundred twenty-two. They accommodate both red and white

wine in the same cellar, with different temperatures from top to bottom. One free-standing model, the Premier Edition, has an amber-tinted, double-paned, contoured glass door framed in either silver or black. The designer series features an elegant, full-view, flush glass door framed in black with silver or black trim. Some of the new models have features such as soft interior lighting and a dual-function LED readout, which provides both automatic temperature settings and thermometer readings. Available in high-end wine catalogs and full-line appliance stores, Haier wine cellars start at $299 and go as high as over $2,000 for the 114-bottle cellar. A free-standing, 30-bottle Haier wine cellar with adjustable leveling legs sells for $299.99 at Sears, while a 30-bottle Haier premier wine cellar with lock and LED read-out retails at $379 at CompactAppliance.com.

In the absence of a straight comparison, a Sanyo 24-bottle, no-frills wine cellar retails at $249.99 while an Avanti 34-bottle deluxe wine cellar sells for $149.

Jemal told a story about a customer to whom he had been trying to sell products for a very long time with no success. It turned out that this customer, a buyer, had a very good relationship with one of Haier's competitors, and did not want to make a switch.

One Sunday, Jemal went to the office to clean out his files, and found the folder of this customer. Jemal looked at the name and hesitated over whether he should call him or just throw the folder out. Because he had tried so hard and made so many efforts, he said to himself, "One more time. I'm going to try just one more time."

So he called this customer the next day. It happened that his contact, who had been the buyer there, had left the company.

Jemal said to the person who answered his phone, "Let me talk to the new buyer."

The answer was "No. I can't switch you, but I'll take a message." Jemal then said, "Okay. Here's my message. I'm sending ten samples, different models. No charge. "

The person at the other end of the phone said, "No, no, no, don't do this."

Jemal said, "I'll send it. No charge. I just want to hear your evaluation. I respect your analysis of the product. If it's good, all you have to do is to tell me it's good. If it's no good, keep it, throw it into the garbage or send it back. I'll pay the freight. I'll pay everything."

The result? Haier America now has a contract with this customer for five years, with a total value of $140 million.

Shawn was very interested in knowing the story of how Haier America was accepted by Wal-Mart, because he had read many different versions of that in the Chinese media, and wanted to hear the "authentic" version from the President of the company.

Haier is among the most reported-on companies in China, and its entry into America has been the focus of much media coverage. In August 2001 alone, one month after Haier's purchase of the Greenwich Savings Bank building on Broadway, eleven major Chinese national media, among them *China Central TV, Xinhua News Agency, People's Daily,* and *The Economic Daily,* ran series of stories about Haier, covering everything from its management style to its overseas operations. Haier's globalization attracted a lot of attention in these reports. For the Chinese, nothing is more exciting than the words "international" and "global." Only the Chinese can know what tremendous joy and ecstasy they felt when Beijing won the right to run the 2008 Olympic Games.

But getting into Wal-Mart was no easy task for Jemal. He said it was nothing but consistent patience and perseverance with phone calls. "It took us a whole year just to get an appointment." Finally, in July 1999, Jemal and his team were offered an appointment to show their room air conditioners. A remarkable salesman, Jemal talked Wal-Mart into agreeing to open its door just a little for Haier.

Wal-Mart subsequently made a lot of tests and checks on Haier refrigerators to make sure that they were of superior quality and met their standards. After testing the Haier products and approving the company, Wal-Mart went to the Haier manufacturing facilities in China. Haier got the highest scores among all the factories they inspected.

Wal-Mart was eventually satisfied with Haier, and placed an initial order for 50,000 room air conditioners. The following year, the Wal-Mart order doubled. In 2002, the total increased to 400,000 units, including compact refrigerators, washing machines and air conditioners.

By all accounts, Wal-Mart was the most difficult chain for Haier to get into. But Jemal sighed, and said that none of the chains had been easy. Each had specific requirements. Office Depot, for example, required that Haier refrigerators have locks, so that college student customers who share their apartments with roommates would not have to worry about the safety of their drinks and whatnot. Some small stores had different requirements, because they could not buy many. So Haier worked out a plan to sell to them through distributors.

Perhaps the easiest chain to get into was Home Depot, whose buyer called Haier to place orders for air conditioners, because they had run out of stock of their usual brand.

On the marketing and promotion side, Haier's marketing department, headed by Vincent Cefalu, identifies the most popular places to advertise. Until 2002, Haier advertising had been primarily targeted at trade buyers, though they also did some advertising aimed at individual consumers. Placing advertisements on the luggage carts at New York's JFK airport is one such effort. Haier rents the space, creates the design, and pays about $200,000 a year.

Jemal was pleased when Haier got encouraging feedback from the luggage-cart advertising. He said that every time he traveled overseas, somebody would tell him that they had seen the Haier cart at JFK. Once, when he was in France, wearing a Haier hat, somebody approached him and said, "Hey, I saw that in the New York airport, the same name. What's up with Haier?"

Haier also advertises on luggage trolleys at Miami airport. Jemal said Haier chose the JFK and Miami trolleys because they target international customers who know Haier. In Arkansas, where Wal-Mart headquarters is located, and in South Carolina, where Haier has a factory, Haier puts up billboards.

When asked about the results of the advertising, Jemal conceded that they were somewhat hard to gauge. "You have to believe the statistics. When people go through airports, a certain number of those who use the carts look at the advertising. The same can be said about any type of advertising that we do. We gauge the results by the positive feedback we receive from our customers and from other people, and also on our own impressions. If our customers ask for more, they must like what we're doing."

As with any product, Jemal believes that the best way to promote Haier is by word of mouth coming from satisfied consumers. "If they have a good experience with our products, they're always going to recommend them, and say good things. That's number one. So our job is always to satisfy our consumers. If they have small or large problems, we'll take care of them. We must have excellent service. We make sure that people who spend one dollar and people who spend a hundred dollars with us get the same satisfaction. That's why word of mouth is best. We also try to focus on our own customers. We spend a lot of time developing our image. We believe that we are Number One. If we believe it, our customers believe it. And that's how we get our message across."

As for costs, Jemal said that, in 2001, Haier America spent roughly six percent of its sales on advertising, just under $10 million. The company has attended a number of trade shows, such as the Consumer Electronics Show (CES), the Housewares Show, and the Kitchen/Bath Industry Show.

Talking about Haier America's competitors in the U.S. market, Jemal offers a special take on the subject.

"In the major-appliances industry, there are GE, Whirlpool, Maytag and Frigidaire. These are the major appliance manufacturers. We don't look to compete with them, because they are much bigger than we are. The way we look at it is that they are really cooperators or customers. We also can call them teachers. I don't consider them competitors. We believe we have our separate position in the market, and they have theirs. They can step on us anytime they want, because we are so small compared to them in the United States. So we don't look to compete. What we do is try to find our own position."

Haier America's position is to develop products that are different, and sell the products that the big makers don't pay much attention to. One of Haier's success stories has to do with supplying an underserved market with its full line of compact refrigerators. The compact refrigerator market is not a very profitable one, because of the narrow margins. Companies like GE and Whirlpool are engaged in head-on competition in the more profitable side-by-side refrigerator market, by and large leaving the compact market to companies like Haier, Avanti and Danby.

Haier's compact refrigerators are of different models and colors, ranging from 1.4 to 5.8 cubic feet. They target primarily the college-student market, hoping the college students will remember Haier and buy more Haier products after they graduate and establish families. By mid 2002, Haier had captured about thirty percent of the American market for compact refrigerators.

The June 3, 2002 issue of the appliance trade magazine *TWICE* listed Haier's 1.8 cubic-foot compact refrigerator as the number one seller in the category. This model features a slide-out wire shelf, a half-width freezer compartment, full-width and half-width door-storage shelves and two-liter door storage with manual defrost. It retails for $78.83 at Wal-Mart stores. The company's other popular refrigerator, a 4.2-cubic-foot model, sells for $180 at Office Depot. Comparable products cost $150 to $200.

Jemal maintains that a company that is going to be successful is not one that only competes and expands a category; it is one that creates a market. The Haier chest freezer is a case in point.

Over the years, the chest freezer has become a loser in many American families, often finding itself banished from the kitchen or even the basement for demanding too much valuable room space and, more importantly, for not providing easy access to, say, the frozen item that cuddles under the thirty-pound turkey in the depths of the white box. What is worse, the popularity of the side-by-side models that offer bigger freezer sections has made the chest freezer even more unpopular, almost irrelevant for today's space- and access-oriented consumers.

Haier has addressed the problem of these consumers, and its solution is the 4.2 cubic-foot, two-compartment Access Plus chest freezer. The top half of this freezer can be accessed through a conventional top-opening lid, but the lower half is a pull-out drawer, which makes accessing any frozen item a piece of cake.

Michael Jemal calls the freezer "the world's only chest freezer that has a pullout drawer." He has good reason to be proud of that because the freezer was his brainchild.

Starting in 2001, the Haier Group began to hold an annual global conference, inviting all the Haier overseas executives and distributors to attend. The 2001 conference took place in Qingdao. During one of the breaks, Jemal walked over to Zhang Ruimin, the Group

Chairman and CEO, took a napkin, and started making some colored lines on it. Jemal was drawing the freezer of his imagination, and Zhang called his engineer over.

Explaining the idea and process, Jemal struggled with the language, trying to convey how he wanted the freezer to be a chest freezer with two compartments, with the temperature to be extra cold on the top and a little bit warmer at the bottom, and the organizer to be of certain height so that the woman, who uses it most, does not hurt her back when she has to empty it. And the temperature on the bottom should be warmer so that people can use it for ice cream. And it should be very energy-efficient.

The Chairman understood him and made some notes. He then turned to the engineer and said, "Let's do this." Seventeen hours later, they brought Jemal back to the room. They had a cover over something. Zhang patted him on the shoulder and lifted up the cover. It was a model chest freezer made from Jemal's blueprint.

Jemal could not believe his eyes. In seventeen hours, they had developed his product! This was the fastest product development he had ever seen in his life.

"Many companies have a lot of ideas. The reason we have the winning strategy is that we have the speed, the innovation and the desire to be the best. You can't find another company that can design a product in seventeen hours." A year later, Michael Jemal was still excited.

Zhang named the chest freezer the "Michael Freezer," in Chinese, and that later became the official name of the product for the Chinese market, though, in the United States market, it is called "Access Plus." Michael Jemal has since become a popular name at Haier Qingdao, and people there generally call him "Mr. Michael."

Haier Industrial Park at Camden, South Carolina

In April 1999, Haier invested thirty million U.S. dollars to open up a wholly-owned manufacturing facility in Camden, South Carolina, to produce refrigerators to be sold on the American market under its own brand name. This act of overseas expansion attracted a lot of media and industry attention, as well as raising some eyebrows among business analysts both in and outside China.

While it is understandable for a foreign company like Haier to set up trading or sales outlets in the U.S., building a factory from the ground up and hiring local people and paying them at ten times the rate the company pays its Chinese workers seemed a bit out of rhythm with conventional wisdom. Some American analysts thought that moving some production to the United States could ease political strains by reining in the growth of China's surplus in its trade with the Americans, but that was clearly not Haier's intention. To Zhang Ruimin, the Haier CEO, the reasons behind it were purely commercial.

An aficionado of books by Michael E. Porter, the Harvard Business School professor whose writings on business competition and strategy have made him an iconic figure among CEOs around the world, Zhang must have found justification in Porter's writing when he was making the Camden investment decision. "Gaining access to sophisticated and demanding buyers in other nations often requires a sequence of steps over a considerable period of time, and it always demands investment...Typically, a subsequent move is to supply relatively simple items in the product line, or products targeted at underserved niches. Investment in some local production may be a further step along the path."

It was obvious that the Camden move was part of Zhang's globalization strategy, which aims to make and market a third of the company's products overseas. If there was anything political in the decision, it must have had to do with Zhang's desire to conquer a piece of American land, and his satisfaction in giving jobs to Americans.

The more intriguing question, then, is, "Why Camden?"

A city of about eight thousand residents, Camden is the seat of Kershaw County, South Carolina. Kershaw County and the City of Camden are in the central part of the state. Columbia, the state capital, is 32 miles southwest, while Charleston, the largest container port on the U.S. Southeast and Gulf coasts, and the fourth largest in the United States for cargo value, is 124 miles south.

Interstate 20 serves Kershaw County with four interchanges. Within a short distance, I-20 connects with Interstate 95, which leads to New York in the north and Florida in the south, and with Interstate 26, which leads to the port of Charleston. The community is served by the Seaboard System Railroad, which also provides access to Amtrak.

The Camden-Kershaw County Airport accommodates mostly private airplanes, but the Columbia Metropolitan Airport, thirty-eight miles away, offers regularly scheduled commercial airline service on Delta, U.S. Air, and American Airlines. In addition, Charlotte International Airport is conveniently located seventy-two miles north of Kershaw County, with service from all the major airlines.

Camden, the oldest existing inland town in South Carolina, was part of a township plan ordered by King George II of England in 1730. The frontier settlement was initially named Fredericksburg Township. In 1758, Joseph Kershaw came to establish a store for a Charleston mercantile firm. His business thrived, and, by 1768, the town had become the number one inland trade center in the colony. At his suggestion, the town changed its name to Camden in honor of Lord Camden, the champion of colonial rights.

The town is best known for a battle during the American Revolution, the Battle of Camden, fought on August 16, 1780, which resulted in the worst American defeat of the Revolution. But in the subsequent Battle of Hobkirk's Hill, fought on April 25, 1781, near Camden, the British won at a heavy price, which forced the Redcoats to withdraw from Camden, heading on to Yorktown and into history.

Traditionally an Anglo-Saxon community, Kershaw County, with a total population of about 50,000, now has a population that is about seventy-two-percent white and twenty-seven-percent African American. People of Asian origin make up about 0.3 percent.

According to Kershaw County statistics, the average annual wage for county employees, in 2000, was $24,576. While the average weekly wage was $512, the average manufacturing weekly wage was $730. The two major employers are the Kershaw County School District, which employs 1,200 people and E.I. DuPont DeNemours, which employs 1,000.

The City of Camden has a council-manager form of municipal government. The four city councilpersons and the mayor are elected at large for four-year terms. The current mayor is Mary Y. Clark, who took office in December 2000.

With its convenient geography and special investment incentives, Kershaw County has successfully attracted foreign investors from around the world to open factories in Camden, where there are four industrial parks.

Prior to the arrival of Haier, there had been about ten foreign companies—two from the United Kingdom, one from Switzerland, two from Canada and three from Japan—that had set up manufacturing facilities in Camden. They employ anywhere from 70 to 318 workers, and make products ranging from fabrics, chemicals, fans and molding, to copper foil, textile synthetic linings, suspension parts and brake disks.

There are some major state and county investment incentive programs to lure the investor in. For example, the state of South Carolina offers job-creation tax credits ranging from $1,500 to $4,500 per job created. Corporate or industrial location in Kershaw County is rewarded through a five-year moratorium on general county taxes. There are also various sales-tax exemptions on things such as machinery, equipment, fuel and electricity, in addition to many kinds of property-tax incentives and fee-in-lieu of property taxes offered for various investments and programs. With the corporate income-tax rate at a low five percent, net operating losses are allowed to be carried forward for a fifteen-year period.

The price of land was fabulous, almost twenty times cheaper than that in China. No exact amount was posted for Haier's purchase of the 110 acres of land upon which they built their three-hundred-thousand-square-foot refrigerator manufacturing facility, but records of an August 2002 Kershaw County government purchase from a private landowner revealed that land price was about $6,000 per acre.

There was one more factor that played an important role in Haier's final decision to move into Camden, the relatively relaxed labor-union environment in South Carolina. Although Federal law protects the right of any and all employees to join a union, South Carolina chose, more than forty years ago, to pass a Right-to-Work law, granting employees in South Carolina the right to work and be free from coercion. Employees in South Carolina have the right to decide freely whether or not they want to join labor unions, and that decision can have no impact on their right to be employed. No company or union can negotiate away that fundamental right.

This puts Haier in a better position in South Carolina than if it had chosen to invest in a state where organized labor-union activities are strong. Haier had initially considered investing in a northern state, but after learning about the strong labor activities there, they dropped the idea, conceding that they had no experience in dealing with American labor unions.

The labor union is a totally different story in China. In almost every Chinese company of respectable size, there is a labor union, but the union is by and large controlled by the Communist Party organization within the company. It is an open secret in China that the Labor Union, like the Women's Federation and the Youth League, is an extended arm of the Communist Party. There is virtually no such thing as perceiving, still less using, the labor union as a bargaining power with the employer, to demand higher wages or improved working conditions. For a long time, especially during the Cultural Revolution (1966 to 1976), the Chinese called labor unions in the West, especially in America, "yellow unions," as compared with the "red unions" in China. The off-color "yellow" showed the disapproval of the Chinese workers toward their Western counterparts, who, they believed, only fought for economic betterment, and never for political rights.

There were, of course, some factors against such an overseas operation. The most obvious was concern about the cost of doing business in the United States. Although South Carolina is among the states where wages are modest, Haier still has to pay about ten times the wages it does in China, not to mention the benefits—paid vacation, health insurance, etc.—and things such as retirement plans and workers' compensation plans. But Zhang argued that the higher wages could be mitigated by avoiding the high cost of shipping finished products, especially large-sized refrigerators, from China.

For example, the cost of shipping a large refrigerator from China to the United States is about forty dollars. If there are 200,000 units to be shipped in a year, the total shipping cost will be eight million dollars. Assuming that Haier pays an average of $30,000 to its 200 employees in Camden, the total wages amount to six million dollars a year. Even if other costs are factored in, they do not alter the difference by very much.

Of course, Haier has to consider the cost of shipping parts from China for assembly in Camden, but they do not add up to as much, because parts, unlike ready-to-sell refrigerators which take up too much container space with their hollow insides, can be packed tightly for space conservation during shipping. Haier has already begun outsourcing local suppliers for reasonably priced plastic parts to save some shipping costs.

The bright side is that Haier can put a "Made-in-U.S.A." sticker on its refrigerators, a rarity now in the American manufacturing industry, as more and more American factories are moving to Mexico and Asia. That position could help Haier as a local manufacturer in bidding for purchases by Uncle Sam, among other things. According to Zhang, other advantages include Haier's ability to recruit local talent, absorb high technology and apply for membership in American trade and industrial organizations.

All things considered, Camden seemed to be a good choice for Haier.

One person who played a pivotal role in bringing Haier to Camden was Charlie Nash, a longtime Kershaw County businessman who had worked as a State Farm insurance agent for thirty-three years. His effort and involvement in the Haier Camden investment were recognized by South Carolina Governor Jim Hodges, who named him 1999 Ambassador for Economic Development. Another person, Nelson Lindsay, director of the Kershaw County Economic Development Office, helped materialize Haier's investment in Camden. Lindsay also helped attract the Japanese company, Yutaka Technologies Inc., to Kershaw County, at almost the same time as Haier.

The Haier venture, called "Haier America Refrigerators Co.," is located in the Steeplechase Industrial Park on Black River Road in Camden. The plant officially brought in its first employees at the end of March 2000, most of them residents of Kershaw County. The company continued an ongoing hiring process for about eighteen months. In August 2002, there were about 200 employees on the company's payroll.

Haier headquarters initially sent some technicians from Qingdao to train the new employees on the equipment, but hired local managers to take care of daily business operations. Michael Jemal told Shawn that the general manager of the Camden factory, Allan

Guberski, reports to him. Every two months, Jemal tries to make a tour of Camden, to make sure that everything is going well.

In an effort to put all Haier employees around the world into one family perspective, Haier headquarters has brought its family-oriented enterprise culture to Camden, along with its strict OEC (see Chapter 3) management style. Walking the factory floors, people will see things such as a board filled with pictures of children and families, and a newspaper clipping announcing an engagement, under the title "Our reasons for working safely."

As in Qingdao, the Camden factory walls are lined with signs, posters and banners in both Chinese and English. One banner warns, "A defective product is a wasted product," while another says, "Innovation is the soul of Haier culture."

The controversial practice of the big pair of footprints was also introduced, and initially caused a lot of dispute and resistance from the American employees, who considered standing on the footprints in order to be criticized a humiliation, at best.

The September 16, 2002 issue of the *Fortune International* magazine ran a cover story on Haier, with a focus on its American operations. Jonathan Sprague, the *Fortune* reporter who wrote the cover story, points out: "Haier's autocratic management style was something of a culture shock to American workers, and the Chinese were surprised at the Americans' surprise. Zhang [Zhang Jinmin, President of the Haier Camden factory, sent from China] explains, 'In China, the leader decides, and the staff do. Here, the leader decides, and the staff respond with questions and suggestions.' Tensions subsided as the two sides got used to each other, and Zhang says he hopes to take some of that two-way management style back to China."

Talking about the Camden employees from his Broadway office in August 2002, Michael Jemal was very excited. "We are very lucky, because we have very good employees. They understand that time is the most important thing. Everybody knows that our brand should be of the best quality. Everybody knows that the Haier brand should be something that, when we go home from work, we can be proud to be a part of. You see and feel the spirit when you go to the factory. The employees we have are very dedicated, and they don't look at their watches."

Jemal also said, with some pride, that Haier Camden were running on a six-day work-week schedule, because they were behind on orders. The next project Haier is going to have in South Carolina will be to bring in their own product designs, something Jemal believes will be very important for the company's success. They have assembled a group of independent sub-contractors to form a strong product-development team, from whom Haier will get fresh and innovative ideas for new products.

The first refrigerators rolled off the Haier Camden assembly lines in March 2000. With a full capacity of 200,000 units per shift per year, in the first phase of development, the factory basically assembles large-sized and some compact refrigerators to be sold in the United States.

The Haier presence in Camden has been viewed positively by the local government and residents. On April 5, 2001, only a few days after an American spy-plane made an emergency landing on China's Hainan island, which caused a strain in relations between the two countries, Mary Y. Clark, Mayor of Camden, offered Zhang, the visiting Haier CEO, two special gifts: the key to the city and a sign naming the Steeplechase Industrial Park road entrance to the Haier manufacturing plant "Haier Boulevard." She said the relationship with Haier gave her the chance to promote Camden to an almost unimaginable audience. Prior to the ceremony, she had given a thirty-minute interview to "Haier Around the World," a China Central TV program, which was to be shown to 1.2 billion people in China, later that month.

The Haier picture began to look rosier in 2002. By mid-year, in addition to major and regional chains such as Wal-Mart, Lowe's, Best Buy, Home Depot, Office Depot, Target, Fortunoff, Menards, Bed Bath & Beyond, BJ's, Fry's, ABC and BrandsMart, there are also over 7,000 independent stores that carry Haier products. A quick search on the Amazon.com website using the search term "Haier" will also yield over a dozen Haier products.

Having access to a strong distribution network will significantly strengthen Haier's position in the American market, and keep them from facing the same problem that the Acer Group, Taiwan's leading computer manufacturer, had faced in America. A well-known

computer brand in Taiwan and many parts of Asia, Acer entered the
U.S. market in the 1980s. At its peak, the company's U.S. share
was 5.4% in late 1995, but in 2001, Acer had to retreat from the
American market because of dwindling sales. One of the reasons
for Acer's withdrawal was that Acer did not have a strong enough
distribution network that operated at both the retail chain and mass
outlet levels.

Haier is in a stronger position because its products are sold both
in appliance retail chains, such as Lowe's and Best Buy, and in
mass outlets, such as Wal-Mart and Home Depot.

In an interview in October 2002 for the Haier America newsletter,
The Haier Life, Gene Russell, Senior Vice President of Sales at
Haier America, said, "It is clear to me that major accounts want to
be a part of the Haier America growth curve, because they sense
something big is happening and do not want to be left out while
their competitors successfully sell Haier products."

That is true, for Sears, the largest appliance retailer chain, has
begun to carry Haier's wine cellars in its stores.

The Haier product lines comprise an array of electrical and
electronic appliances ranging from refrigerators, freezers, wine
cellars, air conditioners and washing machines to microwave ovens,
toasters, irons, flat-screen TVs and DVD players. The lines will
soon be augmented by beer cellars and game machines for children.

According to reports from AHAM, the Association of Home
Appliance Manufacturers, which represents the manufacturers of
household appliances and products and services associated with
household appliances in the United States, Haier's 2001 market share
for apartment refrigerators (from 6.5 to 12.4 cubic feet) was 19.12%.
Its market share for chest freezers (up to 7.0 cubic feet) was 14.49%,
with the up-to-4.4-cubic-foot ones taking up 29.43% in that category.
For compact refrigerators (up to 6.4 cubic feet) Haier's market share
in 2001 was 34.39%, with over half a million units sold.

In the April 2002 issue of the *Appliance Manufacturer* magazine,
an influential trade publication in the field, Haier freezers in the
five-cubic-foot-and-above category ranked third, after Electrolux
and W.C. Wood, in the U.S. market for 2001, taking 8% of the market
share with a total of 177,000 units sold. In the same survey, Haier
room air conditioners ranked fifth, after LG Electronics, Fedders,

Electrolux and Whirlpool, taking nine percent of the market share, with a total of 502,000 units sold.

As for the market share of Haier wine cellars in the U.S., Michael Jemal said that it was about fifty percent in 2001.

Jemal believed that at least five million people in the United States own Haier products. He confirmed that Haier America sales were in the neighborhood of $200 million for 2001. The company now hires about ninety people at its Broadway headquarters, and has sales offices and showrooms in Miami, Chicago, Boston, Atlanta, California and Arkansas. Manufacturing programs in Mexico and Ecuador are also underway. With new advertising campaigns targeted more closely at consumers, Jemal projected that, by 2005, Haier America will reach one billion dollars in sales, and become a household name in America, like Sony.

Michael Jemal's biggest dream is to send Haier products to every home in America. Just as the word "family" is a catchphrase in Haier China, "home" is the buzzword at Haier America. All Haier America's brochures, posters and advertisements bear the tag line "What the World Comes Home To," and its meaning and implication have grown all the more important to Americans, after the turbulent events that happened in September of 2001. Home is the ultimate place where everyone longs to go at the end of a day's work, where men and women, young or old, find relaxation, warmth, comfort, and, most important, peace.

It is good when what the world comes home to is what people at Haier do.

Conclusion:
The Future for Haier

Zhang Ruimin, the Haier Group Chairman and CEO, once said that, if he had a chance to meet with Jack Welch of General Electric, he would ask him two questions: how to make a company grow bigger, and how to do well in the financial market.

The questions reveal the Haier leader's real concern and true ambition. He has to overcome the bottleneck of growing his company into a multinational like GE or Sony, and he wants to shift its direction to the financial market.

Over the past eighteen years, Haier has been growing at an amazing speed, with sales of 3.48 million RMB in 1984, increasing to 72 billion RMB in 2002. The Haier Group ranked sixteenth among the top 500 Chinese businesses for the year 2002 in a survey jointly conducted, in August 2002, by the Federation of Chinese Enterprises and the Association of Chinese Entrepreneurs. In a September 2002 survey conducted by the China Statistics Bureau, Haier ranked eleventh among the 500 largest companies in China for the year 2001. There might be some marginal errors in either survey, but a comparative look at both surveys should yield a realistic assessment of Haier's position in China's business pyramid.

Another basis for assessment can be found in the 2002 market report of the London-based Euromonitor International, the longest-established provider of global strategic research. According to that report, Haier ranked fifth among global white appliance makers, and Haier refrigerators attained a 5.98% market share, ranking first in the world.

Haier has certainly grown big, but not big enough to satisfy Zhang. Like the majority of companies in the top 500 Chinese businesses, Haier is still a small company compared with the *Fortune* 500, the smallest of which had revenues of $10 billion in 2001, $2.7 billion more than Haier's. Although there were eight Chinese companies on the *Fortune* 500 list and three on the *Forbes Global* 500 list for 2001, all of them were state-run conglomerates operating in highly protected fields such as petroleum, telecommunications and commercial banking.

While attending the Future of Asia Forum in Japan in May 2002, Zhang made a pointed comment on the situation: "None of the eleven companies has grown under a competitive environment. Rather, they are state-run enterprises grown with the country's monopoly policies. With their large numbers of employees, they have made the lists, but they are not efficient."

Support for Zhang's argument can be found in the case of China National Petroleum, Number 81 on the *Fortune* 500 list for the year 2001. The company had a workforce of 1,167,129, almost twelve times as large as that of Exxon-Mobile, which had 97,900 employees, but its revenue was $41,499 million, about 22% of Exxon-Mobile's $191,581 million. In terms of productivity per employee, China National Petroleum's was $35,556 while that of Exxon-Mobile was $1,956,905.

With a worldwide workforce of a little over 30,000 and revenues of $7,300 million, Haier's productivity per capita was about $243,000, almost seven times higher than that of China National Petroleum, but still eight times lower than that of Exxon-Mobile.

One of the goals for Haier is to get onto the *Fortune* 500 list in a few years, and that may partly explain why Zhang has been so keen on making his company bigger, in terms of revenues. The fact that GE Capital constituted 40% of GE's total revenue is a great inspiration for Zhang, whose recent actions have shown the clear intention to move full-speed into China's service sectors.

In addition to its effort to diversify into China's financial services, such as life insurance, securities market, and commercial banking (see Chapter 5), Haier has also branched into the retail business. In June 2001, Haier formed a 50-50 joint venture with the German furniture giant OBI, the largest in Germany in the Do-It-Yourself sector, and the second largest in Europe. With over 450 chain stores worldwide, OBI entered China in 1998. Now it has a total of four stores in three Chinese cities, hiring about 1,200 employees. On October 1, 2002, the Haier-OBI joint venture celebrated its grand opening in Shanghai. Haier-OBI plans to open a store in Qingdao in 2003, and between ten and fifteen more in the next two or three years. The goal is to increase the total number of stores to one hundred within a span of ten years.

There have been some indications that Haier will retreat somewhat from the domestic appliance market and focus more on domestic services and international markets. Dwindling profit margins as the result of cutthroat competition in the Chinese home appliance sector have partly contributed to this shift in orientation. In 2000, Haier's net profit margin for home appliance products was 8.78%, but in 2001 it dropped to 5.4%.

Haier's domestic competitors fared even worse. Three of the eight major players in the field had negative profits. Of the four that were profitable, TCL had a 3.04% margin, Guangdong Midea Holding had a 2.38% margin, Sichuan Changhong had a 0.93% margin and Qingdao Hisense had only a 0.47% margin. With strong foreign competitors such as Whirlpool and Electrolux entering the market and grabbing more market share, there will be more fierce competition among appliance makers. Profit margins will further decrease until the Chinese home appliance industry becomes a so-called "chicken-rib business"—not of much value or interest to the manufacturers, who, nevertheless, hesitate to abandon it entirely because of its huge market size.

For the first six months of 2002, Haier made 1.83 million refrigerators, of which 980,000 units were exported, and 1.46 million air conditioners, of which 597,000 units were exported. While the total units made were almost the same as in the same period of the previous year, Haier's net profit decreased by 45% compared with the same period in 2001, further lowering its margin to 3.5%. Haier blamed the profit slide partly on the detrimental domestic competition environment which drove Haier to increase considerably its export of air conditioners to mitigate the impact of domestic competition, and partly on low unit prices on exported products.

The Haier Group's reported worldwide sales in 2002 were 72 billion RMB, or $8.7 billion. Although the figure is 11.8 billion RMB, or $1.43 billion, higher than that for 2001, it shows a decreasing growth rate than the previous two years, from about 50% to about 20%.

After years of mergers and acquisitions, Haier has grown into a conglomerate with a lot of subsidiaries, but all Haier subsidiaries are not listed on the Chinese stock market, which has made it difficulties for people outside Haier to obtain financial information about the company as a whole. Qingdao Haier Co., Ltd., the publicly traded portion of the Haier Group, is primarily its refrigeration operations—including refrigerator, freezer and air conditioner—whose revenues make up less than twenty percent of the Haier Group's worldwide revenues. Haier had used the name "Qingdao Haier Refrigerator Co., Ltd." for this publicly traded subsidiary from 1993 to 2000, but the name was changed to "Qingdao Haier Co., Ltd." in 2001. Though the subsidiary's revenues, profits, and earnings per share were growing at a steady rate by the end of 2001, its stock price has been generally on the decline since 1997, when it reached an all-time high (See Appendix C). Haier blamed the situation on the generally sluggish stock market environment in the wake of the Asian economic crisis that started in 1997.

According to the Annual Report of Qingdao Haier Co., Ltd., the company had revenues of 11.44 billion RMB or $1.38 billion U.S. dollars in 2001, with a profit of $74.6 million. (The reported worldwide revenues of the Haier Group in 2001 were 60.2 billion RMB or $7.3 billion U.S. dollars, but no profit figures were available.) It does not look likely that the Haier Group as a whole will go public any time soon.

Haier's status as one of the most reported companies in China has attracted a lot of media curiosity and attention, both at home and abroad, about its financial situation. Although Haier has no obligation to disclose the financial condition of those non-public subsidiaries, Haier's characteristic shyness in the face of requests for such information has given rise to some speculation about its overall financial health. In some cases, Haier's response to negative views about or criticism of the company has raised some eyebrows, leading to misunderstandings or more speculation.

All things considered, what are Haier's competitive advantages and strategies now and in the future?

Domestically, Haier's competitive advantages still lie in its high-quality products, supported by a strong brand appeal to Chinese consumers. After eighteen years of tireless effort, Haier has acquired almost all the effective management components necessary to run a multinational—high quality and low cost, a wide array of models and features, a lean production system, including Total Quality Control, Just-in-Time manufacturing, design for manufacturability, close supplier relationships, flexible manufacturing and rapid production-cycle time.

But all this does not guarantee that a company the size of Haier can maintain sustained growth and success. In the domestic market, a big challenge for Haier is the question of how to hold tight to its market share without being negatively engaged in what Harvard business professor Michael Porter called "competitive convergence," which means that all the competitors in an industry compete on the same dimensions, such as quality, cycle time, supplier partnerships and after-sale services. Since these are areas that competitors can easily imitate, sooner or later a company will blunt its competitive edge in the race. Many Japanese companies adopted this competitive strategy in the 1980s and 1990s, which ultimately led them to a state in which they were making high-quality products but earning very low or negative profits, a situation the Chinese home-appliance makers are now facing.

Experience has shown that competing just in terms of operational effectiveness, which basically involves improving quality and cost simultaneously, can hardly lead a company to enduring success. Worse yet, competition on operational effectiveness alone, like competition on price, is mutually damaging, and leads business warriors nowhere but into a continuous war of erosion from which even winners take nothing.

A more sensible strategy for companies like Haier seems to be competing on strategy rather than on operational effectiveness alone. While operational effectiveness is concerned with performing the same or similar activities better than competitors, competing on strategy has to do with providing different products or services from one's competitors.

Dell Computer, for example, offers a different approach to selling computers from other major U.S. computer makers such as IBM and Compaq. Their strategy—low inventory, customer focus, and direct sales—has substantially strengthened Dell's competitive advantage.

Another case in point is the competition among the three Japanese video-game producers, Nintendo, Sega and Sony. To avoid head-on competition that would lead to competitive convergence, each of the three companies adopted a strategy that differentiated its computer games from its rivals'. Nintendo emphasized playability, or the ease of running games; Sega focused on enhanced graphics; and Sony offered quality games at lower prices. As a result of their distinct positioning, all three companies came out winners in the competition, with very good returns on earnings.

An even more encouraging outcome was that the benign competition has not only allowed many of its major players to thrive at the same time, but also expanded the total market.

Haier has exhibited some tendency to compete on strategy, as in the case of its insistence on competing on quality and service rather than on price in the domestic appliance market. But without the participation of other major players, Haier finds it hard to maintain its integrity in the recurring and escalating wars on price.

Haier's general strategies for growth are still diversification and globalization, although diversification has focused more on non-manufacturing sectors, such as financial services and retailing. There has been much discussion among industry analysts and entrepreneurs about the necessity and practicality of both diversification and globalization for Chinese companies like Haier. Not a few people have expressed concern over Haier's aggressive diversification programs, especially in areas unrelated to its core business.

While there is no right or wrong about a company's decision to diversify, entering into various unrelated and unfamiliar businesses will certainly not be an easy ride for Haier in the years to come.

Globalization has proved to be the ultimate path for any company to travel if it aspires to be a true multinational. Haier's early-bird strategy in going international has put it in an advantageous position in winning domestic government support and in grabbing national and international media attention.

Haier has been chosen by the Chinese government as one of the six companies to receive all the support necessary to make it to the *Fortune* 500 list.

At the Sixteenth Congress of the Communist Party of China that ended in mid-November 2002, Zhang Ruimin was elected an alternate member of the Party's Central Committee. This is by and large an honorary position with no real responsibility, but only very few entrepreneurs have made it to this decision-making circle in China. At the Fifteenth Congress five years earlier, Ni Runfeng, President of Sichuan Changhong Electric Corp., China's largest TV maker, held the same position.

A movie called *Chief Executive Officer* was released in October 2002, based on Zhang's experiences, with the emphasis on globalization.

The December 26, 2002 issue of the *Far East Economic Review* ranked Haier number one on its list of Top Ten Chinese Multinationals in 2002.

What is more important is that, with more intensified domestic competition and shrinking profit margins, Haier's overseas operations will provide the company a relatively safe haven, where it can expect to generate more revenues.

Toyota, for example, sold 1.74 million vehicles in the U.S. in 2001, more than the 1.71 million sold in Japan. Sony's American operations generated $18.5 billion in 2001, which constituted one third of the company's worldwide sales of $56.9 billion. There is still a long way to go for Haier to attain the status of a truly global brand in the United States and Europe, but, given its history and resources, the company has been doing a tremendous job in building a global brand name and inching into the international spotlight.

What, then, does the future hold for Haier?

From a macro perspective, Haier's ultimate competitiveness lies in its core competencies, which means "the collective learning of the organization, especially the capacity to coordinate diverse production skills and integrate multiple streams of technologies." The concept of core competencies was first put forward by Gary Hamel and C. K. Prahalad in a landmark article titled "The Core Competence of the Corporation," in the *Harvard Business Review* in 1990. It has since become the magazine's most reprinted article.

Core competencies involve shared corporate capabilities that are very hard to imitate, and not physical assets, such as patent, brand name, technologies or corporate structure that may be instrumental in a company's short-term success. Core competencies require corporate leaders to have vision and foresight, so that they can create their own futures, envision new markets and reinvent themselves.

In the case of Haier, neither its brand and services nor its OEC management theory and product technologies is an essential part of its core competencies. Like Dell Computer, Haier does not own many key technologies such as those of refrigerator compressors.

But Dell has been growing at an astronomical speed, supported by its core competencies, which are characterized by the company's collective ability to coordinate low-cost procurement, assembling and selling that offers speedy and personalized services. Dell's competitors have tried to imitate the Dell model, but have not been successful, either because they could not afford the high cost of imitation or because they abandoned the imitation due to its poor result for them.

Likewise, Haier's success in the domestic market has demonstrated that its core competencies lie in the company's collective ability to coordinate a number of diverse production skills, such as Just-In-Time manufacturing, brand name maneuvering and customer services. The fact that almost none of Haier's competitors could beat Haier in those fields combined is not so much due to the ignorance of those companies as to the prohibitive cost of imitation.

A Chinese proverb might well serve as an explanation: "It takes more than one cold day for the river to freeze three feet deep."

Though it remains to be seen what really will happen to Haier's success mix for the next decade or so, there are strong indications that the Haier core competencies that have worked so far should continue to work for the company's sustained growth.

Haier's product structure can be conveniently divided into three groups: profitable core products, such as refrigerators, air conditioners, freezers, washing machines and TVs; new and promising market products, such as computers and mobile phones; and future market opportunities, such as financial services and retailing. The key to future success for the company is whether Haier can keep the momentum for its existing core competencies and smoothly extend the existing core competencies to all three product groups, so that they are capable of coordinating diverse production skills and integrating multiple streams of technologies.

Predictably, Haier's sustained success lies largely in how the company's top management views, defines and creates a future for themselves. Obviously, some work has been done in that regard. In order to create a successful vision of the future, a dedicated Haier senior management has been making a tremendous effort to escape the orthodoxies of the corporation's current concept of self. Haier is building the best possible assumption base about the future, which indicates to its management what changes in the company's products, competencies and consumer interface today are necessary to address customer needs tomorrow. Since 1998, Haier top management has been working extremely hard to edify its middle-level management with teachings that aim at establishing a generation of managers with vision and foresight for tomorrow. This effort is coupled with the company's business process reengineering (BPR) program, the so-called Haier Revolution, which is still unfolding on the Haier landscape, to drive home the notion and spirit of constantly reenergizing and reinventing themselves.

To some, Haier seems to have been overworking itself with what looks like an endless undertaking of deconstruction and reconstruction, but we believe that Haier is moving in the direction of stretching the boundaries surrounding its competitive position of today in order to include competition and changes in customer needs tomorrow. Such a "stretch" between today's capacities and tomorrow's vision ensures that the company constantly innovates in order to keep the momentum of its core competencies, whose strength does not diminish with use.

As the Chinese proverb says, "The strength of a horse is tested by the distance traveled." Time will tell if Haier is a good and strong horse, capable of millions of miles and beyond.

Appendix A: The Haier Chronicle
1984-2002
(Sales Amount in RMB)

1984   Sales: 3.48 million
- In late December, Zhang Ruimin was appointed director of the Qingdao General Refrigerator Factory, predecessor of the Haier Group. The factory was 1.47 million RMB in debt.

1985   Sales: 18 million
- Zhang devised a strategy of first going after quality. In order to bring awareness of product quality to the workers, Zhang ordered the destruction of 76 defective refrigerators with a sledgehammer.

1986   Sales: 80 million
- Haier refrigerators were sold and well received in three large cities in China.

1987   Sales: 140 million
- In a refrigerator bid sponsored by the World Health Organization, Haier refrigerators defeated other brands from over ten countries and won the bid.

1988   Sales: 270 million
- In December, Haier refrigerator won the gold medal in China's first national refrigerator competition, which established Haier's reputation as a leading company in the industry.

1989   Sales: 410 million
- In June, the Chinese refrigerator market had a down-turn. While almost all other brand names slashed their prices, Haier increased its prices by 15% without losing any market share.

1990   Sales: 710 million
- Haier won two national gold medals: the Golden Horse Award in business management and the National Award for Quality Management. Haier products received American UL certification.

1991   Sales: 830 million
- In a national brand name competition, Haier was acknowledged as one of the top 10 brand names in China.
- In December, Haier merged with Qingdao Freezer Factory and Qingdao Air Conditioner Factory to form the Haier Group. Zhang Ruimin became the Group President.

1992   Sales: 1.05 billion
- In May, Haier purchased 5,000 acres of land in the High-Tech Zone in Qingdao to build its first Industrial Park.
- In September, Haier products passed ISO 9001 to qualify Haier as an international supplier.

1993   Sales: 1.49 billion

·   In November, Haier went public on the Shanghai Stock Exchange to raise fund for the construction of the Haier Industrial Park.

1994   Sales: 2.56 billion

·   Haier Industrial Park was under construction. Haier's super freon-free refrigerators were displayed at the World Earth Day Exhibition.

1995   Sales: 4.33 billion

·   In May, Haier's Industrial Park was completed.

·   In July, Haier acquired the Red Star Electric Appliance Company.

1996   Sales: 6.16 billion

·   Haier won a number of domestic quality product awards, which further boosted Haier's brand image.

1997   Sales: 10.8 billion

·   In February, Haier participated in the Electronic Appliance Exhibition in Cologne, Germany.

·   Haier acquired and merged over a dozen factories. Among them were Guangdong Shunde Washing Machine Factory, Shandong Laiyang Iron Factory, Guizhou Fenghua Refrigerator Factory, Hefei Yellow Mountain Television Company, etc.

1998   Sales: 16.8 billion

·   In March, Zhang Ruimin was invited by the Harvard Business School for talks and discussions about the role of Haier's enterprise culture in its mergers and acquisitions.

·   In December, the London-based *Financial Times* ranked Haier seventh among Asia-Pacific's Most Respected Companies.

1999   Sales: 26.86 billion

·   In February, Haier Middle East was formed.

·   In March, Haier America was established.

·   In April, Haier began building its factory in South Carolina, to manufacture refrigerators.

·   In September, Zhang Ruimin was invited to speak at the Fortune Shanghai Annual Conference. Zhang was the only Chinese executive who gave a speech at the conference.

·   In December, *Financial Times* ranked Zhang 26th among the World's 30 Most Respected Business Leaders.

2000   Sales: 40.6 billion

·   In late January, Zhang participated in the 30th World Economic Forum in Davos, Switzerland, at which he gave a speech on Haier innovations.

·   In March, the first Haier refrigerator made in America came off the assembly line.

· In May, Zhang Ruimin changed his position from President to CEO of the Haier Group.

· In October, Zhang was invited by the International Institute for Management Development (IMD) in Lausanne, Switzerland, to give a talk on Haier's management.

· In December, Haier Europe was established.

2001   Sales: 60.2 billion

· In early April, Zhang was invited by Columbia and Wharton Business Schools to speak on management.

· In April, Haier began to build its second overseas industrial park—Haier Pakistan Industrial Park.

· In June, Haier, together with Ericsson, turned out Internet-ready household products using "Bluetooth" technology.

· In June, Haier acquired the Italian refrigerator plant belonging to Meneghetti Equipment.

· In July, Haier spent $14 million to purchase a landmark building in Manhattan to be its U.S. headquarters.

· In December, Haier announced its joint venture with the New York Life Insurance Company to sell life insurance in China.

2002   Sales: 72 billion

· In January, Haier and Japan's Sanyo Electric Co. formed a broad business alliance to gain a stronger foothold in each other's market for electrical appliance products.

· In February, Haier formed a strategic alliance with Taiwan's Sampo Corp. to sell each other's products using the distribution channels each owns in their own markets.

· In April, the American *Appliance Manufacturer* magazine ranked Haier freezers in the five-cubic-foot-and-above category third place, and Haier room air conditioners fifth place, in the U.S. market for 2001.

· In July, AHAM, the Association of Home Appliance Manufacturers in the U.S., reported that the market share for Haier compact refrigerators (up to 6.4 cubic feet) was 34.39% in 2001.

· In October, Euromonitor ranked Haier fifth among the world's largest white appliance makers and first among the largest refrigerator makers in the world.

· In December, the Haier brand was valued at 48.9 billion RMB, becoming the number one national brand in China.

(Sources: Haier Group and media reports)

Appendix B: Haier Sales Chart

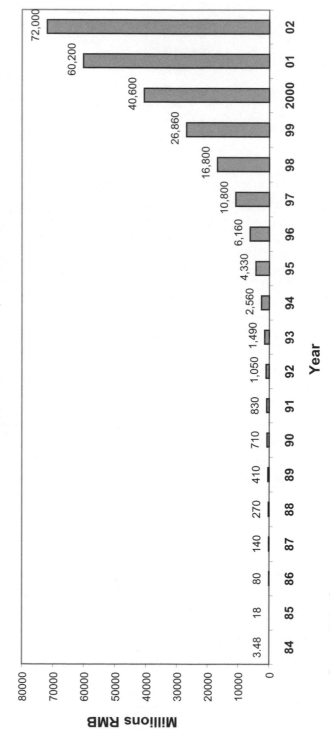

Haier Sales Chart, 1984-2002

Millions RMB

Year

Source: Haier Group

Appendix C: Haier Stock Price Chart

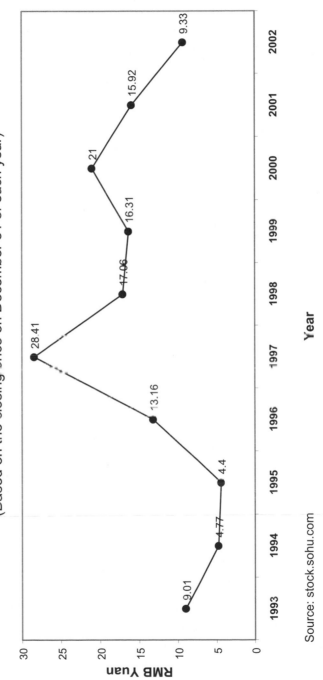

Haier Stock Price Chart, 1993-2002

Traded on the Shanghai Stock Market, Stock No. 600690

(Based on the closing price on December 31 of each year)

Year

RMB Yuan

Appendix D:
Chinese-U.S. Currency Exchange Rate
1982-2002

(Based on Chinese RMB per US Dollar, RMB/US$)

Year	Rate
1982	1.92
1983	1.98
1984	2.79
1985	3.20
1986	3.71
1987	3.72
1988	3.72
1989	4.72
1990	5.23
1991	5.40
1992	5.84
1993	5.81
1994	8.44
1995	8.32
1996	8.33
1997	8.31
1998	8.28
1999	8.28
2000	8.28
2001	8.28
2002	8.28

Sources: Datastream and CIA China fact sheets

Appendix E: Case Study

The Haier Group (B), Harvard Business School

HARVARD BUSINESS SCHOOL
9-398-102
REV: JULY 27, 2001

LYNN SHARP PAINE

The Haier Group (B)

Zhang Ruimin, the CEO of China's Haier Group, concluded the conversation and put down the telephone receiver. It was another caller asking him not to dismiss this or that manager in his effort to remake Red Star, the Group's newly acquired washing machine maker. Rebuilding Red Star was a daunting challenge, but what really troubled Zhang were these calls from friends and government officials seeking special consideration.

Zhang had decided that if Haier was going to expand beyond its base as a middle-sized regional manufacturer, it needed to acquire Red Star. The decision, which was Zhang's alone, was almost universally opposed within the Haier Group. The opportunity, Zhang argued, was just too good to pass up: it was locally based, which meant negotiating with only one set of municipal officials, and its industrial facilities were sound, as was its work force. Indeed, with the exception of the debt and the salary and benefit obligations Haier would inherit, Red Star appeared to be a great bargain, at least to Zhang.

In close consultation with Zhang, who remained hospitalized, Yang Mianmian handled the early stages of the negotiation in June of 1995.

With the aid of Qingdao Mayor Yu Zhengshen, who was a firm believer in the talents and instincts of Zhang, Ms. Yang lobbied key officials in the municipal government and was able to quickly secure their agreement to the acquisition. Though Red Star's top management banded together with the leaders of several other companies in Qingdao and succeeded in creating more doubters, they were not effective in arguing against Zhang and Haier. Zhang's feat of converting Qingdao General Refrigerator Factory into China's number one refrigerator manufacturer still carried immense prestige. Officials in the municipal government were willing to give him another chance. Besides, Red Star was in such critical shape that they were taking a relatively minor risk.

In terms of servicing the debt, paying salaries, and turning Red Star around, Haier would bear the brunt of the acquisition risk. Haier renegotiated Red Star's debt with its banks, including as part of the bargain a three-year grace period on interest payments and a credit line secured by the assets of the whole group. To protect the Haier brand and give Red Star employees an incentive to earn the Haier name, Zhang decided to wait until Red Star reached a certain standard of quality before renaming it the "Haier Washing Machine Company," or HWMC. Zhang immediately began the process of instilling Haier's enterprise culture. "We had to create an environment where [Red Star] employees would recognize what was the right thing to do," he explained.

The Integration Process

On July 4, 1995, the second day after the acquisition, the former vice president of the Haier Group, Ms. Yang, arrived with a group of representatives from each of Haier's five departments: consulting, asset management, planning and development, accounting, and the enterprise culture center. They spoke to the entire company, explaining the general outlines of the Haier "enterprise spirit": "love your job, contribute to the country, and strive for excellence." Ms. Yang explained Haier's emphasis on personal responsibility, its reputation for the highest quality, and its system of accountability. She explained how open competition would help them survive. Ms. Yang nonetheless clearly stated that employees who did not do things the Haier way as measured in evaluations would be fired.

To engage their sense of "face," Ms. Yang asked Red Star employees if they were prepared to follow the Haier way, and then immediately requested that they put their commitment in writing. Though most of the top management would be fired, she emphasized that those who could compete would be kept on. Workers, she reiterated, would not be blamed for Red Star's decline: management was at least 80% responsible. (See **Exhibit 1** for Haier statement of common goal, a Chinese brand.)

In August, Zhang himself went over the same issues with the company's middle managers. He shared his opinion that human capital was the most important factor of production. He highlighted the role of middle managers in developing an enterprise. Zhang urged everyone to start, at that very moment, to plan and apply good management skills to every operation, every employee, and every transaction. Zhang also outlined the specific elements of the strategy for Red Star (See **Exhibit 2** for Zhang's entire speech):

- Focus on the market. Red Star should sell its reputation, not just cheap products, with every step oriented toward customer demand.
- Lower cost to increase profit, maximizing output while minimizing input.
- Make concrete plans and set clear targets for every person, within the overall goal of making Red Star the number one manufacturer of washing machines in China in two to three years, and ultimately making it an internationally recognized brand.

The Haier team next turned to the operational level. First, under the direction of Ms. Su, three educators in Haier's enterprise culture were dispatched, presenting the basics to all employees in small groups. They approached key individuals throughout the organization, in an effort to persuade them that Haier could make Red Star number one in washing machines, just as Zhang had done with Qingdao General Refrigerator Factory. Despite their resistance, Red Star employees were impressed with Zhang's accomplishments and style.

Mr. Chai Yongsen, the newly appointed general manager of the new washing machine division, went immediately to the factory floor. An engineer in his early thirties and former assistant general manager of the refrigerator division—Haier's manufacturing standard bearer—Chai knew he had to get the plant working again to improve morale. By assigning workers to repair the defective units in stock, he created a vehicle to explain why the quality of work was unacceptable. "They understood there were problems in quality for the first time," he said, "and many of them wept in shame, admitting their responsibility and expressing a willingness to change."

Nevertheless, Chai felt more was needed to instill an understanding of Haier's culture. He reflected on an incident involving a quality inspector, Ms. Fan Ping, who had missed some improperly inserted switches and plugs. As was normal, Ms. Fan had been fined 50 Rmb for the oversight, and the matter dropped. Chai, however, thought Ms. Fan's supervisors should take some responsibility for what happened. He was considering how best to develop their sense of managerial responsibility. One possibility was to launch a discussion of the issue in the company newspaper.

Exhibit 1 Excerpt from Company Newsletter: "For a Common Goal: Our Chinese Brand" (July 12, 1995)

Many of the original Red Star employees disagreed with the decision of the Qingdao City government to merge Red Star with Haier. Because Red Star was a large company that should be able to develop business on its own, they believed it was unnecessary for Red Star to come under Haier's leadership.

Based on the concerns of Red Star's staff, top Haier managers commented:

- As Red Star had existed independently for more than 30 years, it was understandable that Red Star employees felt a sense of loss.
- However, "an invisible hand" controlled the market. The Qingdao City government realized that, given the demands of the market economy, a merger was necessary for Red Star to become profitable again. During the process, there was a certain degree of involvement and guidance by the government.

- The goal of joining forces with Haier was to build a national brand. If the two companies were not united, Red Star would be devoured by foreign competitors. While Haier had established national recognition over the previous 10 years, the merger with Red Star would strengthen Haier's ability to protect a national industry and to compete with foreign companies.

Source: *Haier News* #188.

Exhibit 2 Excerpts from Company Newsletter: Zhang's Speech—"A Special Lesson (A Small Rice Bowl) for the Washing Machine Co." (August 15, 1995)

On August 15, 1995, after the Washing Machine Co. merger, Zhang Ruimin (CEO) and Yang Mianmian (Executive Director) participated in a monthly, group self-evaluation meeting of the middle management.

To boost morale and put an end to confusion about the new company, Zhang stressed three requirements to middle management: (1) evaluate yourself objectively; (2) pay more attention to the operation of the company; and (3) envision future goals.

Evaluating yourself. Zhang said: "Everyone attending this meeting should feel ashamed of the poorly managed washing machine operation. Middle and upper management should lead by example, bringing superior performance to the employees of the company. Management bears 80% of the responsibility for company performance, while employees bear 20%. There are two basic prerequisites for our management: the first is devotion, meaning willingness to contribute to the company and help your subordinates; the second is the spirit of teamwork. In other words, team leaders should lead, motivating their teams to solve problems. It is unsuitable for management to wait for problems to develop, to blame them for disappointing performance, or to avoid dealing with them.

Paying more attention to the operations of the company. According to Zhang, "Every department is directly responsible for low profits, which indicates that operations are improperly run. For example, the raw material department should have a competitive bidding system for purchasing supplies. A competitive system should be established within the company."

Envisioning the future. "Our ultimate goal," Zhang said, "would be to create well-known products, both domestically and internationally, and to achieve 100 billion Rmb in sales. Within the next two to three years, our biggest challenge is to produce the highest quality washing machines for the domestic market."

During the meeting, Chief Coordinator and General Manager Chai Yongsen announced the results of an evaluation of middle management performance in July: seven middle managers were openly commended and some of the others were criticized. This was the first public evaluation of management in the company.

Source: *Haier News.*

Appendix F: Case Study
Building Market Chains at Haier
International Institute for Management Development

IMD

INTERNATIONAL

LAUSANNE - SWITZERLAND

CEIBS

GM 939

13.06.2000

BUILDING MARKET CHAINS AT HAIER

Professor William A. Fischer, of IMD, with the assistance of Ge Jun and Li Yun Lu, of CEIBS, prepared this case as a basis for class discussion rather than to illustrate either effective or ineffective handling of an administrative situation. At the time the case research was undertaken, Professor Fischer was the Dean of CEIBS.

> An enterprise is like a ball being pushed up a slope. Under the pressure of market competition and internal stress, the ball needs a strong braking force to prevent it from rolling back down. This braking force is the internal management infrastructure.[1]

At the end of 1999, after 20 years of strong and fairly consistent economic growth that had resulted in the almost total transformation of the lives of nearly a quarter of the world's population, the consumer appetites of the Chinese people were apparently still not satiated. Despite two years of relatively sluggish consumer purchases, 30% of China's consumers still planned to purchase a color TV within the next two years, 22% a washing machine, 21% a refrigerator, 14% an air-conditioner and 10% a microwave oven.[2] Such estimates should have been music to the ears of China's home appliance manufacturers, yet in the face of uncertainty regarding the softening of China's consumer economy, the unpredictable future promised by the inevitability of state-owned enterprise reforms, and the fears associated with China's likely accession to the WTO, caution, more than elation, was the norm in the domestic industry.

Throughout China, after decades, if not centuries, of scarcity characterizing the prevailing economic order in nearly all industry segments (either as a result of industrial backwardness, or the failures of central planning), the mid-1990s witnessed a profound and disruptive shift to more balance between supply and demand. Such relative parity brought with it enormous trauma associated with market shake-outs. One of the hardest-hit was the home appliance industry, where the nature of rivalry reached levels that could only be described as hyper-competitive. According to China's Business Information Center, by late 1997 supply exceeded demand for 55.3% of 36 various household electrical appliance categories.

One particularly vivid illustration of what such numbers meant to the actual players in the marketplace, could be seen in the refrigerator industry, where:

> [...] The top four refrigerator producers in the 1980s were Snowflake Refrigerator in Beijing, Wan Bao in Guangzhou, Xiang Xue Hai in Suzhou, and Shuanglu in Shanghai. But in the 1990s these four had been displaced by new players. The top four had been unable to sustain their competitiveness in a rapidly changing and increasingly competitive business environment.[3]

In fact, none of the top four from the 1980s had even remained among the top six brands in the mid-1990s!

In home air-conditioners, a similar situation had emerged following, in mid-1998, the lowering of China's import duties on such products, and the consequential increase in the success of foreign brands, which achieved a market share of over 30%, and even 40% when domestic foreign invested enterprises production were added. In fact, the power of the foreign brands was evident in an apparent domestic consumer preference for such products:

> When imported [air-conditioner] merchandise costs 50% to 60% more than domestic merchandise, the consumer selection rate is 30% to 40%. But, when foreign prices are 20% to 40% higher than domestic products, this selection rate soars to 60% to 70%.

To make matters even more confusing, the nature of competition was so unpredictable that even well-known international brands were not spared the trauma of the market shake-outs. Whirlpool, for example, found itself withdrawing from two of its four China joint-ventures (including air-conditioners) in 1998, largely because it had underestimated the strength of the Chinese domestic manufacturers' reaction to Whirlpool's market entry.

The net result of all of this was broad uncertainty throughout the home appliance industry, and hesitancy, if not paralysis, within many of the Chinese domestic enterprises that sold in these markets. One exception was the Haier Group, located in Qingdao, in Shandong province in northeast China, which had grown from an essentially bankrupt producer of poor-quality electric appliances in 1984, to one of China's premier brands in the late-1990s, after accumulating more than 18 bankrupt producers of home appliances along the way. In the eyes of many observers, the leadership of Mr. Zhang Ruimin had been essential to this success. It was his belief that sustainable competitive success is achievable only through the full-utilization of the talents of the workforce. In a comment he made at the Harvard Business School in March 1998, he put it this way: "In the present conditions of China, the key to success is to provide an arena in which everyone can bring his or her talents into full play. In this way, you will always be more advanced than your counterparts in the market."[4]

Haier Group

In early 2000, the Haier Group was a collectively owned enterprise, consisting of more than 90 plants and companies, and employing more than 20,000. In November 1993, its core enterprise, Haier Refrigerator Stock Company Limited, listed on the Shanghai Stock Exchange, allowed it the resources to build China's largest home electronics production and export base. As of mid-1999, it exported to 87 countries and regions and had 62 dealerships abroad, as well as manufacturing operations in several foreign countries, including a new factory under construction in South Carolina, to serve the North American market, which was scheduled to open in 2000. Haier produced 42 types of appliances, with over 8,600 specifications. Between 1984 and 1999, it had achieved an annual average sales increase of 82.8%. According to corporate statements:

> Haier Group aims at being a multi-national company with an internationally well-known brand. Presently, Haier Group is poised as a multi-national company both in management philosophy and enterprise culture and in production, business, science and technology.
>
> [...] Haier provides people with high-tech products and internationalized services, constantly improving products, functions, and designs to meet the requirements of each customer. Customer satisfaction is the standard by which we judge our work.

As of December 1998, Haier had a 39.7% share of China's domestic market, with 1,000 large stores (50% freezers, 37.1 % air-conditioners, and 34.8% washing machines). In addition, Haier, which had only introduced color TVs in September 1997, was one of the top four producers in China.[5]

Despite all of its success, Haier Group president Mr. Zhang Ruimin was not complacent about the future:

> We are fully preparing for WTO. There will be big differences! Survival will be hard in Chinese enterprises that cannot internationalize. At Haier, we are using a model of "three one-thirds": 1/3 of what we produce will be made in China for the local market; 1/3 will be made in China for export; and 1/3 will be produced outside of China for foreign markets. We are putting ourselves in a position where it will actually make little difference whether China enters the WTO or not. Our strategy is to internationalize, and whatever happens with WTO will not change our strategy. The main thing is to develop our competencies so that we can compete.

Changing Mindsets: The Market Chain Concept

For some time it has been fashionable in China to speak of having to change the mindset of the Chinese organization as a prerequisite for being able to develop competitive competencies in the face of an increasingly open and difficult market. This is thought to be most challenging in state-owned enterprises (SOEs), which have long benefited from the so-called iron rice bowl (*da guo fan*), which was unbreakable no matter how many mistakes the enterprise made. At Haier, Mr. Zhang Ruimin believed that a major competitive advantage had stemmed from the company being a collective and not an SOE:

> Because we are a collective and not an SOE, the government has no investment in us. So, we've always been in the market. From the beginning, we've had to learn how to settle our own problems, and we've always regarded the market as the primary part: we devote all of our energies to the market.

The story of Haier is replete with examples of total customer focus. Early in his tenure as president of Haier, Mr. Zhang Ruimin gained national attention by having his workers smash 76 refrigerators with sledge-hammers because their quality was inferior. This, despite the prevailing mentality of the time, which was that, due to the scarcity of products such as refrigerators in the mid-1980s, anything made could be sold. *Fortune*, in introducing Haier's achievements, pointed out that Mr. Zhang Ruimin's action in smashing refrigerators was similar to Henry Ford's changing the discharge-valve production-procedure into 21 steps, or Akio Morita's producing the first section of magnetic tape in a saucepan."[6] Early in Mr. Zhang Ruimin's transformation of Haier, the concept of OEC emerged, and began to evolve. OEC stands for: Overall, Every, Control and Clear. Overall refers to all dimensions. Every means Everyone, Everyday, and Everything, which means all people, all the time and all things. Control and Clear means to manage and deal with the overall control and clearing up of everything by everyone everyday to ensure that everything is under control all the time. This implies that everyone has his or her work responsibility or, in other words, "today's work finished today and work improved day by day." The concept grew out of Haier's desire for overall optimization, and added-on elements of Japanese management philosophy, American innovation concepts, and Chinese traditional culture, as well as Haier's own management practices. It served the need to transform the status quo of "extensive" management, which was popular among Chinese enterprises, into a more intensive one, with everyday, everyone and every moment observed. "Haier insists that 'today's work must be finished today; today's accomplishment must be better than yesterday's; and tomorrow's goal must be higher than today's.'"[7]

The continuing dedication of enterprise energies to the market was particularly evident in Haier's success at building a national market presence and a national brand in a country where such accomplishments were still relatively unusual:

> We built up our own brand reputation by ourselves. We divided the market into specific markets and, in different places, we design and supply different products. Our sales networks are also different: we do not use distributors, but set-up our own sales networks and our own retailers. So, we control our own distribution.

In addition, Haier had been cited as opposing the common Chinese practice of offering markets in exchange for technology. According to one observer, in this regard Haier's strategy was "to introduce advanced technology and equipment, and assimilate it as rapidly as possible by way of imitation, and at the same time take the initiative to cultivate and train its own technological personnel. Haier wishes to narrow the gap it has with advanced international enterprises as quickly as possible."[8]

In late 1998 Haier began to experiment with a market chain strategy to reinforce the market focus that Mr. Zhang Ruimin often spoke of. The market chain had been inspired by Michael Porter's value chain, but was, in fact, quite different in both philosophy and in objectives. According to Mr. Zhang Ruimin:

> The concept of value chain developed by Porter emphasizes marginal income and aims to realize profit maximization, while we regard maximum customer satisfaction as our goal. We take customers as being most important, so in our market chain everybody is a market, and everybody has a market. This way, inside-employees can begin to feel market pressures even though they are inside the organization: Everybody faces the market, and everybody supplies their best procedures!

The essence of the market chain was that every unit, every operation and everyone was linked directly to a customer, and every unit/operation/ body was also someone else's customer. In this way, everybody in the enterprise, no matter how deep inside the firm, felt market pressure directly. As an example, the environmental testing laboratory was depicted as having the design department as a customer. Design expected that the laboratory would provide timely service, meet time deadlines, and show integrity in the testing it performed and the data it produced. Production, in turn, was seen as being a customer of design, depending on design for manufacturable products. In another example, Mr. Wang Yangmin, director of manpower resource development for the Haier Group, was portrayed as having the job of "finding ideas and solutions to settle productivity problems of the factories. In this way, the factories are his customers." He was also the customer of top management to the extent that they needed to develop group-wide policies pertaining to manpower development. Madame Shi Chunjie, information center director within the Haier Group's plan and development center, was described as heading-up a group that had formerly been directors of the whole group (planning and development had effectively played that role in the centrally planned economy which had preceded the reforms), but that now had to sell its planning services to others within Haier, who then become its customers.

The management of facilities in Haier was also described in market chain terms: The integrated technical facilities department set the standard charges for equipment management, which was responsible mainly for reducing downtime according to customers, i.e., product divisions. It integrated the equipment management in the group and provided the third party's integrated services of purchasing, maintenance and preparation of spare parts. After negotiations between the technical facilities department and product divisions, the standard charges were written in a contract. The technical facilities department was thus the supplier to the product divisions, providing equipment management with its equipment managers as executors, while the product divisions were the users of equipment and the market of the technical facilities department.

Haier University, which was scheduled to open in December 1999 for the internal training of Haier's staff and management team, was described as both a customer and a supplier for the production functions. The University was expected to respond as a supplier to two major customers—the production functions and senior management—in creating educational offerings that met their needs, and would be, in turn, a customer of the production functions to the extent that the production functions wanted it to add new capabilities to their existing portfolios.

One of the appeals of market chains to Chinese managers, according to Mr. Zhang Ruimin, was that "the traditional Chinese approach to being a manager is different from that of the West. In China, people would rather be a big manager in a small company, than a small manager in a big company." In other words, "Better be the head of a dog than the tail of a lion...Chinese managers want to do everything with their own ideas." Mr. Zhang Ruimin believed that market chains made it possible for Haier employees to approach being big managers in a small company, even though they were in the very middle of a 20,000 employee organization. In a sense, everybody was the senior manager of his or her own target market. Or, generally speaking, "Everyone is a boss!"

Market chains were also useful in overcoming the dysfunctional nature of hierarchy and relationships based on mutual obligations (*guanxi*), which have historically characterized Chinese organizations, and which, in the words of Mr. Zhang Ruimin, were "usually speed-absorbers":

> Since we are not an SOE, relationships are not so important to us. Also, we say that 'Haier is a race-track,' and we want everyone to race to see if they have the ability to rise to the top. Everyone shows their ability through competition. We continuously redesign our group structures to make our firm more market-oriented.

SST: Claim Compensation, Claim Payment, Stop!

Aside from the idea of using the chain metaphor to reinforce the requirement for everybody at Haier to be customer-focused, the market chain concept also had a second major element to make it work effectively, and which was referred to as SST. The acronym SST was derived from the sounds of three Chinese words that defined how the market chain should work:

- *S (Suo Chou): Claim for compensation*
  If you can do your job well, you should claim compensation from the employees after you (your customers downstream in the market chain);

- *S (Suo Pei): Claim for payment*
  If you cannot do a good job, the employees after you (your customers downstream in the market chain) should claim payment from you;

- *T (Tiao Zha):*
  If there is neither a claim for compensation nor a claim for payment, [computer] systems will take it as of no record. This is the so-called Stop!, which means that the immediate downstream process cannot go on. In case of Stop!, the responsible party should pay the claims.

An example of how SST worked could be seen in the relationship between Haier University and a production function. If the production function asked for a certain training course to be designed for its people, and the University delivered a high-quality program, it could expect to be paid for this service, at the negotiated rate, even if the production function chose not to do the program but still used some of the ideas anyway. If the University failed, it should not expect to be paid, and the customer might even claim some compensation for being unsatisfied. The final decision as to whether or not to pay, however, was up to the customer— and the customer is always right! As a service provider, Haier University's words, in this instance, don't count; only the customer's do. This leads one manager to observe that "within Haier, we treat service as a product."

The need for Stop! originated from the recognition that Haier Group had been growing at 80% per year, but that the quality of its human capital had not been increasing that fast. So, it needed some sort of standard to monitor the first two Ss in SST. Thus, the rationale behind the T was: "If you don't meet the standard: Stop! This standard was set-up by the customers, and if the customers believed that the product or service was not meeting the standard, they could stop the process."

To some extent, the origins of some of the SST philosophy might be traceable to the so-called Fan Ping incident of July 12, 1995, following

Haier's acquisition of Qingdao Red Star Electrical Appliance Factory. At that time, the factory had already changed its name to the Haier Washing Machine Co., Ltd. The quality control inspector, Fan Ping, was fined 50 *yuan* for a failing in her job. Her case showed that loopholes existed in management. Thus, managers from the Haier Group held that it was not only Fan Ping but also her supervisor who should carry the responsibility. This judgment aroused an enthusiastic discussion in the Haier Journal because none of the bosses had ever been fined for problems in quality control before. In the end, the person in charge at the higher level fined himself 300 *yuan* after handing over a written self-criticism.[9]

At the beginning of the launch of SST, there was considerable resistance to it because of issues of *face* and *guanxi*. These have gradually been overcome, however. According to one manager:

> We overcame face and *guanxi* resistance because now we have to claim compensation for performance. In the past we were all good friends, and we didn't want to claim compensation from a friend, so we always tolerated mediocre performance. Now, however, if my product does not satisfy my customers, they will claim compensation from me; so I am forced to ensure that my suppliers do a good job. In other words, the market chain idea is working because of 'popularization through necessity.'

Issues of Implementation

One manager at Haier observed that:

> The traditional Chinese mentality is not to be innovative. We are content with maintaining the status quo, and we would prefer to stay on a team and never move—to have something stable. In the beginning, people were concerned about *face* and *guanxi* but, step-by-step, they realized that they are all in the chain, so relations became harmonious.

This same manager believes that a year into the experiment,

> The benefits include the pushing of everyone into the marketplace, so that they have to think about the needs of their customers, and they are forced to be innovative. The system also encourages leadership, because if you are in more chains, you can claim more compensation, so leadership leads to larger salaries.

How to allocate overhead, always a sticky issue in such pricing schemes, was determined by negotiations between suppliers and customers. The negotiations were based on the previous year's status quo, i.e., "the bottom line." As for each project, less input for more output was encouraged. Returning to the equipment management example:

> A contract established by the technical facilities department and product divisions clearly specified that for product divisions, 1 minute above the defined downtime limit agreed by the two parties, should result in a penalty of 1 *yuan*, while 1 minute saved can be rewarded with 1 *yuan*. It also defined service projects that, if completed by product divisions, would result in the technical facilities department paying them. After the service contract had been established, the technical facilities department changed its original concept and approaches to equipment management, and dis-aggregated the objectives required by product divisions, (i.e., markets) down to every equipment manager, maintenance worker and piece of equipment, as well as to every month, every day and every moment. It tied each person's performance to his or her wages so as to ensure clear objectives and responsibilities. Every month, the technical facilities department charged product divisions according to the total downtime, while equipment managers and maintenance workers got compensated according to the downtime and services within their functional areas. Likewise, if the technical facilities department was not doing a good job, product divisions could claim compensation and also source outside equipment management service. As a result, the technical facilities department had to provide superior services and a satisfactory price. In this way, what we've done is to take a seemingly isolated transaction, deep inside the organization, and make it into a big chain connected to the market place.

Next Steps

The next steps in Haier's market chains concept was to expand the dimensions that were covered. A senior manager put it this way:

> We'd like to establish a multidimensional matrix structure to create flows: material flows, cash flows, overseas flows and knowledge flows—all of which would be market chains. This is administratively very complicated, and we are presently thinking about how to do it.

Notes:

[1] "Haier Law," as quoted in "Haier's Goal—Fortune Global 500," *China Daily, Business Weekly*, August 15-21, 1999, p.6.

[2] These numbers come from the Gallup Organization's Third Survey of Consumer Attitudes and Lifestyles in the People's Republic of China, as reported in Brian Palmer, "What the Chinese Want," *Fortune*, October 11, 1999, p.80.

[3] Arthur Yeung, *Haier Group: The Making of a Global Firm from China*, case published by CEIBS.

[4] Li Xia, "Haier Enterprise Culture: The Key to Success," *China Today*, August 1999, pp. 15-16. It is interesting to note that in a separate interview, Mr. Zhang Ruimin reflected on his life as a government bureaucrat, and remarked: "I had not been able to get a chance to use my talents to the full." In Li Xia and Xue Lisheng, "Creating Miracles with Ancient Culture," *China Today*, August 1999, p.21.

[5] Li Xia. "Haier's Road to Success," *China Today*, August 1999, pp.11-14.

[6] Anthony Paul, "China's Haier Power," *Fortune*. February 15, 1999, as cited in Li Xia, "Haier's Road to Success," pp.11-14.

[7] Li Xia, "Haier's Road to Success," p.12.

[8] Ibid., p.13.

[9] Li Xia, "Haier Enterprise Culture," p.16.

References and Bibliography

English Language Books

Bacal, Robert. *Performance Management*. New York: McGraw-Hill, 1999.

Bedbury, Scott, with Stephen Fenichell. *A New Brand World*. New York: Viking, 2001.

Bernstein, Richard. *Ultimate Journey: Retracing the Path of an Ancient Buddhist Monk Who Crossed Asia in Search of Enlightenment*. New York: Vintage, 2001.

Bunnell, David. *Making the Cisco Connection: The Story Behind the Real Internet Superpower*. New York: John Wiley & Sons, 2000.

Burstein, Daniel, and Arne De Keijzer. *Big Dragon: China's Future: What It Means for Business, the Economy, and the Global Order*. New York: Simon & Schuster, 1998.

Capodagli, Bill. *The Disney Way: Harnessing the Management Secrets of Disney in Your Company*. New York: McGraw-Hill, 1999.

Champy, James. *Reengineering Management: The Mandate for New Leaders Reengineering the Corporation*. New York: HarperBusiness, 1995.

Chen, Ming-Jer, *Inside Chinese Business. A Guide for Managers Worldwide*. Boston: Harvard Business School Press, 2001.

Confucius. *The Analects*. New York: Alfred A. Knopf, 2000.

_____. *The Wisdom of Confucius*. Lin, Yutang, ed. and trans. New York: The Modern Library, 1938.

Drucker, Peter Ferdinand. *Management Challenges for the 21st Century*. New York: HarperBusiness, 1999.

_____. *Managing in the Next Society*. New York: St. Martin's Press, 2002.

Drucker, Peter Ferdinand, and Isao Nakauchi. *Drucker on Asia: A Dialogue Between Peter Drucker and Isao Nakauchi*. Oxford: Butterworth-Heinemann, 1997.

Forden, Sara Gay. *The House of Gucci: A Sensational Story of Murder, Madness, Glamour, and Greed*. New York: William Morrow, 2000.

Fung, Hung-gay, and Kevin H. Zhang, eds. *Financial Markets and Foreign Direct Investment in Greater China*. Armonk, NY: M.E. Sharpe, 2002.

Gates, Bill, with Collins Hemingway. *Business @ the Speed of Thought: Using a Digital Nervous System*. New York: Warner Books, 1999.

Greising, David. *I'd Like the World to Buy a Coke: The Life and Leadership of Roberto Goizueta*. New York: John Wiley and Sons, 1998.

Gross, Daniel, and the editors of *Forbes* magazine. *Greatest Business Stories of All Time*. New York: John Wiley & Sons, 1996.

Hammer, Michael and James Champy. *Reengineering the Corporation: A Manifesto for Business Revolution*. New York: HarperBusiness, 1993.

Henderson, Callum. *China on the Brink*, New York: McGraw-Hill, 1999.

Iacocca, Lee, with William Novak. *Iacocca: An Autobiography*. Toronto: Bantam Books, 1984.

Imai, Masaaki. *Kaizen, The Key to Japan's Competitive Success*. New York: Random House Business Division, 1986.

_____. *Gemba Kaizen: A Commonsense Low-cost Approach to Management*. New York: McGraw-Hill, 1997.

Kotler, Philip. *Kotler on Marketing: How to Create, Win, and Dominate Markets*, New York: Free Press, 1999.

_____. *Marketing Management*. Upper Saddle River, N.J: Prentice Hall, 2000.

Kotler, Philip, and Gary Armstrong. *Principles of Marketing*. 8th ed., Upper Saddle River, NJ: Prentice Hall, 1999.

Kotter, John. *Matsushita Leadership: Lessons from the 20th Century's Most Remarkable Entrepreneur*. New York: Free Press, 1997.

Kotter, John, and James Heskett. *Corporate Culture and Performance*. New York: Free Press, 1992.

Lao Tzu. *Tao-Te Ching*. Washington, DC: Counterpoint, 2000.

Legge, James. *The Chinese Classics*. Taipei, Taiwan: SMC Publishing, 1991.

Liang, Congjie, and Todd Lappin, ed. *The Great Thoughts of China: 3,000 Years of Wisdom That Shaped a Civilization*. New York: John Wiley & Sons, 1996.

Lin, Yutang. *The Wisdom of China and India*, New York. Random house, 1942.

Lowe, Janet. *Jack Welch Speaks: Wisdom from the World's Greatest Business Leader*. New York: John Wiley & Sons, 1998.

_____. *Welch: An American Icon*, New York: John Wiley & Sons, 2001.

McGregor, Douglas. *The Human Side of Enterprise*. New York: McGraw-Hill, 1960.

Maslow, Abraham H. *Motivation and Personality*. 3rd ed., New York: Harper and Row, 1987.

Morita, Akio, with Edwin M. Reingold, and Mitsuko Shimomura. *Made in Japan: Akio Morita and Sony*. New York: Dutton, 1986.

Nathan, John. *Sony: The Private Life.* New York: Houghton Mifflin, 1999.

O'Boyle, Thomas. *At Any Cost: Jack Welch, General Electric, and the Pursuit of Profit.* New York: Alfred A. Knopf, 1998.

Porter, Michael E. *Competitive Advantage: Creating and Sustaining Superior Performance.* New York: Free Press, 1985.

_____. *The Competitive Advantage of Nations.* New York: Free Press, 1990.

Porter, Michael E., Hirotaka Takeuchi, and Mariko Sakakibara. *Can Japan Compete?* Basingstoke: Macmillan, 2000.

Rosen, Robert, et al. *Global Literacies: Lessons on Business Leadership and National Cultures: A Landmark Study of CEOs from 28 Countries.* New York: Simon & Schuster, 2000.

Sheff, David. *China Dawn: The Story of a Technology and Business Revolution.* New York: HarperBusiness, 2002.

Short, Philip. *Mao: A life.* New York: Henry Holt, 2000.

Slater, Robert. *Jack Welch and the GE Way.* New York: McGraw-Hill, 1999.

Stross Randall E. *The Microsoft Way: The Real Story of How the Company Outsmarts Its Competition.* Reading, MA: Addison-Wesley Pub. Co., 1996.

Studwell, Joe. *The China Dream: The Quest for the Last Untapped Market on Earth.* New York: Atlantic Monthly Press, 2002.

Stuttard, John. *The New Silk Road: Secrets of Business Success in China Today.* New York: John Wiley & Sons, 2000.

Sun Tzu. *The Art of War: A New Translation.* Boston: Shambhala, 2001.

Taylor, Frederick Winslow. *The Principles of Scientific Management.* New York: Norton, 1947.

Tsang, Cheryl D. *Microsoft First Generation: The Success Secrets of the Visionaries Who Launched a Technology Empire.* New York: John Wiley & Sons, 2000.

Ulrich, Dave, Jack Zenger, and Norm Smallwood. *Results-Based Leadership: How Leaders Build the Business and Improve the Bottom-line.* Boston: Harvard Business School Press, 1999.

Welch, Jack, with John A. Byrne. *Jack: Straight from the Gut.* New York: Warner Books, 2001.

English Language Newspapers and Magazines

Abu-Shalback, "Turning Up the Heat." *Appliance,* June 2001.

Arndt, Michael. "Can Haier Freeze Out Whirlpool and GE?" *BusinessWeek International,* April 11, 2002.

Balfour, Frederik. "A Global Shopping Spree for the Chinese: Mainland Companies Are Snapping Up More Overseas Assets." *BusinessWeek International*, November 18, 2002.

Bayark, Richard J. "First Step: The Journey to the Connected Future Begins at a Deliberate Pace." *Appliance Manufacture*, October 2001.

Beatty, Gerry. "Landmark Property on Broadway to Give Haier a Higher Profile." *HFN*, July 30, 2001.

Biers, Dan. "Taking the Fight to the Enemy: China's Top Appliance Maker, Haier, Breaks into the U.S. Market Using a Combination of Quality, Price and Local Manufacturing." *Far Eastern Economic Review*, March 29, 2001.

Chen, Kathy. "China Thinks It Can Become an Export Powerhouse; Haier Leads the Way." *Wall Street Journal*, September 17, 1997.

Cheng, Allen T. "Defrosting China-Taiwan Trade: With $7.5 billion in Revenues, Haier Has the Capacity to Wipe Out Every Rival in Taiwan." *Fortune International*, March 18, 2002.

Clifford, Mark L. "China's Fading Free-Trade Fervor." *BusinessWeek*, June 5, 2002.

Clifford, Mark L., et al. "Moving Up the Ladder: From Cheap Labor to Skilled Workers." *BusinessWeek*, November 6, 2000.

Dawson, Chester, et al. "The Americanization of Toyota." *BusinessWeek*, April 15, 2002.

Dolven, Ben. "The Perils of Delivering the Goods." *Far Eastern Economic Review*, July 25, 2002.

Dunlap, David W. "Chinese Group Buys Landmark Site." *New York Times*, July 25, 2001.

Flannery, Russell. "China Goes Global: The Ambitious Haier Leads an International Brand Push by Mainland Multinationals." *Forbes Global*, August 6, 2001.

Flannery, Russell, et al. "Another Look: Haier and Higher." *Forbes Global*, February 4, 2002.

Iritani, Evelyn. "Chinese Firms See U.S. as Land of Opportunity." *Los Angeles Times*, November 6, 2001.

Kunii, Irene M., et al. "Can Sony Regain the Magic?" *BusinessWeek*, March 11, 2002.

Kynge, James. "China's Modest Entrepreneur." *Financial Times*, December 7, 1999.

Landler, Mark. "In China, a Management Maverick Builds a Brand." *New York Times*, July 23, 2000.

Lee, Charles S. "Acer's Last Stand? After Flaming out in the U.S., Stan Shih Is Pointing His Company Straight at China." *Fortune International*, June 10, 2002.

Lynch, David J. "CEO Pushes China's Haier as Global Brand." *USA Today*, January 2, 2003.

Paul, Anthony. "China's Haier Power." *Fortune International*, February 15, 1999.

Pomfret, John. "Chinese Industry Races to Make Global Name for Itself." *Washington Post*, April 23, 2000.

Powell, Bill. "The Legend of Legend." *Fortune International*, September 16, 2002.

Prasso, Sheri. "Chinese Fridges Made in South Carolina." *BusinessWeek International*, May 6, 1999.

_____. "We Want to Become a Global Company." *BusinessWeek International*, June 14, 1999.

_____. "Zhang Ruimin, CEO, Haier Group, China." *BusinessWeek International*, June 14, 1999.

Roberts, Dexter. "Baby Steps for a Chinese Giant." *BusinessWeek International*, July 17, 2002.

Roberts, Dexter, et al. "Haier's Tough Trip from China: The Mainland's Top Appliance Maker Aims to Go Global." *BusinessWeek International*, April 1, 2002.

Sprague, Jonathan. "Haier Reaches Higher." *Fortune International*, September 16, 2002.

_____. "China's Manufacturing Beachhead." *Fortune*, October 28, 2002.

Wolf, Alan. "Asian Invasion Adds to Domestic Makers' Woes," *TWICE*, May 28, 2001.

Wysocki, Bernard, Jr. "Chinese Multinationals Aim to Be Just That." *Wall Street Journal*, January 28, 2002.

Chinese Language Books

Fan, Zhiyu. *Marketing Strategies (cuxiao celue)*. Shanghai: Shanghai People's Publishing House, 1999.

Hu, Angang, ed. *A Road Map for China's Strategies (zhongguo zhanlue gouxiang)*. Hangzhou, Zhejiang: Zhejiang People's Publishing House, 2002.

Li, Ren, ed. *Toward a Global Business (dazao quanqiu lingxian baye)*. Beijing: The Publishing House of All-China Federation of Industry and Commerce, 2001.

Li, Xuefeng. *The Taiji Wisdom: Sun Tzu's Art of War and Modern Enterprise Strategy Management (taiji zhihui: sunzi bingfa yu xiandai qiye zhanlue guanli)*. Beijing: China International Radio Press, 2002.

Li, Yining. *Facing the Road of Reform (miandui gaige zhilu)*. Beijing: China Development Publishing House, 1999.

Li, Yongheng. *WTO and China's Economic Development (WTO yu zhongguo jingji fazhan)*. Beijing: China Financial and Economic Publishing House, 2000.

Liu, Yonghao, et al. *The Wisdom of Chinese CEOs (zongcai de zhihui)*. Beijing: Central Compilation and Translation Press, 2002.

Lu, Taihong, ed. *Marketing in China: 2001 Marketing Report (yingxiao zai zhongguo: 2001 yingxiao baogao)*. Guangzhou: Guangzhou Publishing House, 2001.

Shen, Zhikun. *A Survey of Enterprise Laws of China (qiyefa tonglun)*. Hangzhou, Zhejiang: Hangzhou University Press, 1995.

Sun, Jian. *The Corporation Strategy of Haier (haier de qiye zhanlue)*. Beijing: Enterprise Management Publishing House, 2002.

Tang, Renwu. *Trends in the World Economy: China, East Asia and the World in the 21st Century (shijie jingji daqushi yanjiu: 21 shiji zhongguo dongya yu shijie)*. Beijing: The Publishing House of Beijing Normal University, 2001.

Wu, Jinglian. *Reform: We Are Going Through an Ordeal (gaige: women zhengzai guo daguan)*. Beijing: Joint Publishing Co., 2001.

Yan, Jianjun, and Hu Yong. *Haier: Made in China (haier zhongguo zhao)*. Haikou, Hainan: Hainan Publishing House, 2001.

Ye, Kuangshi. *The General Manager's Underclothes: A Probe into the Nature of Management (zongjingli de neiyi: toushi guanli de benzhi)*. Beijing: China Social Science Documentation Publishing House, 2001.

Zhang, Haitang, and Song Junying, eds. *The Chinese You Should Know About in the 21st Century (21 shiji ni ying guanzhu de zhongguoren)*. Beijing: China Society Press, 2000.

Zhang, Junli. *Structural Adjustment: Issues on China's Economic Development (jiegou tiaozheng: zhongguo jingji de fazhan zhuti)*. Beijing: Enterprise Management Publishing House, 1998.

Zhang, Weiying. *Enterprise Theory and China's Enterprise Reform (qiye lilun yu zhongguo qiye gaige)*. Beijing: Peking University Press, 2000.

Zhao, Huayong, ed. *Fortune Dialogue (caifu duihua)*. Beijing: World Publishing Corporation, 1999.

Chinese Language Newspapers and Magazines

Cao, Jianwei, and Yin Xiaoshan. "Haier's Incomplete Revolution" (*haier fei wanzheng geming*). *World of IT Managers*, June 26, 2001.

Chen, Yi. "Foreign Multinationals in China" (*kuaguo gongsi zai zhongguo*). *China Entrepreneur*, July 2001.

Fan, Zeshun. "Beyond the Blue Sea: Stories Told by Zhang Ruimin and Haier [I, II and III]" (*kuayue weilan, zhang ruimin he haier gaoshu women de gushi [shang, zhong, xia]*). *Qingdao Daily*, August 6-8, 2001.

Haier Enterprise Culture Center. *Haier Magazine (haier ren zazhi)*. Vols. 1-5, 2001, Qingdao, China.

Haier Enterprise Culture Center. *Haier News, Combined Issues 2000 (haier ren hedingben 2000)*. Qingdao, China.

Hong, Tao. "Six Questions for Haier" (*liu wen haier*). *South Wind Window*, July 7, 2002.

Hu, Kaoxu, and Liu Cheng. "Cloning a Group of 'Foreign' Haiers" (*kelong yiqun 'yang' haier*). *Economic Daily*, August 7, 2001.

Jiang, Ruxiang. "The Riddle of Haier's Future" (*haier de weilai zhimi*). *Global Entrepreneur*, March 4, 2002.

Lin, Hong. "'Made in China' Challenges the World" (*zhongguo zhizao tiaozhan shijie*). *China Business Monthly/New Economy*, December 2001.

Shi, Xinghui. "The Global Competitiveness of the Chinese Business Leaders" (*zhongguo qiye lingxiu quanqiu jingzhengli pingjia*). *China Entrepreneur*, December, 2001.

Su, Min. "Nurturing a 'Strong' Haier" (*peiyu yige 'qiang' haier*). *Economic Daily*, August 6, 2001.

Wang, Yantian, and Song Xuechun. "Set Sail on a Long Voyage, Haier Series Reports I" (yangfan yuanhang ying dahai—ji zai gaige kaifang zhong jueqi de haier [shang]). *People's Daily*, August 6, 2001.

_____. "Management: Cornerstone of a Great Undertaking, Haier Series Reports II" (*guanli: wengu daye de jishi—ji zai gaige kaifang zhong jueqi de haier [zhong]*). *People's Daily*, August 7, 2001.

_____. "Creativity: Soul of Enterprise Growth, Haier Series Reports III" (*chuangxin: qiye fazhan de linhun—ji zai gaige kaifang zhong jueqi de haier [xia]*). *People's Daily*, August 8, 2001.

Zhang, Nianqing. "Is China the Manufacturing Center? Tricks behind the Numbers of the Manufacturing Industry" (*zhongguo shi zhizaoye zhongxin ma? zhizaoye shuzi yincang youhuan*). *Beijing Youth Daily*, July 29, 2002.

Zhang, Shuhong. "Recreating a 'New' Haier" (*zaizao yige 'xin' haier*). *Economic Daily*, August 8, 2001.

Index

More Titles from Homa & Sekey Books

Ink Paintings by Gao Xingjian, the Nobel Prize Winner
ISBN: 1-931907-03-X, Hardcover, Art, $34.95

Splendor of Tibet: The Potala Palace, Jewel of the Himalayas
By Phuntsok Namgyal, ISBN: 1-931907-02-1, Hardcover
Art/Architecture, $39.95

Flower Terror: Suffocating Stories of China
By Pu Ning, ISBN 0-9665421-0-X, Fiction, Paperback, $13.95

The Peony Pavilion: A Novel
By Xiaoping Yen, Ph.D., ISBN 0-9665421-2-6, Fiction, Paperback, $16.95

Butterfly Lovers: A Tale of the Chinese Romeo and Juliet
By Fan Dai, Ph.D., ISBN 0-9665421-4-2, Fiction, Paperback, $16.95

Always Bright: Paintings by American Chinese Artists 1970-1999
Edited by Xue Jian Xin, et al. ISBN 0-9665421-3-4, Art, Hardcover, $49.95

Always Bright, Vol. II: Paintings by Chinese American Artists
Edited by Eugene Wang, Ph.D., et al. ISBN: 0-9665421-6-9
Art, Hardcover, $50.00

Dai Yunhui's Sketches
By Dai Yunhui, ISBN: 1-931907-00-5, Art, Paperback, $14.95

Musical Qigong: Ancient Chinese Healing Art from a Modern Master
By Shen Wu, ISBN: 0-9665421-5-0, Health, Paperback, $14.95

Surfacing Sadness: A Centennial of Korean-American Literature 1903-2003
Edited by Yearn Hong Choi, Ph. D. & Haeng Ja Kim, ISBN: 1-931907-09-9
Literary Anthology, Hardcover, $25.00

www.homabooks.com

Order Information: U.S.: $5.00 for the first item, $1.50 for each additional item. **Outside U.S.**: $10.00 for the first item, $5.00 for each additional item. All major credit cards accepted. You may also send a check or money order in U.S. fund (payable to Homa & Sekey Books) to: Orders Department, Homa & Sekey Books, 138 Veterans Plaza, P.O. Box 103, Dumont, NJ 07628 U.S.A. Tel: 201-384-6692; Fax: 201-384-6055; Email: info@homabooks.com